Praise for *The Seven Habits of Highly Effective People* by Stephen R. Covey, which introduced the philosophy of Principle-Centered Leadership

"Stephen Covey is an American Socrates, opening your mind to the 'permanent things'—values, family, relationships, communicating."
—BRIAN TRACY
author of *Psychology of Achievement*

"It's powerful reading. His principles of vision, leadership, and human relations make it a practical teaching tool for business leaders today. I highly recommend it."
—NOLAN ARCHIBALD
President and CEO, Black & Decker

"Stephen Covey's deliberate integration of life and principles leads to squaring inner thought and outward behavior, resulting in personal as well as public integrity."
—GREGORY J. NEWELL
former U.S. Ambassador to Sweden

"The difference between principle and preference is rarely understood, much less explained in clear, understandable language. Stephen both understands and explains the difference with examples that give the reader confidence that there is more to this book than a description of the latest management fad."
—BRUCE L. CHRISTENSEN
President, Public Broadcasting Service

"When Stephen Covey talks, executives listen."
—*Dun's Business Month*

Praise for *Executive Excellence* magazine copublished by The Institute for Principle-Centered Leadership

"I appreciate the quality and content of *Executive Excellence*."
—*John Naisbitt*
author of *Megatrends 2000*

"*Executive Excellence* is outstanding. Your readership is a very important one to us, and I'm very pleased to have had the opportunity to contribute to reaching it."
—Curt W. Reimann
Director for Quality Programs
Malcolm Baldrige National Quality Award
United States Department of Commerce
National Institute of Standards
and Technology

"I look forward to receiving a new issue of *Executive Excellence* each month."
—Barron Hilton
Hilton Hotels

"Excellent! This is one of the finest newsletters I've seen in the field."
—Thomas J. Peters
author of *In Search of Excellence*

"*Executive Excellence* is the best executive advisory newsletter anywhere in the world—it's just a matter of time before a lot more people find that out."
—Kenneth Blanchard
author of *The One Minute Manager*

"You are doing a great job with the newsletter. I greatly admire you for what you're doing, I think it's possibly one of the most powerful forces for good in our country today."
—Don Williams
Managing Partner, Trammell Crow

Also by

STEPHEN R. COVEY

The 7 Habits of Highly Effective People
The 7 Habits of Highly Effective Families
Daily Reflections for Highly Effective People
Spiritual Roots of Human Relations
How to Succeed with People
Marriage and Family Insights
The Divine Center

With

A. ROGER MERRILL

First Things First

STEPHEN R. COVEY

PRINCIPLE-CENTRED LEADERSHIP

POCKET
BOOKS

LONDON · SYDNEY · NEW YORK · TORONTO

To inspired principle-centered leaders and thinkers of the past and present
for their timeless wisdom, and to our clients and their organizations for
the challenge to bridge the gap between the theoretical and the practical.

First published in Great Britain by Simon & Schuster UK Ltd, 1992
This edition first published by Pocket Books, 2002
An imprint of Simon & Schuster UK Ltd
A CBS COMPANY

2

Simon & Schuster UK Ltd
1st Floor
222 Gray's Inn Road
London WC1X 8HB

www.simonandschuster.co.uk

Simon & Schuster Australia
Sydney

A CIP catalogue record for this book is
available from the British Library

ISBN-13: 978-0-7434-6860-2

Printed and bound in India by
Replika Press Pvt. Ltd.

CONTENTS

Preface

A Principle-Centered Approach

In my seminars I often invite people to share their toughest problems or ask their hardest questions. Inevitably these deal with conflicts or dilemmas that can't be resolved using conventional approaches. Here are just a couple of examples:

- How do I balance personal and professional areas of life in the middle of constant crises and pressures?
- How can I be genuinely happy for the successes and competencies of another?
- How do we maintain control, yet give people the freedom and autonomy they need to be effective in their work?
- How do we internalize the principles of total quality and continuous improvement at all levels and in all people when they are so cynical in the wake of all the past programs of the month?

Perhaps you have asked yourself these questions as you have grappled with real-life challenges in your personal life and in your organizations. As you read this book you will gain an understanding of the basic principles of effective leadership.

Give a man a fish, and you feed him for a day. Teach him how to fish, and you feed him for a lifetime.

With understanding you will be empowered to answer these and other tough questions by yourself. Without understanding you will tend to use hit-and-miss, seat-of-the-pants approaches to living and problem-solving.

In recent years, since the publication of my book *The 7 Habits of Highly Effective People*, I have worked with many wonderful individuals who are seeking to improve the quality of their lives and the quality of their products, services, and organizations. But, sadly, I have seen that many use a variety of ill-advised approaches in sincere attempts to improve their relationships and achieve desired results.

Often these approaches reflect the inverse of the habits of effective people. In fact, my brother, John Covey, who is a master teacher, sometimes refers to them as the seven habits of *ineffective* people:

- *Be reactive: doubt yourself and blame others.*
- *Work without any clear end in mind.*
- *Do the urgent thing first.*
- *Think win/lose.*
- *Seek first to be understood.*
- *If you can't win, compromise.*
- *Fear change and put off improvement.*

Just as personal victories precede public victories when effective people progress along the maturity continuum, so also do private failures portend embarrassing public failures when ineffective people regress along an *immaturity continuum*—that is, when they go from a state of *dependency*, where others must provide their basic needs and satisfy their wants and desires, to a state of *counterdependency*, where they engage in fight-or-flight behaviors, to a state of *codependency*, where they cooperate in rather destructive ways with each other.

Now, how can people break such habits and replace them with new ones? How can you and I escape the pull of the past and re-create ourselves and achieve meaningful change in our personal lives and in our organizations?

That's what this book attempts to answer. In section 1, I deal with the personal and interpersonal applications of the principles of effectiveness; in section 2, I deal with the managerial and organizational applications.

Some Observations of the Problem

Let me share with you some examples of the problem we all face in personal and professional life. Then I will suggest a principle-centered solution.

• Some people justify heavy-handed means in the name of virtuous ends. They say that "business is business" and that "ethics" and "principles" sometimes have to take a backseat to profits. Many of these same people see no correlation between the quality of their personal lives at home and the quality of their products and services at work. Because of the social and political environment inside their organizations and the fragmented markets outside, they think they can abuse relationships at will and still get results.

• The head coach of a professional football team told me that some of his players don't pay the price in the off season. "They come to camp out of shape," he said. "Somehow they think they can fool me and Mother Nature, make the team, and play great in the games."

• When I ask in my seminars, "How many of you would agree that the vast majority of the work force possess far more capability, creativity, talent, initiative, and resourcefulness than their present jobs allow or require them to use?" the affirmative response is about 99 percent. In other words, we all admit that our greatest resources are being wasted and that poor human resource management hurts our bottom lines.

• Our heroes are often people who make a lot of money. And when some hero—an actor, entertainer, athlete, or other professional—suggests that we can get what we want by living life by our own rules, then we listen to them, especially if social norms reinforce what they say.

• Some parents don't pay the price with their kids, thinking they can fake it for the public image and then shout and yell and slam the door. They are then shocked to see that their teenage kids experiment with drugs, alcohol, and sex to fill the void in their lives.

• When I invited one executive to involve all his people and take six months to write a corporate mission statement, he said, "You don't understand us, Stephen. We will whip this baby out this weekend." I see people trying to do it all over a weekend—trying to rebuild their marriage on a weekend, trying to rebuild an alienated relationship with their son on a weekend, trying to change a company culture on a weekend. But some things just can't be done on a weekend.

• Many parents take teenage rebellion and rejection personally, simply because they are too emotionally dependent upon their children's acceptance of them, so a state of collusion is established, where they need each other's weaknesses to validate their perceptions of each other and to justify their own lack of production.

• In management everything is often reduced to measurement. July belongs to the operators, but December belongs to the comptrollers. And figures are often manipulated at the end of the year to make them look good. The numbers are supposed to be precise and objective, but most know they are based on subjective assumptions.

• Most people are turned off by "motivational" speakers who have nothing more to share than entertaining stories mingled with "motherhood and apple pie" platitudes. They want substance; they want process. They want more than aspirin and a Band-Aid for acute pain. They want to solve their chronic problems and achieve long-term results.

• I once spoke to a group of senior executives at a training conference and discovered that they were bitter because the CEO had "forced" them to "come and sit for four days to listen to a bunch of abstract thoughts." They were part of a paternalistic, dependent culture that saw training as an expense, not an investment. Their organization managed people as things.

• In school we ask students to tell us what we told them; we test them on our lectures. They figure out the system, party and procrastinate, then cram and feed it back to us to get the grades. They often think all of life operates on the same short-cut system.

Some habits of ineffectiveness are rooted in our social conditioning toward quick-fix, short-term thinking. In school many of us procrastinate and then successfully cram for tests. But does cramming work on a farm? Can you go two weeks without milking the cow and then get out there and milk like crazy? Can you "forget" to plant in the spring or goof off all summer and then hit the ground real hard in the fall to bring in the harvest? We might laugh at such ludicrous approaches in agriculture, but then in an academic environment we might cram to get the grades and degrees we need to get the jobs we want, even if we fail to get a good general education.

THE SOLUTION: CENTER ON NATURAL PRINCIPLES

These are problems that common approaches can't solve. The quick, easy, free, and fun approach won't work on the farm because there we're subject to natural laws or governing principles. Natural laws, based upon principles, operate regardless of our awareness of them or our obedience to them.

The only thing that endures over time is the law of the farm: I must prepare the ground, put in the seed, cultivate it, weed it, water it, then gradually nurture growth and development to full maturity. So also in a marriage or in helping a teenager through a difficult identity crisis—there is no quick fix, where you can just move in and make everything right with a positive mental attitude and a bunch of success formulas. The law of the harvest governs. Natural laws, principles, operate regardless. So get these principles at the center of your life, at the center of your relationships, at the center of your management contracts, at the center of your entire organization.

If I try to use manipulative strategies and tactics to get other people to do what I want—while my *character* is flawed or my *competency* is questionable—then I can't be successful over time. Rhetoric and good intentions aside, if there is little or no *trust*, there is no foundation for permanent success. But if we learn to manage things and lead people, we will have the best bottom line because we will unleash the energy and talent of people.

We often think of change and improvement coming from the outside in rather than from the inside out. Even if we recognize the need for change within, we usually think in terms of learning new skills, rather than showing more integrity to basic principles. But significant breakthroughs often represent internal breaks with traditional ways of thinking. I refer to these as *paradigm shifts*.

Principle-centered leadership introduces a new paradigm—that we center our lives and our leadership of organizations and people on certain "true north" principles. In this book I will deal with *what* those principles are, *why* we need to become principle-centered, and *how* we attain this quality. (Incidentally, these chapters first appeared as separate articles in *Executive Excellence* magazine, copublished by our Institute for Principle-Centered Leadership. Over the past eight years in *Executive Excellence*, some 500 contributing writers, representing the best thinking on management in America, have validated the paradigm of principle-centered leadership.)

Our effectiveness is predicated upon certain *inviolate principles*— natural laws in the human dimension that are just as real, just as unchanging, as laws such as gravity are in the physical dimension. These principles are woven into the fabric of every civilized society and constitute the roots of every family and institution that has endured and prospered.

Principles are not invented by us or by society; they are the laws of the universe that pertain to human relationships and human organizations. They are part of the human condition, consciousness, and conscience. To the degree people recognize and live in harmony with such basic principles as fairness, equity, justice, integrity, honesty, and trust, they move toward either survival and stability on the one hand or disintegration and destruction on the other.

My experience tells me that people instinctively trust those whose personality is founded upon correct principles. We have evidence of this in our long-term relationships. We learn that technique is relatively unimportant compared to trust, which is the result of our trustworthiness over time. When trust is high, we communicate easily, effortlessly, instantaneously. We can make mistakes and others will still capture our meaning. But when trust is low, communication is exhausting, time-consuming, ineffective, and inordinately difficult.

It's relatively easy to work on personalities: all we have to do is learn some new skill, rearrange language patterns, adopt human relations technologies, employ visualization affirmations, or strengthen our self-esteem. But it's comparatively hard to change habits, develop virtues, learn basic disciplines, keep promises, be faithful to vows, exercise courage, or be genuinely considerate of the feelings and convictions of others. Nonetheless, it's the true test and manifestation of our maturity.

To value oneself and, at the same time, subordinate oneself to higher purposes and principles is the paradoxical essence of highest humanity and the foundation of effective leadership.

LEADERSHIP BY COMPASS

Correct principles are like compasses: they are always pointing the way. And if we know how to read them, we won't get lost, confused, or fooled by conflicting voices and values.

Principles are self-evident, self-validating natural laws. They don't change or shift. They provide "true north" direction to our lives when navigating the "streams" of our environments.

Principles apply at all time in all places. They surface in the form of values, ideas, norms, and teachings that uplift, ennoble, fulfill, empower, and inspire people. The lesson of history is that to the degree people and civilizations have operated in harmony with correct principles, they have prospered. At the root of societal declines are foolish practices that represent violations of correct principles. How many economic disasters, intercultural conflicts, political revolutions, and civil wars could have been avoided had there been greater social commitment to correct principles?

Principle-centered leadership is based on the reality that we cannot violate these natural laws with impunity. Whether or not we believe in them, they have been proven effective throughout centuries of human history. Individuals are more effective and organizations more empowered when they are guided and governed by these proven principles. They are not easy, quick-fix solutions to personal and interpersonal problems. Rather, they are foundational principles that when applied consistently become behavioral habits enabling fundamental transformations of individuals, relationships, and organizations.

Principles, unlike values, are objective and external. They operate in obedience to natural laws, regardless of conditions. Values are subjective and internal. Values are like maps. Maps are not the territories; they are only subjective attempts to describe or represent the territory. The more closely our values or maps are aligned with correct principles—with the realities of the territory, with things as they really are—the more accurate and useful they will be. However, when the territory is constantly changing, when markets are constantly shifting, any map is soon obsolete.

A value-based map may provide some useful description, but the principle-centered compass provides invaluable vision and direction. An accurate map is a good management tool, but a compass set on "true north" principles is a leadership and empowerment tool. When pointing to true north, the needle reflects alignment with natural laws. If we are locked in to managing by maps, we will waste many resources by wandering aimlessly or by squandering opportunity.

Our values often reflect the beliefs of our cultural background. From childhood we develop a value system that represents a combination of cultural influences, personal discoveries, and family scripts. These become the "glasses" through which we look at the world. We evaluate, assign priorities, judge, and behave based on how we see life through these glasses.

One common reactive pattern is to live life in value-based compartments, where our behavior is largely the product of expectations built in to certain roles: spouse, parent, child, business executive, community leader, and so on. Because each of these compartments carries its own value system, reactive people often find themselves trying to meet conflicting expectations and living by differing values according to the role or the environment they are in at any particular time.

When people align their personal values with correct principles, they are liberated from old perceptions or paradigms. One of the characteristics of authentic leaders is their humility, evident in their ability to take off their glasses and examine the lens objectively, analyzing how well their values, perceptions, beliefs, and behaviors align with "true north" principles. Where there are discrepancies (prejudice, ignorance, or error), they make adjustments to realign with greater wisdom. Centering on unchanging principles brings permanency and power into their lives.

Four Dimensions

Centering life on correct principles is the key to developing this rich internal power in our lives, and with this power we can realize many of our dreams. A center secures, guides, empowers. Like the hub of a wheel, it unifies and integrates. It's the core of personal and organizational missions. It's the foundation of culture. It aligns shared values, structures, and systems.

Whatever lies at the center of our lives becomes the primary source of our life-support system. In large measure, that system is represented by four fundamental dimensions: security, guidance, wisdom, and power. Principle-centered leadership and living cultivates these four internal sources of strength.

ALTERNATE LIFE CENTERS

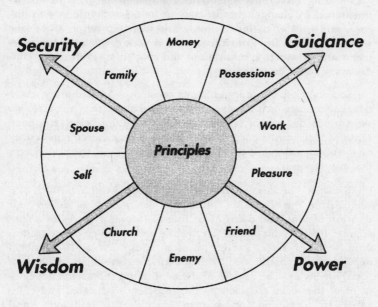

Focusing on alternative centers—work, pleasure, friends, enemies, spouse, family, self, church, possessions, money, and so on)—weakens and disorients us. For example, if we are focused on the social mirror, we empower circumstances and the opinions of others to guide and control us. Lacking security and self-esteem, we tend to be emotionally dependent on others. Lacking wisdom, we tend to repeat past mistakes. Lacking guidance, we tend to follow trends and fail to finish what we start. Lacking power, we tend to reflect what happens to us and react to external conditions and internal moods.

But when we center our lives on correct principles, we become more balanced, unified, organized, anchored, and rooted. We have a foundation for all activities, relationships, and decisions. We also have a sense of stewardship about everything in our lives, including time, talents, money, possessions, relationships, our families, and our bodies. We recognize the need to use them for good purposes and, as a steward, to be accountable for their use.

Centering on principles provides sufficient security to not be threatened by change, comparisons, or criticisms; guidance to discover our mission, define our roles, and write our scripts and goals; wisdom to learn from our mistakes and seek continuous improvement; and power to communicate and cooperate, even under conditions of stress and fatigue.

• *Security*. Security represents our sense of worth, identity, emotional anchorage, self-esteem, and personal strength. Of course, we see various degrees of security—on a continuum between a deep sense of high intrinsic worth on one end and an extreme insecurity on the other, wherein a person's life is buffeted by all the fickle forces that play upon it.

• *Guidance*. Guidance is the direction we receive in life. Much of it comes from the standards, principles, or criteria that govern our decision making and doing. This internal monitor serves as a conscience. People who operate on the low end of the guidance continuum tend to have strong physical addictions and emotional dependencies, conditioned by their centering on selfish, sensual, or social life-styles. The middle of the continuum represents development of the social conscience—the conscience educated and cultivated by centering on human institutions, traditions, and relationships. On the high end of the continuum is the spiritual conscience, wherein guidance comes from inspired or inspiring sources—a compass centered on true principles.

• *Wisdom*. Wisdom suggests a sage perspective on life, a sense of balance, a keen understanding of how the various parts and principles apply and relate to each other. It embraces judgment, discernment, comprehension. It is a oneness, an integrated wholeness. At the low end of the wisdom continuum are inaccurate maps, which cause people to base their thinking on distorted, discordant principles. The high end represents an accurate and complete life compass wherein all the parts and principles are properly related to each other. As we move toward the high end, we have an increasing sense of the ideal (things as they should be) as well as a sensitive, practical approach to realities (things as they are). Wisdom also includes the ability to discern pure joy as distinct from temporary pleasure.

• *Power*. Power is the capacity to act, the strength and courage to accomplish something. It is the vital energy to make choices and decisions. It also represents the capacity to overcome deeply embedded habits and to cultivate higher, more effective habits. At the low end of the power continuum we see people who are essentially powerless, insecure, products of what happens or has happened to them. They are largely dependent on circumstances and on others. They are reflections of other people's opinions and directions; they have no real comprehension of true joy and happiness. At the high end of the continuum we see people with vision and discipline, whose lives are functional products of personal decisions rather than of external conditions. These people make things happen; they are proactive; they choose their responses to situations based upon timeless principles and universal standards. They take responsibility for their feelings, moods, and attitudes as well as their thoughts and actions.

These four factors—security, guidance, wisdom, and power—are interdependent. Security and well-founded guidance bring true wisdom, and wisdom becomes the spark or catalyst to release and direct power. When these four factors are harmonized, they create the great force of a noble personality, a balanced character, a beautifully integrated individual.

Organizational Centers

Principle-centered leadership incorporates the Seven Habits of Highly Effective People and related principles, application practices, and processes. Because principle-centered leadership focuses on fundamental principles and processes, genuine cultural transformations often transpire.

Once you get principles at the center, you realize that the only way to treat people is how you want them to treat you. You see your competition as a learning source, as friends who can keep you sharp and teach you where your weaknesses are. Your identity is not threatened by them or by other external conditions because you have an anchor and a compass. Even in a sea of turbulent change, you maintain perspective and judgment. And you are always empowered from within.

ALTERNATE ORGANIZATIONAL CENTERS

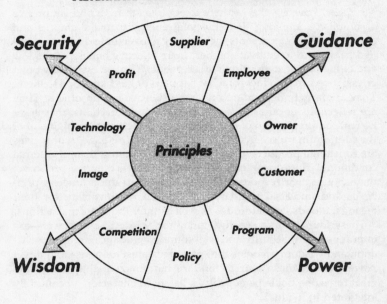

Alternate organizational centers—profit, supplier, employee, owner, customer, program, policy, competition, image, and technology—are flawed compared with a principle-centered paradigm. As with individuals, principle-centered companies enjoy a greater degree of security, guidance, wisdom, and power.

For example, if the security of an organization comes from its image or cash flow or from comparisons with competitors or from the opinions of customers, its leaders tend either to overreact or to underact to the news and events of the day. Moreover, they tend to see business (and life) as a zero sum game; to be threatened by the success and recognition of others; and to delight in the failures of competitors. If our security is founded on the weaknesses of others, we actually empower those weaknesses to control us.

Real empowerment comes from having both the principles *and* the practices understood and applied at all levels of the organization. Practices are the *what to do's*, specific applications that fit specific circumstances. Principles are the *why to do's*, the elements upon which applications or practices are built. Without understanding the principles of a given task, people become incapacitated when the situation changes and different practices are required to be successful. When training people, we often teach skills and practices, the specific *how to* of a given task. But when we teach practices without principles, we tend to make people dependent on us or others for further instruction and direction.

Principle-centered leaders are men and women of character who work with competence "on farms" with "seed and soil" on the basis of natural principles and build those principles into the center of their lives, into the center of their relationships with others, into the center of their agreements and contracts, into their management processes, and into their mission statements.

The challenge is to be a light, not a judge; to be a model, not a critic.

PERSONAL and INTERPERSONAL EFFECTIVENESS

INTRODUCTION

I HAVE LONG ADVOCATED a natural, gradual, day-by-day, step-by-step, sequential approach to personal development. My feeling is that any product or program—whether it deals with losing weight or mastering skills—that promises "quick, free, instant, and easy" results is probably not based on correct principles. Yet virtually all advertising uses one or more of these words to entice us to buy. Small wonder many of us are addicted to "quick fix" approaches to personal development.

In this section I suggest that real character and skill development is irrevocably related to natural laws and governing principles; when we observe these, we gain the strength to break with the past, to overcome old habits, to change our paradigms, and to achieve primary greatness and interpersonal effectiveness.

Of course, we do not live alone on islands, isolated from other people. We are born into families; we grow up in societies; we become students of schools, members of other organizations. Once into our professions, we find that our jobs require us to interact frequently and effectively with others. If we fail to learn and apply the principles of interpersonal effectiveness, we can expect our progress to slow or stop.

So in this section I also deal with the attitudes, skills, and strategies for creating and maintaining trustful relationships with other people. In effect, once we become relatively independent, our challenge is to become effectively interdependent with others. To do this we must practice empathy and synergy in our efforts to be proactive and productive.

RESOLVING DILEMMAS

Throughout history, the most significant breakthroughs have been breaks with the old ways of thinking, the old models and paradigms. Principle-centered leadership is a breakthrough paradigm—a new way of thinking that helps resolve the classic dilemmas of modern living:

- How do we achieve and maintain a wise and renewing balance between work and family, personal and professional ambitions, in the middle of constant crises and pressures?
- How do we adhere to simplicity in the thick of terrible complexity?
- How do we maintain a sense of direction in today's wilderness, where well-developed road maps (strategies and plans) are rendered useless by rapid change that often hits us from the blind side?
- How do we look at human weakness with genuine compassion and understanding rather than accusation and self-justification?
- How do we replace prejudice (the tendency to prejudge and categorize people in order to manipulate them) with a sense of reverence and discovery in order to promote learning, achievement, and excellence in people?
- How can we be empowered (and empower other people) with confidence and competence to solve problems and seize opportunities—without being or fearing loose cannons?
- How do we encourage the desire to change and improve without creating more pain than gain?
- How can we be contributing members of a complementary team based on mutual respect and the valuing of diversity and pluralism?
- Where do we start, and how do we keep recharging our batteries to maintain momentum for learning, growing, and improving?

As you read this section, you will gain an understanding of the basic principles of effective personal leadership, and this new understanding will empower you to resolve these and other tough questions by yourself.

Four Levels, Four Principles

Principle-centered leadership is practiced from the inside out on four levels: 1) *personal* (my relationship with myself); 2) *interpersonal* (my relationships and interactions with others); 3) *managerial* (my responsibility to get a job done with others); and 4) *organizational* (my need to organize people—to recruit them, train them, compensate them, build teams, solve problems, and create aligned structure, strategy, and systems).

Each level is "necessary but insufficient," meaning we have to work at all levels on the basis of certain master principles. In this section, I will focus on the first two principles:

• *Trustworthiness* at the *personal level*. Trustworthiness is based on *character*, what you are as a person, and *competence*, what you can do. If you have faith in my character but not in my competence, you still wouldn't trust me. Many good, honest people gradually lose their professional trustworthiness because they allow themselves to become "obsolete" inside their organizations. Without character *and* competence, we won't be considered trustworthy, nor will we show much wisdom in our choices and decisions. Without meaningful ongoing professional development, there is little trustworthiness or trust.

• Trust at the *interpersonal level*. Trustworthiness is the foundation of trust. Trust is the emotional bank account between two people that enables them to have a win-win performance agreement. If two people trust each other, based on the trustworthiness of each other, they can then enjoy clear communication, empathy, synergy, and productive interdependency. If one is incompetent, training and development can help. But if one has a character flaw, he or she must make and keep promises to increase internal security, improve skills, and rebuild relationships of trust.

Trust—or the lack of it—is at the root of success or failure in relationships and in the bottom-line results of business, industry, education, and government.

FOUR LEVELS OF PRINCIPLE-CENTERED LEADERSHIP WITH KEY PRINCIPLES

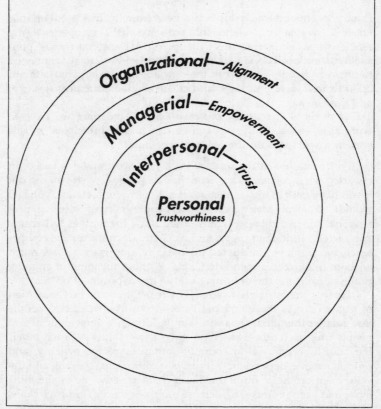

Organizational—Alignment

Managerial—Empowerment

Interpersonal—Trust

Personal
Trustworthiness

Chapter 1

CHARACTERISTICS OF
PRINCIPLE-CENTERED LEADERS

FROM STUDY AND OBSERVATION and from my own strivings, I have isolated eight discernible characteristics of people who are principle-centered leaders. These traits not only characterize effective leaders, they also serve as signs of progress for all of us. I will briefly discuss each in turn.

THEY ARE CONTINUALLY LEARNING

Principle-centered people are constantly educated by their experiences. They read, they seek training, they take classes, they listen to others, they learn through both their ears and their eyes. They are curious, always asking questions. They continually expand their competence, their ability to do things. They develop new skills, new interests. They discover that the more they know, the more they realize they don't know; that as their circle of knowledge grows, so does its outside edge of ignorance. Most of this learning and growth energy is self-initiated and feeds upon itself.

You will develop your abilities faster by learning to make and keep promises or commitments. Start by making a small promise to yourself; continue fulfilling that promise until you have a sense that you have a little more control over yourself. Now take the next level of challenge. Make yourself a promise and keep it until you have established control at that level. Now move to the next level; make the promise, keep it. As you do this, your sense of personal worth will increase; your sense of self-mastery will grow, as will your confidence that you can master the next level.

Be serious and intent in the whole process, however, because if you make this commitment to yourself and then break it, your self-esteem will be weakened and your capacity to make and keep another promise will be decreased.

THEY ARE SERVICE-ORIENTED

Those striving to be principle-centered see life as a mission, not as a career. Their nurturing sources have armed and prepared them for service. In effect, every morning they "yoke up" and put on the harness of service, thinking of others.

See yourself each morning yoking up, putting on the harness of service in your various stewardships. See yourself taking the straps and connecting them around your shoulders as you prepare to do the work assigned to you that day. See yourself allowing someone else to adjust the yoke or harness. See yourself yoked up to another person at your side—a co-worker or spouse—and learning to pull together with that person.

I emphasize this principle of service or yoking up because I have come to believe that effort to become principle-centered without a load to carry simply will not succeed. We may attempt to do it as a kind of intellectual or moral exercise, but if we don't have a sense of responsibility, of service, of contribution, something we need to pull or push, it becomes a futile endeavor.

THEY RADIATE POSITIVE ENERGY

The countenances of principle-centered people are cheerful, pleasant, happy, Their attitude is optimistic, positive, upbeat. Their spirit is enthusiastic, hopeful, believing.

This positive energy is like an energy field or an aura that surrounds them and that similarly charges or changes weaker, negative energy fields around them. They also attract and magnify smaller positive energy fields. When they come into contact with strong, negative energy sources, they tend either to neutralize or to sidestep this negative energy. Sometimes they will simply leave it, walking away from its poisonous orbit. Wisdom gives them a sense of how strong it is and a sense of humor and of timing in dealing with it.

Be aware of the effect of your own energy and understand how you radiate and direct it. And in the middle of confusion or contention or negative energy, strive to be a peacemaker, a harmonizer, to undo or reverse destructive energy. You will discover what a self-fulfilling prophecy positive energy is when combined with the next characteristic.

THEY BELIEVE IN OTHER PEOPLE

Principle-centered people don't overreact to negative behaviors, criticism, or human weaknesses. They don't feel built up when they discover the weaknesses of others. They are not naive; they are aware of weakness. But they realize that behavior and potential are two different things. They believe in the unseen potential of all people. They feel grateful for their blessings and feel naturally to compassionately forgive and forget the offenses of others. They don't carry grudges. They refuse to label other people, to stereotype, categorize, and prejudge. Rather, they see the oak tree in the acorn and understand the process of helping the acorn become a great oak.

Once my wife and I felt uneasy about the labels we and others had attached to one of our sons, even though these labels were justified by his behavior. By visualizing his potential, we gradually came to see him differently. When we believed in the unseen potential, the old labels vanished naturally, and we stopped trying to change him overnight. We simply knew that his talent and potential would come in its own time. And it did, to the astonishment, frankly, of others, including other family members. We were not surprised because we knew who he was.

Truly, believing is seeing. We must, therefore, seek to believe in the unseen potential. This creates a *climate for growth and opportunity.* Self-centered people believe that the key lies in them, in their techniques, in doing "their thing" to others. This works only temporarily. If you believe it's "in" them, not "in" you, you relax, accept, affirm, and let it happen. Either way it is a self-fulfilling prophecy.

THEY LEAD BALANCED LIVES

They read the best literature and magazines and keep up with current affairs and events. They are active socially, having many friends and a few confidants. They are active intellectually, having many interests. They read, watch, observe, and learn. Within the limits of age and health, they are active physically. They have a lot of fun. They enjoy themselves. They have a healthy sense of humor, particularly laughing at themselves and not at others' expense. You can sense they have a healthy regard for and honesty about themselves.

They can feel their own worth, which is manifest by their courage and integrity and by the absence of a need to brag, to drop names, to borrow strength from possessions or credentials or titles or past achievements. They are open in their communication, simple, direct, nonmanipulative. They also have a sense of what is appropriate, and they would sooner err on the side of understatement than on the side of exaggeration.

They are not extremists—they do not make everything all or nothing. They do not divide everything into two parts, seeing everything as good or bad, as either/or. They think in terms of continuums, priorities, hierarchies. They have the power to discriminate, to sense the similarities and differences in each situation. This does not mean they see everything in terms of situational ethics. They fully recognize absolutes and courageously condemn the bad and champion the good.

Their actions and attitudes are proportionate to the situation—balanced, temperate, moderate, wise. For instance, they're not workaholics, religious zealots, political fanatics, diet crashers, food bingers, pleasure addicts, or fasting martyrs. They're not slavishly chained to their plans and schedules. They don't condemn themselves for every foolish mistake or social blunder. They don't brood about yesterday or daydream about tomorrow. They live sensibly in the present, carefully plan the future, and flexibly adapt to changing circumstances. Their self-honesty is revealed by their sense of humor, their willingness to admit and then forget mistakes, and to cheerfully do the things ahead that lie within their power.

They have no need to manipulate through either intimidating anger or self-pitying martyrdom. They are genuinely happy for others' successes and do not feel in any sense that these take anything from them. They take both praise and blame proportionately without head trips or overreactions. They see success on the far side of failure. The only real failure for them is the experience not learned from.

THEY SEE LIFE AS AN ADVENTURE

Principle-centered people savor life. Because their security comes from within instead of from without, they have no need to categorize and stereotype everything and everybody in life to give them a sense of certainty and predictability. They see old faces freshly, old scenes as if for the first time. They are like courageous explorers going on an expedition into uncharted territories; they are really not sure what is going to happen, but they are confident it will be exciting and growth producing and that they will discover new territory and make new contributions. Their security lies in their initiative, resourcefulness, creativity, willpower, courage, stamina, and native intelligence rather than in the safety, protection, and abundance of their home camps, of their comfort zones.

They rediscover people each time they meet them. They are interested in them. They ask questions and get involved. They are completely present when they listen. They learn from them. They don't label them from past successes or failures. They see no one bigger than life. They are not overawed by top government figures or celebrities. They resist becoming any person's disciple. They are basically unflappable and capable of adapting virtually to anything that comes along. One of their fixed principles is flexibility. They truly lead the abundant life.

THEY ARE SYNERGISTIC

Synergy is the state in which the whole is more than the sum of the parts. Principle-centered people are synergistic. They are change catalysts. They improve almost any situation they get into. They work as smart as they work hard. They are amazingly productive, but in new and creative ways.

In team endeavors they build on their strengths and strive to complement their weaknesses with the strengths of others. Delegation for results is easy and natural to them, since they believe in others' strengths and capacities. And since they are not threatened by the fact that others are better in some ways, they feel no need to supervise them closely.

When principle-centered people negotiate and communicate with others in seemingly adversarial situations, they learn to separate the people from the problem. They focus on the other person's interests and concerns rather than fight over positions. Gradually others discover their sincerity and become part of a creative problem-solving process. Together they arrive at synergistic solutions, which are usually much better than any of the original proposals, as opposed to compromise solutions wherein both parties give and take a little.

THEY EXERCISE FOR SELF-RENEWAL

Finally, they regularly exercise the four dimensions of the human personality: physical, mental, emotional, and spiritual.

They participate in some kind of balanced, moderate, regular program of aerobic exercise, meaning cardiovascular exercise—using the large leg muscles and working the heart and lungs. This provides endurance—improving the capacity of the body and brain to use oxygen—along with many other physical and mental benefits. Also valuable are stretching exercises for flexibility and resistance exercises for strength and muscle tone.

They exercise their minds through reading, creative problem-solving, writing, and visualizing. Emotionally they make an effort to be patient, to listen to others with genuine empathy, to show unconditional love, and to accept responsibility for their own lives and decisions and reactions. Spiritually they focus on prayer, scripture study, meditation, and fasting.

I'm convinced that if a person will spend one hour a day on these basic exercises, he or she will improve the quality, productivity, and satisfaction of every other hour of the day, including the depth and restfulness of sleep.

No other single hour of your day will return as much as the hour you invest in sharpening the saw—that is, in exercising these four dimensions of the human personality. If you will do this daily, you will soon experience the impact for good on your life.

Some of these activities may be done in the normal course of the day; others will need to be scheduled into the day. They take some time, but in the long run they save us a great deal of time. We must never get too busy sawing to take time to sharpen the saw, never too busy driving to take time to get gas.

I find that if I do this hour of exercise early in the morning, it is like a private victory and just about guarantees public victories throughout the day. But if I take the course of least resistance and neglect all or part of this program, I forfeit that private victory and find myself uprooted by public pressures and stresses through the day.

These principles of self-renewal* will gradually produce a strong and healthy character with a powerfully disciplined, service-focused will.

* If you would like to receive a complimentary, self-scoring profile to help you evaluate your current level of effectiveness, please call 1-800-255-0777.

Chapter 2

SEVEN HABITS REVISITED

SEVEN UNIQUE HUMAN ENDOWMENTS

One way to revisit the Seven Habits of Highly Effective People is to identify the unique human capability or endowment associated with each habit.

Those associated with Habits 1, 2, and 3 are *primary* human endowments. And if those endowments are well exercised, *secondary* endowments are bequeathed to the person through the exercise of Habits 4, 5, and 6. And the endowment associated with Habit 7 renews the process of growth and development.

The primary human endowments are 1) self-awareness or self-knowledge; 2) imagination and conscience; and 3) volition or will-power. The secondary endowments are 4) an abundance mentality; 5) courage and consideration; and 6) creativity. The seventh endowment is self-renewal. All are unique human endowments; animals don't possess any of them. But they are all on a continuum of low to high levels.

• Associated with *Habit 1: Be Proactive* is the endowment of *self-knowledge* or *self-awareness*—an ability to choose your response (response-ability). At the low end of the continuum are the ineffective people who transfer responsibility by blaming other people, events, or the environment—anything or anybody "out there" so that they are not responsible for results. If I blame you, in effect I have empowered you. I have given my power to your weakness. Then I can create evidence that supports my perception that you are the problem.

At the upper end of the continuum toward increasing effectiveness

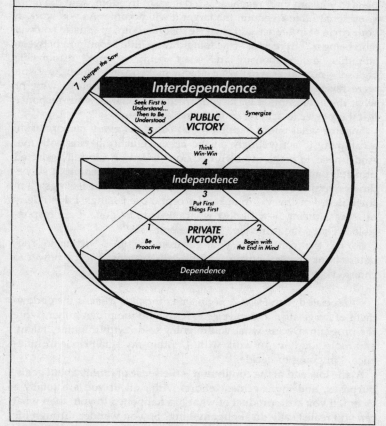

SEVEN HABITS MATURITY CONTINUUM

Interdependence

7 Sharpen the Saw

Seek First to Understand... Then to Be Understood
5

PUBLIC VICTORY

Synergize
6

Think Win-Win
4

Independence

3

Put First Things First

1

Be Proactive

PRIVATE VICTORY

Begin with the End in Mind
2

Dependence

© 1991 Covey Leadership Center

is self-awareness: "I know my tendencies, I know the scripts or programs that are in me, but I am not those scripts. I can rewrite my scripts." You are aware that you are the creative force of your life. You are not the victim of conditions or conditioning. You can choose your response to any situation, to any person. Between what happens to you and your response is a degree of freedom. And the more you exercise that freedom, the larger it will become. As you work in your circle of influence and exercise that freedom, gradually you will stop being a "hot reactor" (meaning there's little separation between stimulus and response) and start being a cool, responsible chooser—no matter what your genetic makeup, no matter how you were raised, no matter what your childhood experiences were or what the environment is. In your freedom to choose your response lies the power to achieve growth and happiness.

Imagine what might happen if you could get every person inside a company to act willingly on the belief "Quality begins with me. And I need to make my own decisions based on carefully selected principles and values." Proactivity cultivates this freedom. It subordinates your feelings to your values. You accept your feelings: "I'm frustrated, I'm angry, I'm upset. I accept those feelings; I don't deny or repress them. Now I know what needs to be done. I am responsible." That's the principle "I am *response-able*."

So on the continuum you go from being a victim to self-determining creative power through self-awareness of the power to choose your response to any condition or conditioning.

• Associated with *Habit 2: Begin with the End in Mind* is the endowment of *imagination* and *conscience*. If you are the programmer, write the program. Decide what you're going to do with the time, talent, and tools you have to work with: "Within my small circle of influence, I'm going to decide."

At the low end of the continuum is the sense of futility about goals, purposes, and improvement efforts. After all, if you are totally a victim, if you are a product of what has happened to you, then what can you realistically do about anything? So you wander through life hoping things will turn out well, that the environment may be positive, so you can have your daily bread and maybe some positive fruits.

At the other end is a sense of hope and purpose: "I have created the future in my mind. I can see it, and I can imagine what it will be like." Animals can't do that. They may instinctively gather nuts for the winter, but they can't create a nut-making machine, nor do they ask, "Why do I do nuts? Why don't I get someone else to gather nuts for me?" Only humans examine such questions. Only people have the capability to imagine a new course of action and pursue it conscientiously.

Why conscience? Because to be highly effective, your conscience must monitor all that you imagine, envision, and engineer. Those who attempt to exercise creativity without conscience inevitably create the unconscionable. At the very least, they exchange their creative talents for "canned goods," using their creativity—their applied imagination and visual affirmations—to win material things or social rewards. Then they become hopelessly imbalanced. They may speak the lines of the life balance script, but in reality their constitutions are written on the fleshy tablets of their spleen.

It is reaffirming to me to see that winners of the Academy Awards, for the most part, exhibit creativity with conscience. For example, Kevin Costner's *Dances with Wolves* made a beautiful statement about Native Americans. The academy knows that the film industry has enormous influence, and with that creative power must come conscientious social responsibility.

Practice using these two unique human capacities: first, see yourself going to the office this afternoon, or home tonight, and finding it in a terrible situation. The house is a total disaster. No one has done his or her job; all the commitments made have been unfulfilled. And you're tired and beat up.

Now, imagine yourself responding to that reality in a mature, wise, self-controlled manner. See the effect that has on someone else. You didn't confess their sins. You started to pitch in. You were cheerful, helpful, pleasant. And your behavior will prick the conscience of others and allow the consequences agreed upon to happen.

You just used two unique human capacities: *imagination and conscience*. You didn't rely on memory; if you had relied on memory or history, you might have lost your cool, made judgments of other people, and exacerbated conditions. Memory is built into your past responses to the same or similar stimuli. Memory ties you to your past. Imagination points you to your future. Your potential is unlimited, but to potentiate is to actualize your capabilities no matter what the conditions.

In the book *Man's Search for Meaning*, Viktor Frankl, the Austrian psychiatrist imprisoned in the death camps of Nazi Germany in World War II, tells how he exercised the power to choose his response to his terrible conditions. One day he was subjected to experiments on his body. And he discovered, "I have the power to choose." And he looked for meaning. He believed that if you have a meaning (purpose or cause), if you have a *why*, you can live with any *what*.

The development of his professional life came out of that one insight. He was raised in the Freudian tradition of psychic determinism. He learned it was a lie. It wasn't based on science. It came from the study of sick people—neurotics and psychotics—not from the study of healthy, creative, effective people. He didn't go to his memory, he went to his imagination and conscience.

You, too, can progress along the continuum from futility and old habits to faith, hope, and inner security through the exercise of conscience and imagination.

• Associated with *Habit 3: Put First Things First* is the endowment of *willpower*. At the low end of the continuum is the ineffective, flaky life of floating and coasting, avoiding responsibility and taking the easy way out, exercising little initiative or willpower. And at the top end is a highly disciplined life that focuses heavily on the highly important but not necessarily urgent activities of life. It's a life of leverage and influence.

You go from victim to creative resource, from futility to hope and anchorage, and from flaky to disciplined—Habits 1, 2, and 3. Habit 1 draws on self-awareness or self-knowledge; 2 draws on conscience and imagination; and 3 draws on willpower. These are unique human endowments that animals don't possess. On the continuum, you go from being driven by crises and having *can't* and *won't* power to being focused on the important but not necessarily urgent matters of your life and having the *willpower* to realize them.

FROM PRIMARY TO SECONDARY ENDOWMENTS

The exercise of primary human endowments empowers you to use the secondary endowments more effectively.

• Associated with *Habit 4: Think Win/Win* is the endowment of an *abundance mentality*. Why? Because your security comes from principles. Everything is seen through principles. When your spouse makes a mistake, you're not accusatory. Why? Your security does not come from your spouse's living up to your expectations. If your son, your husband, your friend, or your boss makes a mistake, you don't become accusatory, you look with compassion. Why? Your security does not come from them. It comes from within yourself. You're principle-centered.

As people become increasingly principle-centered, they love to share recognition and power. Why? It's not a limited pie. It's an ever-enlarging pie. The basic paradigm and assumption about limited resources is flawed. The great capabilities of people are hardly even tapped. The abundance mentality produces more profit, power, and recognition for everybody.

On the continuum, you go from a scarcity to an abundance mentality through feelings of intrinsic self-worth and a benevolent desire for mutual benefit.

• Associated with *Habit 5: Seek First to Understand, Then to Be Understood* is the endowment of *courage balanced with consideration*. Does it take courage and consideration to *not* be understood first? Think about it. Think about the problems you face. You tend to think, "You need to understand me, but you don't understand. I understand you, but you don't understand me. So let me tell you my story first, and then you can say what you want." And the other person says, "Okay, I'll try to understand." But the whole time they're "listening," they're preparing their reply. They're just pretending to listen, selectively listening. When you show your home movies or tell some chapter of your autobiography—"Let me tell you my experience"— the other person is tuned out unless he feels understood.

What happens when you truly listen to another person? The whole relationship is transformed: "Someone started listening to me, and they seemed to savor my words. They didn't agree or disagree, they just were listening, and I felt as if they were seeing how I saw the world. And in that process, I found myself listening to myself. I started to feel a worth in myself."

The root cause of almost all people problems is the basic communication problem—people do not listen with empathy. They listen from within their autobiography. They lack the skill and attitude of empathy. They need approval; they lack courage. Within their frame of reference, they say, "What can I do to please that person? He has this high need for control. Wait a minute, I'm the manager in control. I didn't come to listen—I came to tell. When I want your opinion, I'll give it to you." The ability to listen first requires restraint, respect, and reverence. And the ability to make yourself understood requires courage and consideration. On the continuum, you go from fight and flight instincts to mature two-way communication where courage is balanced with consideration.

• Associated with *Habit 6: Synergize* is the endowment of *creativity*—the creation of something. How? By yourself? No, through two respectful minds communicating, producing solutions that are far better than what either proposed originally. Most negotiation is positional bargaining and results at best in compromise. But when you get into synergistic communication, you leave position. You understand basic underlying needs and interests and find solutions to satisfy them both.

Two Harvard professors, Roger Fisher and William Ury, in their book *Getting to Yes*, outline a whole new approach to negotiation. Instead of assuming two opposing positions—"I want that window open." "No, closed." "No, open."—with occasional compromise (half-open half the time) they saw the possibility of synergy. "Why do you want it open?" "Well, I like the fresh air." "Why do you want it closed?" "I don't like the draft." "What can we do that would give the fresh air without the draft?" Now, two creative people who have respect for each other and who understand each other's needs might say, "Let's open the window in the next room. Let's rearrange the furniture. Let's open the top part of the window. Let's turn on the air-conditioning." They seek new alternatives because they are not defending positions.

Whenever there's a difference, say, "Let's go for a synergistic win/win. Let's listen to each other. What is your need?" "Well, I'm in just the mood for this kind of a movie. What would you like?" Maybe you can find a movie or some other activity that would satisfy both. And you get people thinking. And if you get the spirit of teamwork, you start to build a very powerful bond, an emotional bank account, and people are willing to subordinate their immediate wants for long-term relationships.

One of the most important commitments in a family or a business is never to bad-mouth. Always be loyal to those who are absent, if you want to retain those who are present. And if you have problems, go directly to the person to resolve them. If you refuse to bad-mouth someone behind his back to another person, what does that person know? When somebody bad-mouths him behind his back, you won't join in.

For example, during times of death, divorce, and remarriages, there are typically many strained feelings in families over the settlements. Family members who feel slighted or cheated often say nasty things about other family members. Think how much pain and anguish might be spared if members of the family would adhere to two basic principles: 1) People and relationships in our family are more important than things (people on their death bed never talk about spending more time at the office—they talk about relationships); and 2) When we have any difficulty or difference, we will go directly to the person. We are responsible for our own attitudes and behaviors, and we can choose our responses to this circumstance. With courage and consideration, we will communicate openly with each other and try to create win-win solutions.

On the continuum, you go from defensive communication to compromise transactions to synergistic and creative alternatives and transformations.

• Associated with *Habit 7: Sharpen the Saw* is the unique endowment of *continuous improvement or self-renewal* to overcome entropy. If you don't improve and renew yourself constantly, you'll fall into entropy, closed systems and styles. At one end of the continuum is entropy (everything breaks down), and at the other end is continuous improvement, innovation, and refinement.

My hope in revisiting the Seven Habits is that you will use the seven unique human endowments associated with them to bless and benefit the lives of many other people.

Chapter 3

THREE RESOLUTIONS

EVERY ORGANIZATION—and individual—struggles to gain and maintain alignment with core values, ethics, and principles. Whatever our professed personal and organizational beliefs, we all face restraining forces, opposition, and challenges, and these sometimes cause us to do things that are contrary to our stated missions, intentions, and resolutions.

We may think that we can change deeply imbedded habits and patterns simply by making new resolutions or goals—only to find that old habits die hard and that in spite of good intentions and social promises, familiar patterns carry over from year to year.

We often make two mistakes with regard to New Year's resolutions: *First, we don't have a clear knowledge of who we are.* Hence, our habits become our identity, and to resolve to change a habit is to threaten our security. We fail to see that we are not our habits. We can make and break our habits. We need not be a victim of conditions or conditioning. We can write our own script, choose our course, and control our own destiny.

Second, we don't have a clear picture of where we want to go; therefore our resolves are easily uprooted, and we then get discouraged and give up. Replacing a deeply imbedded bad habit with a good one involves much more than being temporarily "psyched up" over some simplistic success formula, such as "Think positively" or "Try harder." It takes deep understanding of self and of the principles and processes of growth and change. These include assessment, commitment, feedback, and follow-through.

We will soon break our resolutions if we don't regularly report our progress to somebody and get objective feedback on our performance. Accountability breeds *response-ability*. Commitment and involvement produce change. In training executives, we use a step-by-step, natural, progressive, sequential approach to change. In fact, we require executives to set goals and make commitments up front; teach and apply the material each month; and return and report their progress to each other.

If you want to overcome the pull of the past—those powerful restraining forces of habit, custom, and culture—to bring about desired change, count the costs and rally the necessary resources. In the space program, we see that tremendous thrust is needed to clear the powerful pull of the earth's gravity. So it is with breaking old habits.

Breaking deeply imbedded habits—such as procrastinating, criticizing, overeating, or oversleeping—involves more than a little wishing and willpower. Often our own resolve is not enough. We need reinforcing relationships—people and programs that hold us accountable and responsible.

Remember: *Response-ability* is the ability to choose our response to any circumstance or condition. When we are response-able, our commitment becomes more powerful than our moods or circumstances, and we keep the promises and resolutions we make. For example, if we put mind over mattress and arise early in the morning, we will earn our first victory of the day—*the daily private victory*—and gain a certain sense of self-mastery. We can then move on to more public victories. And as we deal well with each new challenge, we unleash within ourselves a fresh capacity to soar to new heights.

UNIVERSAL RESOLUTIONS

In our lives, there are powerful restraining forces at work to pull down any new resolution or initiative. Among those forces are 1) appetites and passions; 2) pride and pretension; and 3) aspiration and ambition. We can overcome these restraining forces by making and keeping the following three resolutions:

· *First, to overcome the restraining forces of appetites and passions, I resolve to exercise self-discipline and self-denial.* Whenever we over-indulge physical appetites and passions, we impair our mental processes and judgments as well as our social relationships. Our bodies are ecosystems, and if our economic or physical side is off balance, all other systems are affected.

That's why the habit of *sharpening the saw regularly* is so basic. The principles of temperance, consistency, and self-discipline become foundational to a person's whole life. Trust comes from trustworthiness—and that comes from competence and character. Intemperance adversely affects our judgment and wisdom.

I realize that some people are intemperate and still show greatness, even genius. But over time it catches up with them. Many among the "rich and famous" have lost fortunes and faith, success and effectiveness, because of intemperance. Either we control our appetites and passions or they control us.

Many corporations and cities have aging inventories and infrastructures; likewise, many executives have aging bodies, making it harder to get away with intemperance. With age the metabolism changes. Maintaining health requires more wisdom. The older we become, the more we are in the crosscurrents between the need for more self-discipline and temperance and the desire to let down and relax and indulge. We feel we've paid our dues and are therefore entitled to let go. But if we get permissive and indulgent with ourselves—overeating, staying up late, or not exercising—the quality of our personal lives and our professional work will be adversely affected.

If we become slaves to our stomachs, our stomachs soon control our mind and will. To knowingly take things into the body that are harmful or addicting is foolishness. More people in America die of overeating than of hunger. "I saw few die of hunger—of eating, a hundred thousand," observed Ben Franklin. When I overeat or over-indulge, I lose sensitivity to the needs of others, become angry with myself, and tend to take that anger out on others at the earliest provocation.

Many of us succumb to the longing for extra sleep, rest, and leisure. How many times do you set the alarm or your mind to get up early, knowing all of the things you have to do in the morning, anxious to get the day organized right, to have a calm and orderly breakfast, to have an unhurried and peaceful preparation before leaving for work?

But when the alarm goes off, your good resolves dissolve. It's a battle of mind versus mattress! Often the mattress wins. You find yourself getting up late, then beginning a frantic rush to get dressed, organized, and fed and be off. In the rush, you grow impatient and insensitive to others. Nerves get frayed, tempers are short. And all because of sleeping in.

A chain of unhappy events and sorry consequences follows not keeping the first resolution of the day—to get up at a certain time. That day may begin and end in defeat. The extra sleep is hardly ever worth it. In fact, considering the above, such sleep is terribly tiring and exhausting.

What a difference if you organize and arrange your affairs the night before to get to bed at a reasonable time. I find that the last hour before retiring is the best time to plan and prepare for the next day. Then, when the alarm goes off, you get up and prepare properly for the day. Such an early morning private victory gives you a sense of conquering, overcoming, mastering—and this sense propels you to conquer more public challenges during the day. Success begets success. Starting a day with an early victory over self leads to more victories.

• *Second, to overcome the restraining forces of pride and pretension, I resolve to work on character and competence.* Socrates said, "The greatest way to live with honor in this world is to be what we pretend to be"—to be, in reality, what we want others to think we are. Much of the world is image conscious, and the social mirror is powerful in creating our sense of who we are. The pressure to appear powerful, successful, and fashionable causes some people to become manipulative.

When you are living in harmony with your core values and principles, you can be straightforward, honest, and up-front. And nothing is more disturbing to people who are full of trickery and duplicity than straightforward honesty—that's the one thing they can't deal with.

I've been on an extended media tour with my book, *The Seven Habits of Highly Effective People,* and I've become aware of how everyone is very anxious about the entertainment value of the program. Recently I was in San Francisco, and I thought I would make my interview more controversial by getting into the political arena. But my comments threw the whole conversation off on a tangent. All the call-ins commented on political points. I lost the power to present my own theme and represent my own material.

Whenever we indulge appetites and passions, we are rather easily seduced by pride and pretension. We then start making appearances, playing roles, and mastering manipulative techniques.

If our definition or concept of ourselves comes from what others think of us—from the social mirror—we will gear our lives to their wants and their expectations; and the more we live to meet the expectations of others, the more weak, shallow, and insecure we become. A junior executive, for example, may desire to please his superiors, colleagues, and subordinates, but he discovers that these groups demand different things of him. He feels that if he is true to one, he may offend the other. So he begins to play games and put on appearances to get along or to get by, to please or appease. In the long run he discovers that by trying to become "all things to all people," he eventually becomes nothing to everyone. He is found out for who and what he is. He then loses self-respect and the respect of others.

If a junior executive neglects her professional development and continuing education, she can easily and quickly become obsolete in a world changing at dizzying rates. Hoping to "rest" for a season after years of rigorous schooling, she might opt to enjoy a more pleasurable, less demanding life-style. The seasons soon multiply, however, and with the passing of time she finds that she has less intellectual vigor, less self-discipline, and less confidence, and she begins to suffer the consequences of obsolescence, a hardening of the mental arteries. To her shock, when she is called to perform when it counts, she is hard-pressed to meet the rising expectations of her boss, notwithstanding her increased time on the job.

Effective people lead their lives and manage their relationships around principles; ineffective people attempt to manage their time around priorities and their tasks around goals. Think effectiveness with people; efficiency with things.

When we examine anger, hatred, envy, jealousy, pride and prejudice—or any negative emotions or passions—we often discover that at their root lies the desire to be accepted by, approved of, and esteemed by others. We then seek a short cut to the top. But the bottom line is that there is no short cut to lasting success. The law of the harvest still applies, in spite of all the talk of "how to beat the system."

Several years ago a student visited me in my office when I was a faculty member at the Marriott School of Management, Brigham Young University. He asked me how he was doing in my class. After developing some rapport, I confronted him directly: "You didn't really come in to find out how you are doing in the class. You came in to find out how I think you are doing. You know how you are doing in the class far better than I do, don't you?"

He said that he did, so I asked him, "How are you doing?" He admitted that he was just trying to get by. He had a host of reasons and excuses for not studying as he ought, for cramming and taking short cuts. He came in to see if it was working.

If people play roles and pretend long enough, giving in to their vanity and pride, they will gradually deceive themselves. They will be buffeted by conditions, threatened by circumstances and other people. They will then fight to maintain their false front. But if they come to accept the truth about themselves, following the laws and principles of the harvest, they will gradually develop a more accurate concept of themselves.

The effort to be fashionable puts one on a treadmill that seems to go faster and faster, almost like chasing a shadow. Appearances alone will never satisfy; therefore, to build our security on fashions, possessions, or status symbols may prove to be our undoing. Edwin Hubbell Chapin said: "Fashion is the science of appearances, and it inspires one with the desire to *seem* rather than to *be*."

Certainly we should be interested in the opinions and perceptions of others so that we might be more effective with them, but we should refuse to accept their opinions as facts and then act or react accordingly.

• *Third, to overcome the restraining forces of unbridled aspiration and ambition, I resolve to dedicate my talents and resources to noble purposes and to provide service to others*. If people are "looking out for number one" and "what's in it for me," they will have no sense of stewardship—no sense of being an agent for worthy principles, purposes, and causes. They become a law unto themselves, a princi*pal*.

They may talk the language of stewardship, but they will always figure out a way to promote their own agenda. They may be dedicated and hardworking, but they are not focused on stewardship—the idea that you don't *own* anything, that you give your life to higher principles, causes, and purposes. Rather, they are focused on power, wealth, fame, position, dominion, and possessions.

The ethical person looks at every economic transaction as a test of his or her moral stewardship. That's why humility is the mother of all other virtues—because it promotes stewardship. Then everything else that is good will work through you. But if you get into pride—into "my will, my agenda, my wants"—then you must rely totally upon your own strengths. You're not in touch with what Jung calls "the collective unconscious"—the power of the larger ethos that unleashes energy through your work.

Aspiring people seek their own glory and are deeply concerned with their own agenda. They may even regard their own spouse or children as possessions and try to wrest from them the kind of behavior that will win them more popularity and esteem in the eyes of others. Such possessive love is destructive. Instead of being agents or stewards they interpret everything in life in terms of "what it will do for me." Everybody then becomes either a competitor or conspirator. Their relationships, even intimate ones, tend to be competitive rather than cooperative. They use various methods of manipulation—threats, fear, bribery, pressure, deceit, and charm—to achieve their ends.

Until people have the spirit of service, they might say they love a companion, company, or cause, but they often despise the demands these make on their lives. Double-mindedness, having two conflicting motives or interests, inevitably sets us at war with ourselves—and an internal civil war often breaks out into war with others. The opposite of double-mindedness is self-unity or integrity. We achieve integrity through the dedication of ourselves to selfless service of others.

IMPLICATIONS FOR PERSONAL GROWTH

Unless we control our appetites, we will not be in control of our passions and emotions. We will instead become victims of our passions, seeking or aspiring our own wealth, dominion, prestige, and power.

I once tried to counsel a junior executive to be more committed to higher principles. It appeared futile. Then I began to realize that I was asking him to conquer the third temptation before he had conquered the first. It was like expecting a child to walk before crawl. So I changed the approach and encouraged him first to discipline his body. We then got great results.

If we conquer some basic appetites first, we will have the power to make good on higher level resolutions later. For example, many people would experience a major transformation if they would maintain normal weight through a healthy diet and exercise program. They would not only look better, they would also feel better, treat others better, and increase their capacity to do the important but not necessarily urgent things they long to do.

Until you can say "I am my master," you cannot say "I am your servant." In other words, we might profess a service ethic, but under pressure or stress we might be controlled by a particular passion or appetite. We lose our temper. We become jealous, envious, lustful, or slothful. Then we feel guilty. We make promises and break them, make resolutions and break them. We gradually lose faith in our own capacity to keep any promises. Despite our ethic to be the "servant of the people," we become the servant or slave of whatever masters us.

This reminds me of the plea of Richard Rich to Thomas More in the play, *A Man for All Seasons*. Richard Rich admired More's honesty and integrity and wanted to be employed by him. He pleaded, "Employ me."

More answered, "No."

Again Rich pleaded, "Employ me!" and again the answer was no.

Then Rich made this pitiful yet endearing promise: "I would be steadfast!"

Sir Thomas, knowing what mastered Richard Rich, answered, "Richard, you couldn't answer for yourself even so far as tonight," meaning, "You might profess to be faithful now, but all it will take is a different circumstance, the right bribe or pressure, and you will be so controlled by your ambition and pride that you could not be faithful to me."

Sir Thomas More's prognosis came to pass that very night, for Richard Rich betrayed him!

The key to growth is to learn to make promises and to keep them. Self-denial is an essential element in overcoming all three temptations. "One secret act of self-denial, one sacrifice of inclination to duty, is worth all the mere good thoughts, warm feelings, passionate prayers, in which idle men indulge themselves," said John Henry

Newman. "The worst education which teaches self-denial is better than the best which teaches everything else and not that," said Sterling.

Making and keeping these three universal resolutions will accelerate our self-development and, potentially, increase our influence with others.

Chapter 4

PRIMARY GREATNESS

IN HIS WORK AND WRITINGS, Erich Fromm has observed that self-alienation is largely a fruit of how oriented we are to the human personality market, to selling ourselves to others.

He notes: "Today we come across an individual who behaves like an automaton, who does not know or understand himself, and the only person that he knows is the person that he is supposed to be, whose meaningless chatter has replaced communicative speech, whose synthetic smile has replaced genuine laughter, and whose sense of dull despair has taken the place of genuine pain."

Positive personality traits, while often essential for success, constitute secondary greatness. To focus on personality before character is to try to grow the leaves without the roots.

If we consistently use personality techniques and skills to enhance our social interactions, we may truncate the vital character base. We simply can't have the fruits without the roots. Private victory precedes public victory. Self-mastery and self-discipline are the roots of good relationships with others.

If we use human influence strategies and tactics to get other people to do what we want, we may succeed in the short-term; but over time our duplicity and insincerity will breed distrust. Everything we do will be perceived as manipulative. We may have the "right" rhetoric, style, and even intention, but without trust we won't achieve primary greatness or lasting success. To focus on technique is like cramming your way through school. You sometimes get by, perhaps even get good grades, but if you don't pay the price, day in and day out, you never achieve true mastery of the subjects. Could you ever "cram" on the farm—forget to plant in the spring, play all summer, and then race in the fall to bring in the harvest? No, because the farm is a natural system. You must pay the price and follow the process. You reap what you sow; there is no short cut.

The law of the harvest also operates in long-term human relationships. In a social or academic system, you may get by if you learn how to "play the game." You may make favorable first impressions through charm; you may win through intimidation. But secondary personality traits alone have no permanent worth in long-term relationships. If there isn't deep integrity and fundamental character strength, true motives will eventually surface and human relationships will fail.

Many people with secondary greatness—that is, social status, position, fame, wealth, or talent—lack primary greatness or goodness of character. And this void is evident in every long-term relationship they have, whether it is with a business associate, a spouse, a friend, or a teenage child. It is character that communicates most eloquently. As Emerson once put it, "What you are shouts so loud in my ears I cannot hear what you say."

Of course, people may have character strength but lack key communication skills—and that undoubtedly affects the quality of their relationships as well. But in the last analysis, what we are communicates far more eloquently than anything we say or do.

How We See Ourselves

The view we have of ourselves affects not only our attitudes and behaviors, but also our views of other people. In fact, until we take how we see ourselves—and how we see others—into account, we will be unable to understand how others see and feel about themselves and their world. Unaware, we will project our intentions on their behavior and think ourselves objective.

If the vision we have of ourselves comes from the social mirror—from the opinions, perceptions, and paradigms of the people around us—our view of ourselves is like a reflection in the crazy mirror at the carnival. Specific data is disjointed and out of proportion:

"You're never on time."

"Why can't you ever keep things in order?"

"This is so simple. Why can't you understand it?"

Such data is often more projection than reflection. It projects the concerns and character weaknesses of people giving the input, rather than accurately reflecting what we are.

When the basic source of a person's definition of himself is the social mirror, he may confuse the mirror reflection with his real self; in fact, he may begin to believe and accept the image in the mirror, even rejecting other, more positive views of himself unless they show the distortions he has come to accept.

From time to time I conduct a little experiment. I ask people to list others' perceptions of them and then compare these with their own self-concept. Typically more than half are shocked to realize that to a large degree, their self-image has come from the social mirror. It has come slowly, gradually, imperceptibly. And unless it changes, it will severely handicap them for life.

The antidote for a poisoned self-image is the affirmation of your worth and potential by another person. In the musical *Man of La Mancha*, Don Quixote slowly changes the self-concept of the prostitute by constantly, unconditionally affirming her. When she starts to see herself differently, she starts to act differently. He even gives her a new name, Dulcinea, so that she will ever be reminded of her new identity and potential.

To affirm a person's worth or potential, you may have to look at him with the eye of faith and treat him in terms of his potential, not his behavior. Goethe put it this way: "Treat a man as he is, and he will remain as he is; treat a man as he can and should be, and he will become as he can and should be." This isn't to say that we trust him unconditionally, but it does mean that we treat him respectfully and trust him conditionally.

Some people say that you have to like yourself before you can like others. Okay, but if you don't know yourself, if you don't control yourself, if you don't have mastery over yourself, it's very hard to like yourself, except in some superficial way.

Real self-respect comes from dominion over self, from true independence and win-win interdependence. If our motives, words, and actions come from human relations techniques (the personality ethic) rather than from our own inner core (the character ethic), others will sense that insecurity or duplicity. We simply won't be able to create and sustain effective, win-win relationships.

The place to begin building any relationship is inside ourselves, inside our circle of influence, our own character.* As we become independent—proactive, centered in correct principles, value-driven, and able to organize and execute around the priorities in our life with integrity—we can choose to become interdependent: capable of building rich, enduring, productive relationships with other people.

ACUTE AND CHRONIC PAIN

Although our relationships with other people open up tremendous possibilities for increased productivity, service, contribution, growth, and learning, they may also cause us the greatest pain and frustration—and we're very aware of that pain because it's acute.

We may live for years with chronic pain caused by a lack of vision, leadership, or management in our personal lives. We may feel vaguely uneasy and uncomfortable and occasionally take steps to ease the pain; yet because the pain is chronic, we get used to it, gradually learning to live with it.

But when we have problems in our relationships with other people, we're very aware of the pain—it's often intense and acute, and we want it to go away. That's when we try to treat the symptoms with quick-fix techniques—the Band-Aid adhesives of the personality ethic. We don't understand that the acute pain is an outgrowth of a deeper, chronic problem. And until we stop treating the symptoms and start treating the problem, our efforts will be counterproductive. We will only obscure the chronic pain even more.

Personal effectiveness is the foundation of interpersonal effectiveness. Private victory precedes public victory. Strength of character and independence form the foundation for authentic, effective interaction with others.

Dag Hammarskjöld, past secretary-general of the United Nations, once made a profound, far-reaching statement: "It is more noble to give yourself completely to one individual than to labor diligently for the salvation of the masses."

* For a complimentary audiotape by Stephen R. Covey on programming oneself for change, please call 1-800-255-0777. There is no cost to you.

In other words, I could devote eight, ten, or twelve hours a day, five, six, or seven days a week, to the thousands of people and projects "out there" and still not have a deep, meaningful relationship with my own spouse, teenage son, or close working associate. And it would take more nobility of character—more humility, courage, and strength—to rebuild that one relationship than it would to continue putting in all those hours for all those people and causes.

Many problems in organizations stem from poor relationships at the very top—between two partners in a firm, between the owner and president of a company, between the president and an executive vice president. And it takes more nobility of character to confront and resolve those issues than it does to work diligently for the many people and projects "out there."

THREE CHARACTER TRAITS

The following three character traits are essential to primary greatness:

· *Integrity.* I define integrity as the value we place on ourselves. As we clearly identify our values and proactively organize and execute around our priorities on a daily basis, we develop self-awareness and self-value by making and keeping meaningful promises and commitments. If we can't make and keep commitments to ourselves as well as to others, our commitments become meaningless. We know it, and others know it. They sense our duplicity and become guarded.

· *Maturity.* I define maturity as the balance between courage and consideration. If a person can express his feelings and convictions with courage balanced with consideration for the feelings and convictions of another person, he is mature. If he lacks internal maturity and emotional strength, he might try to borrow strength from his position, power, credentials, seniority, or affiliations.

While courage may focus on getting bottom-line results, consideration deals more with the long-term welfare of other stake holders. In fact, the basic mission of mature management is to increase the standard of living and the quality of life for all stake holders.

· *Abundance Mentality.* Our thinking is that there is plenty out there for everybody. This abundance mentality flows out of a deep sense of personal worth and security. It results in sharing recognition, profits, and responsibility. It opens up creative new options and alternatives. It turns personal joy and fulfillment outward. It recognizes unlimited possibilities for positive interaction, growth, and development.

Most people are deeply scripted in the scarcity mentality. They see life as a finite pie: if someone gets a big piece of the pie, it means less for everybody else. It's the zero-sum paradigm of life. People with a scarcity mentality have a hard time sharing recognition, credit, power, or profit. They also have a tough time being genuinely happy for the success of other people—even, and sometimes especially, members of their own family or close friends and associates. It's almost as if something were being taken from them when someone else receives special recognition or success.

A character rich in integrity, maturity, and the abundance mentality has a genuineness that goes far beyond technique. Your character is constantly radiating, communicating. From it, people come to trust or distrust you. If your life runs hot and cold, if you're both caustic and kind, if your private performance doesn't square with your public performance, people won't open up to you, even if they want and need your love or help. They won't feel safe enough to expose their opinions and tender feelings.

INSIDE-OUT VS. OUTSIDE-IN

Lasting solutions to problems, lasting happiness and success, come from the inside out. What results from the outside in is unhappy people who feel victimized and immobilized, focused on all the weaknesses of other people and the circumstances they feel are responsible for their own stagnant condition.

Members of our family have lived in three of the world's trouble spots—South Africa, Israel, and Ireland—and I believe that the source of the continuing problems in each of these places is the dominant social paradigm of outside-in.

Inside-out suggests that if you want to have a happy marriage, be the kind of person who generates positive energy and sidesteps negative energy. If you want to have a more cooperative teenager, be a more understanding parent. If you want to have more freedom or more latitude in your job, be more responsible and make a greater contribution.

Inside-out suggests that if we want to develop the trust that results in win-win agreements and synergistic solutions, we must control our own lives and subordinate short-term desires to higher purposes and principles. Private victories precede public victories. Making and keeping promises to ourselves precedes making and keeping promises to others. And it's a continuing process, an upward spiral of growth that leads to progressively higher forms of independence and interdependence.

The deep, fundamental problems we face cannot be solved on the superficial level on which they were created. We need a new level of thinking—based on principles of effective management—to solve these deep concerns. We need a principle-centered, character-based, "inside-out" approach.

Inside-out means to start first with self—to start with the most *inside* part of self—with your paradigms, your character, and your motives. So if you want to *have* a happy marriage, *be* the kind of person who generates positive energy and sidesteps negative energy. If you want to *have* a more pleasant, cooperative teenager, *be* a more understanding, empathic, consistent, loving parent. If you want to *have* more freedom, more latitude in your job, *be* a more responsible, helpful, contributing employee. If you want to be trusted, *be* trustworthy. If you want the secondary greatness of public recognition, focus first on primary greatness of character.

The inside-out approach says that private victories precede public victories, that making and keeping promises to ourselves precedes making and keeping promises to others. Inside-out is a continuing process of renewal, an upward spiral of growth that leads to progressively higher forms of responsible independence and effective interdependence.

In all of my experience, I have never seen lasting solutions to problems, lasting happiness and success, come from the outside in. Outside-in approaches result in unhappy people who feel victimized and immobilized, who focus on the weaknesses of other people and the circumstances they feel are responsible for their own stagnant situation. I've seen unhappy marriages, where each spouse wants the other to change, where each is confessing the other's "sins," where each is trying to shape up the other. I've seen labor-management disputes where people spend tremendous amounts of time and energy trying to create legislation that would force people to act as if trust were really there.

The primary source of continuing problems in many companies

and cultures has been the dominant social paradigm of outside-in. Everyone is convinced that the problem is "out there" and if "they" (others) would "shape up" or suddenly "ship out" of existence, the problem would be solved.

The principles of effectiveness are deeply scripted within us, in our conscience and in our quiet reflection on life experience. To recognize and develop them and to use them in meeting our deepest concerns, we need to think differently, to shift our paradigms to a new, deeper, "inside-out" level.

EDUCATING AND OBEYING THE CONSCIENCE

The key to working from the inside out, the paradigm of primary greatness, is to educate and obey the conscience—that unique human endowment that senses congruence or disparity with correct principles and lifts us toward them.

Just as the education of nerve and sinew is vital to the athlete and education of the mind is vital to the scholar, education of the conscience is vital to primary greatness. Training the conscience, however, requires even more discipline. It requires honest living, reading inspiring literature, and thinking noble thoughts. Just as junk food and lack of exercise can ruin an athlete's condition, things that are obscene, crude, or pornographic can breed an inner darkness that numbs our highest sensibilities and substitutes the social conscience of "Will I be found out?" for the natural conscience of "What is right and wrong?"

The education of conscience begins in the family in one's earliest months and continues there indefinitely through parental example and precept. But when a person becomes converted to the need, he seeks to advance that education himself. He finds that moving along the upward spiral involves learning, committing, and doing—and learning, committing, and doing again at increasingly higher levels.

People with primary greatness have a sense of stewardship about everything in life, including their time, talents, money, possessions, relationships, family, and even their bodies. They recognize the need to use all their resources for positive purposes, and they expect to be held accountable.

People with primary greatness return kindness for offense, patience for impatience. They bring out the best in those around them by seeking to bless when being cursed, to turn the other cheek, to go the second mile, to forgive and forget, to move on in life with cheerfulness, believing in the potential goodness of people and the eventual triumph of truth.

The moment a person attempts to become his own advocate, seeking to defend or justify himself or to return in kind the treatment he receives, he becomes caught up in the exchange of negative energy. He and his enemy are then on the same turf, and they will either fight or flee in such destructive ways as manipulation, violence, withdrawal, indifference, litigation, or political battles.

As we give grace to others, we receive more grace ourselves. As we affirm people and show a fundamental belief in their capacity to grow and improve, as we bless them even when they are cursing or judging us—we build primary greatness into our personality and character.

BUILD ON THE FOUNDATION

You can't have empowerment without first having trust. If you don't trust the people you are working with, then you must use control rather than empowerment. If you do trust them and have performance agreements with them, you can work toward empowerment and alignment of structure and systems. In aligned organizations, everything serves to help the individual be productive and effective in meeting the objectives of the win-win performance agreement. If there is misalignment of structure and systems, you will not have empowerment or trust.

In my seminars I often ask managers, "How many of you have been trained in empowerment or participative management?" Most people raise their hands. Then I ask, "And what happens when you try to empower people when there is no trust?" They all say, "It just doesn't work. You have to go back to a hard MBO approach or some other control approach to keep a semblance of order in the work environment."

Then I ask them, "Why continue to focus then on management training? You give the illusion of solving the problem when you're just treating the symptoms—you may get temporary relief from acute pain, but you aren't treating the chronic problem."

And then I ask about the organizational level: "How many of you see the big solution is to get reorganized, to get alignment?" Half raise their hands. "How many see the big solution is to redo the systems?" One-third raise their hands. Then I ask, "What are the consequences of working at those levels when you haven't worked at the personal and interpersonal levels?" And the answer: "Disaster."

The consensus is that we're working with an ecosystem, a whole environment. And if you approach a problem with something other than principle-centered leadership on all four levels, your efforts will be "necessary but insufficient."

If owners and managers lack character and competence, they won't give power and profit and recognition to others. If they do, they feel that they are at risk personally. They must use the inside-out approach and first work on character and competence to build trust so that they can have empowerment—then they can solve the problems with structure and systems.

Until individual managers have done the inside-out work, they won't solve the fundamental problems of the organization, nor will they truly empower others, even though they might use the language of empowerment. Their personality and character will manifest itself eventually.

We must work on character and competence to solve structural and systemic problems. Remember: Work first on the programmer if you want to improve the program. People produce the strategy, structure, systems, and styles of the organization. These are the arms and hands of the minds and hearts of people.

Chapter 5

A BREAK WITH THE PAST

ALMOST EVERY SIGNIFICANT BREAKTHROUGH is the result of a courageous break with traditional ways of thinking.

In scientific circles, dramatic transformations, revolutions of thought, great leaps of understanding, and sudden liberations from old limits are called "paradigm shifts." These offer distinctively new ways of thinking about old problems.

The word *paradigm* is from the Greek word *paradigma*: a pattern or map for understanding and explaining certain aspects of reality. While a person may make small improvements by developing new skills, quantum leaps in performance and revolutionary advances in technology require new maps, new paradigms, new ways of thinking about and seeing the world.

For example, some 500 years ago people had a certain map that reflected their understanding of the world at that time. It wasn't changed until an expert navigator and courageous seaman, Christopher Columbus (1451–1506), challenged the conventional wisdom by sailing due west in hopes of discovering a new route to the Indies. Although he failed to discover the Indies, he certainly changed the map, the paradigm, of the world. And his break-with resulted in a most significant breakthrough in world history.

Once Columbus was invited to a banquet, where he was assigned the most honorable place at the table. A shallow courtier who was meanly jealous of him asked abruptly: "Had you not discovered the Indies, are there not other men in Spain who would have been capable of the enterprise?"

Columbus made no reply but took an egg and invited the company to make it stand on end. They all attempted, but in vain; whereupon he tapped it on the table, denting one end, and left it standing.

"We all could have done it that way!" the courtier accused.

"Yes, if you had only known how," retorted Columbus. "And once I showed you the way to the New World, nothing was easier than to follow it."

With the 500-year anniversary of the voyage of Columbus, I celebrate with all Americans the spirit of exploration and renaissance—a spirit that distinguishes the best organizations in the world.

A SET OF PRINCIPLES AT THE CENTER

Another renaissance man, Nicolaus Copernicus (1473–1543), developed a new map for the stars, as Columbus had developed a new map of the seas.

At the time, astronomers generally accepted the theory of Egyptian astronomer Ptolemy—that the earth was the center of the universe and had no motion. Copernicus proved that the earth moved rapidly through space and that the sun was at the center. Although his sun-at-the-center paradigm was considered scientific heresy by some and spiritual blasphemy by others, Copernicus bravely broke with tradition and started a revolution that marks the beginning of modern science.

In his writings *De Revolutionibus Orbium Caolestium*, Copernicus noted, "To ascribe movement to the earth must seem absurd to those who for centuries have consented that the earth is placed immovably as the central point of the universe. But I shrink not from any man's criticism. By long and frequent observations and by following a set of fixed principles, I have discovered not only that the earth moves, but also that the orders and magnitudes of all stars and spheres, nay, the heavens themselves, are so bound together that nothing in any part thereof could be moved from its place without producing confusion in all the parts of the Universe as a whole."

Throughout history leaders have used various models and "maps" to manage people. These range from the primitive "carrot-and-stick" paradigm, where rewards and punishments are used to generate productivity, to more sophisticated human relations and human resource models based on influence strategies and involvement techniques.

My hope is to help bring about a paradigm shift in management training by focusing not just on another map, but on a new compass, "Principle-Centered Leadership." Using this paradigm, leaders can expect to transform their organizations and their people by communicating vision, clarifying purposes, making behavior congruent with belief, and aligning procedures with principles, roles, and goals. People may then achieve a heightened sense of personal contribution through their commitment to the organization's mission.

Often we can't embrace a new paradigm until we let go of the old one. Likewise, until we drop unwarranted assumptions about people, we can't expect to bring about lasting improvements in our organizations: we can't magnify our human resources using manipulative management techniques any more than we can repair Humpty Dumpty with more horses and more men. Nevertheless, in this topsy-turvy world, matters often get turned around. We confuse efficiency with effectiveness, expediency with priority, imitation with innovation, cosmetics with character, or pretense with competence.

Ultimately the leadership style one adopts springs from one's core ideas and feelings about the nature of man. Whatever a person has at the center of his life—work or pleasure, friend or enemy, family or possessions, spouse or self, principles or passions—will affect his perception. And it is perception that governs beliefs, attitudes, and behaviors.

I endorse the idea "I teach them correct principles, and they govern themselves" as an enlightened approach to management and leadership. Individuals and organizations ought to be guided and governed by a set of proven principles. These are the natural laws and governing social values that have gradually come through every great society, every responsible civilization, over the centuries. They surface in the form of values, ideas, norms, and teachings that uplift, ennoble, fulfill, empower, and inspire people.

Like the paradigm shift in science, this shift in management pattern can completely change one's outlook on the world and eventually transform one's organization. While managers must focus on the bottom line, leaders must look to the top line for clear vision and direction.

Where there is no vision, says the proverb, people perish. That's because they select goals and begin pursuing them—climbing the proverbial ladder of success—before they define mission and clarify values. Consequently, upon reaching the top rung, they often discover to their dismay that the ladder is leaning against the wrong wall.

Processes for Releasing Potential

In physics, Newton neatly packaged the laws of force and gravity into an all-inclusive theory, adequate for his day. But the enormous energy locked within the atom remained untapped until Albert Einstein (1879–1955) found the key. His principle of relativity treated matter and energy as exchangeable, not distinct, and revolutionized scientific thought with new conceptions of time, space, mass, motion, and gravitation.

In his *Autobiographical Notes*, Einstein writes: "Newton, forgive me. You found the only way that, in your day, was at all possible for a man of the highest powers of intellect and creativity. The concepts that you created still dominate the way we think in physics, although we now know that they must be replaced by others further removed from the sphere of immediate experience if we want to try for a more profound understanding of the way things are interrelated."

Of course, when the tiny atom was split, enormous energy and power were unleashed. Likewise, the aim of any human resource development program ought to be to release the tremendous creative power and potential of people by involving them in a meaningful change and development process.

Principle-centered leadership suggests that the highest level of human motivation is a sense of personal contribution. It views people as the most valuable organizational assets—as stewards of certain resources—and stewardship as the key to discovering, developing, and managing all other assets. Each person is recognized as a free agent, capable of immense achievement, not as a victim or pawn limited by conditions or conditioning.

The training design that matches this paradigm is process-, not product-, oriented. The organizational development process is first, to gather and diagnose the data; second, to select priorities, values, and objectives; third, to identify and evaluate alternatives; fourth, to plan and decide action steps; and fifth, to compare results with original goals and objectives.

The following development process should be an integral part of any ongoing training program: First, capture the content of the material, the essence of what is presented—seeking first to understand the basic principles. Second, expand on what you have learned—adding your own ideas and thoughts. Third, teach the material—sharing what you have learned with others to increase understanding, to create a common vocabulary for change, and to unlock the perceptions that others have of you. Fourth, apply the principles—putting them to the test in your immediate circumstances. And fifth, monitor the results.

All real growth is characterized by this step-by-step developmental process. When individuals are trained in management principles through this process, they are liberated from old limits, old habit patterns, and are increasingly motivated and directed from within. And when people in organizations are thus trained, they find ways to make their structure, systems and style increasingly congruent with their mission, values, roles, and goals.

PROGRAMS FOR BREAKING BARRIERS

Pilot Chuck Yeager (1923–   ) launched an era of supersonic flight on October 14, 1947, when he cracked the sound barrier and its "invisible brick wall." Some prominent scientists had "hard data" that the barrier was impenetrable. Others direly predicted that both pilot and plane would disintegrate at Mach 1 or that the pilot would lose his voice, revert in age, or be severely buffeted. Notwithstanding, on that historic day Yeager attained an air speed of 700 miles per hour (Mach 1.06) in his Bell Aviation X-1 plane. Three weeks later he streaked to Mach 1.35; six years later he flew at an incredible 1,612 miles per hour (Mach 2.44), putting to rest the myth of an impenetrable barrier.

In his autobiography he writes: "The faster I got, the smoother the ride. Suddenly the Mach needle began to fluctuate. It went up to .965 Mach—then tipped right off the scale. I thought I was seeing things! We were flying supersonic, and it was as smooth as a baby's bottom: Grandma could be sitting up there sipping lemonade. I was thunderstruck. After all the anxiety, after all the anticipation, breaking the sound barrier was really a let-down. The sonic barrier, the unknown, was just a poke through Jell-O, a perfectly paved speedway. Later I realized that this mission had to end in a let-down because the real barrier wasn't in the sky, but in our knowledge and experience of supersonic flight."

Having broken the "sound barrier," we yet face what many consider an even more imposing obstacle to progress—the "human barrier." For many managers today, breaking the "human barrier" or status quo performance is as difficult as breaking the "sound barrier" was for aeronautical engineers four decades ago.

Why? Because people are often seen as limitations, if not liabilities, rather than advantages and assets. Thus low performance is often institutionalized in the structure and systems, procedures and processes, of the organization. Some executives pilot their single-engine, propeller-driven firms at slow speeds and low altitudes, cocksure that anything smacking of high performance would cause them to lose control and crash.

Meanwhile, a few well-trained and courageous managers are breaking the mythical human barrier and proving that gains in human performance of 500 percent—not just 5 percent—are possible, without anyone losing his voice, reverting to adolescence, or experiencing violent buffeting. In fact, people in high-performing organizations tend to be much healthier and happier. Because they are treated as the most valuable resource of the organization, they assist each other in making quantum leaps in quality and productivity. They also seek training in the principles and practices of supersonic management and have simple faith in the soaring potential of their people.

Training and development programs should evolve naturally from the company's vision, mission, and principles. Programs should attempt to empower people to soar, to sail, to step forward bravely into the unknown, being guided more by imagination than memory, and ultimately to reach beyond their fears and past failures. Many individuals and companies need to make a quantum leap in performance, a healthy change of habits, a major shift in patterns; otherwise it's business as usual—and that's simply not cutting it anymore.

OVERCOMING THE PULL OF THE PAST

To succeed at breaking old habits and making new ones, learn how to handle the restraining forces and harness the driving forces to achieve the daily private victory.

Overcoming the pull of the past is in large part a matter of having clear identity and strong purpose—of knowing who you are and what you want to accomplish. Poor performance can often be attributed to poor prioritization and organization. Weak resolve is easily uprooted by emotion, mood, and circumstance.

Highly effective people carry their agenda with them. Their schedule is their servant, not their master. They organize weekly, adapt daily. However, they are not capricious in changing their plan. They exercise discipline and concentration and do not submit to moods and circumstances. They schedule blocks of prime time for important planning, projects, and creative work. They work on less important and less demanding activities when their fatigue level is higher. They avoid handling paper more than once and avoid touching paperwork unless they plan to take action on it.

I define discipline as the ability to make and keep promises and to honor commitments. It's the key to overcoming the pull of the past. If we begin small, we can gradually strengthen our sense of personal honor and build our capacity to make and keep large promises. Eventually our sense of personal honor becomes stronger than our moods. We will then make promises sparingly because we keep the ones we make.

It often helps to write commitments down and keep them in front of us. I recently developed my own tool for doing that—the Seven Habits Organizer. Recording our roles and goals strengthens our resolve and reminds us to budget time and other resources to fulfill promises.*

You might start this process by promising to get up at a certain time in the morning, regardless of how you feel. Next, promise that you will use that first waking hour in a very profitable way—planning and preparing for the day. And then do it. You will find that there is enormous power in the principle of keeping promises and honoring commitments. It leads to strong self-esteem and personal integrity, the foundation of all true success.

Three Great Forces

In astronautics we learn that more power and energy is expended during lift-off and in clearing the earth's gravity than in navigating a million miles and returning again to earth.

* If you would like a free one-month supply of weekly worksheets from the Seven Habits Organizer, please call 1-800-255-0777.

Similarly, we expend more effort and energy in starting a new behavior. Old habits exert a powerful pull. We may one day resolve to break the habit of overeating, for example, only to renew the resolve the very next day. We may promise to stop procrastinating by writing those overdue letters and getting at those important but not urgent projects, only to break the resolve and start the circular, self-defeating habit of making resolutions only to break them again. We may then begin to wonder if it's worth making any commitments.

How can we break bad habits and form healthy new ones? We must first sit down and count the costs, lest we make a public statement and lay the foundation but are not able to finish. If we do not finish what we start, we are mocked, either by others or by ourselves. We simply must sit down first and count the costs and calculate the restraining forces to ensure that we have sufficient thrust.

Force-field analysis teaches us that in every environment there are powerful restraining forces at work to pull down any new thrust. Any serious effort to change a habit should take these forces into account. For example, if we resolve to change our diet, we should consider the times and places and situations where we slip. We can then avoid those things that trip us and add things that help us to progress and carry out resolutions.

Old habits have a tremendous pull. Breaking deeply imbedded habits of procrastination, criticism, overeating, or oversleeping involves more than a little willpower. We may be dealing with basic character issues and need to achieve some fundamental reorientation or transformation.

Often our own resolve and willpower are not enough. We may need the transforming power of an alliance with other people who are similarly committed—relationships where we contract to do something. The success of groups like Alcoholics Anonymous attests to the power of reinforcing associations.

Still, change will be difficult at first. Once we decide to change, to lift off, we may have to sacrifice our "freedom" to do as we please or to do what comes naturally until new habits are firmly formed and our desires for the old ways have abated. We'll go through withdrawal—dealing with cravings and routines and tendencies. And just as astronauts are buffeted by the forces of nature as they clear the pull of "g-forces" of gravity, so must we experience some rigors as we attempt to overcome the pull of the past.

Grounding us to our bad habits are the three great forces of appetite, pride, and ambition. Although we discussed these in chapter 3, let's briefly review them here.

• *First, appetites and passions.* We all succumb at times to the pull of appetites—our physiological cravings and longings for food and drink, for example. Many people are slaves to their stomach and to their addictions. Their stomach controls their mind and body, not without consequence. When we overindulge, we are less sensitive to the needs of others. We become angry with ourselves and take that anger out on others, sometimes at the slightest provocation. Hence, when we are controlled by our appetites and passions, we inevitably have relationship problems.

Sir Walter Scott noted, "He who indulges his sense in any excess renders himself obnoxious to his own reason; and to gratify the brute in him, displeases the man and sets his two natures at variance."

• *Second, pride and pretension.* If we are not secure in our self-definition, we look to the social mirror for our identity and approval. Our concept of ourselves comes from what others think of us. We find ourselves gearing our lives to meet their expectations. The more we live what others expect of us, the more insecure and pretentious we become. Expectations change. Opinion is fickle. And as we go on playing games and roles, giving in to vanity and pride, we deceive ourselves and, feeling threatened, fight to maintain the false front.

• *Third, aspiration and ambition.* When we are blinded by ambition, we seek first to be understood and to get glory, position, power, and promotion rather than looking at time, talents, and possessions as a stewardship for which we must account. Aspiring individuals are deeply possessive. They interpret everything in terms of what it will do for them. Everyone becomes a competitor. Their relationships—even close, intimate ones—tend to be competitive. They use various methods of manipulation to achieve their ends.

The Daily Private Victory

If we can overcome the pull of the flesh to arise early in the morning—putting mind over mattress—we will experience our first victory of the day. We can then move on to other things. For by small means are great things accomplished.

Such an early morning victory gives a sense of conquering, of overcoming, of mastering—and this sense propels one to further conquer difficulties and clear hurdles throughout the day. Starting the day with a private victory over self is one good way to break old habits and make new ones.

Our ability to do more and perform better will increase as we exercise the discipline of doing important and difficult work first, when we are fresh, and deferring routine jobs to other times. In this way we are products of our decisions, goals, and plans, not of our moods and circumstances.

All of us have our private battles. And we all have the chance to live out our public battles in our minds before we ever come to them in fact. In this way we can actually live out the challenges of our day before they come. We can deal with aspirations, selfishness, negative inclinations, impatience, anger, procrastination, and irresponsibility —fight these things out and win the battle vicariously before we do in fact.

Then when the public battles come—the pressures and stresses that descend upon our lives—we will have the internal strength to deal with them from a set of correct principles. Winning the private battle before going into the public arena is another key to breaking old habits and making new ones. I have learned that we do not have lasting public victories until we have a successful private victories.

CONDITIONING IS ALL IMPORTANT

We increase our capacity to make and break habits much as we increase our lung capacity—we begin with a program of aerobics.

Certainly we can't run faster than we have strength. We must build up gradually. Aerobics means an active exercise program based on the idea of an incremental buildup of reserve power in the body to supply necessary resource to the systems. Anyone who leads a sedentary life-style and is then physically put to the test finds that his body cries for oxygen. But his circulatory system is underdeveloped, and a serious deficiency may bring stroke, heart attack, or death.

So the principle is to build up regularly, gradually, through daily exercise of emotional fiber. Build reserves of emotional stamina to be called on in times of stress.

With regard to making new habits, the aerobic exercise I recommend is to do two things daily: 1) gain perspective, and 2) make some decisions and commitments in light of that perspective. People have the capability to transcend themselves, to rise above the moment and see what's happening and what should be happening. We need to take time to plan and make some decisions in light of this understanding. As Goethe put it, "Things which matter most must never be at the mercy of things which matter least." Careful planning helps us maintain a sense of perspective, purpose, and ordered priorities.

FIVE SUGGESTIONS

If we will do the following five things, we will have the strength to be strong in hard moments, in testing times.

- Never make a promise we will not keep.
- Make meaningful promises, resolutions, and commitments to do better and to be better—and share these with a loved one.
- Use self-knowledge and be very selective about the promises we make.
- Consider promises as a measure of our integrity and faith in ourselves.
- Remember that our personal integrity or self-mastery is the basis for our success with others.

One simple practice can propel you forward in your long-term quest for excellence and in your struggle for true maturity (courage balanced with consideration) and for integrity. It is this: Before every test of your new habit or desired behavior, stop and get control. Plumb and rally your resources. Set your mind and heart. Choose your mood. Proactively choose your response. Ask, "How can I best respond to this situation?" Choose to be your best self, and that choice will arrest your ambivalence and renew your determination.

When everything is ready for takeoff, the astronauts say, "All systems go." That means everything is in proper balance and working order. They can have a launch from the pad, or they can make some significant maneuvers in space because everything is coordinated, harmonized, and prepared to move ahead.

"All systems go" might be a good expression for us to indicate that all systems are ready to take us to the height planned. When our habit system and value system are not synchronized, we are subject to internal doubts and resistance, and often the mission is aborted. Active, positive behavior reinforces our good intentions and resolutions. Actions—actual doing—can change the very fiber of our nature. Doing changes our view of ourselves. Our personal behavior is largely a product of such self-made fuel.

Consequently if a person makes a promise but does not fulfill that promise, there is a danger of a basic breakdown in his character. His honor and integrity are threatened. His self-esteem tends to diminish. He eventually creates a different picture of himself and conforms his behavior to that picture. But if we deal well with each new challenge and overcome it, we unleash within ourselves a new kind of freedom, power, and capacity to soar to heights previously undreamed of.

Chapter 6

SIX DAYS OF CREATION

ALL REAL GROWTH and progress is made step by step, following a natural sequence of development. For example, as recorded in Genesis, the earth was created in six days. Each day was important, each in its own time: the light, the land, the plants and animals, and finally man. This sequential development process is common to all of life.

- As children, we learn to turn over, to sit up, to crawl, then to walk and run. Each step is important. No step can be skipped.
- In school we study mathematics before algebra, algebra before calculus. We simply can't do calculus until we understand algebra.
- In construction we build a strong foundation before doing any framing and finishing work.

We know and accept this step-by-step process in physical and intellectual areas because things are seen and constant evidence supplied. But in other areas of human development and in social interaction we often attempt to short-cut natural processes—substituting expediency for priority, imitation for innovation, cosmetics for character, style for substance, and pretense for competence. We often skip some vital steps to save time and effort and still hope to reap the desired rewards.

But such hope is vain. There are no short cuts in the development of professional skills, of talents such as piano playing and public speaking, or of our minds and characters. In all of life there are stages or processes of growth and development, and at every step the concept of *the six days of creation* applies.

For example, what happens when a person attempts to short-cut this day-by-day process in developing his or her tennis game? If a person is an average tennis player—at *day three*—but decides one day to play at *day six* to make a better impression, what will result? Or what would happen if you were to lead your friends to believe you could play the piano at *day six*, while your actual present skill was at *day two*? If you are at *day three* in golf and competing against someone at *day five*, would positive thinking alone beat him?

The answers are obvious. It is simply impossible to violate, ignore, or short-cut this development process. It is contrary to nature, and any attempt to seek such a short-cut will result in confusion and frustration. If I am at *day two* in any field, and desire to move to *day five*, I must first take the step toward *day three*. No bypassing, no short-cutting, no pretending or appearing, no making impressions, no amount of "dressing for success," will compensate for lack of skill and judgment.

Progress involves accepting the fact that I am currently at *day two* and refusing to pretend to be anywhere else.

If students won't let a teacher know what level they are on—by asking a question or revealing their ignorance—they will not learn or grow. People cannot pretend for long; eventually they will be found out. Often an admission of ignorance is the first step in our education.

INTERNAL GROWTH

Now, instead of considering skill or knowledge growth, let us consider the internal growth of an individual. For example, suppose that a particular person is at *day five* intellectually but at *day two* emotionally. Everything is okay when the sun is shining or when things go well. But what happens when fatigue, marital problems, financial pressure, uncooperative teenagers, screaming kids, and ringing telephones join together?

The emotionally immature person may find himself or herself absolutely enslaved by the emotions of anger, impatience, and criticalness. Yet in public, when things are going well, one may never detect this internal deficiency, this immaturity.

Short-circuiting the natural development process is not always obvious in emotional, social, and spiritual areas. We can "pose," and we can pretend. And for a while we can get by on "one-night stands." We might even deceive ourselves. Yet most of us know what we really are inside, as do some of those we live with and work around.

To relate effectively with our colleagues, spouse, or children requires emotional strength, because we must learn to listen. Listening involves patience, openness, and the desire to understand. When we are open, we run the risk that we may be changed—we may be influenced. And if we are sure that we are right, we don't want to change. We find it easier to be closed and to tell and dictate. It is easier to operate from our *day two* emotional level and to give *day six* advice.

POSSESSING PRECEDES GIVING

I once tried to teach the value of sharing to my daughter at a time when she was not ready to receive it. In effect I was attempting to move her from *day two* to *day five* on command.

One day I returned home to my daughter's third-year birthday party only to find her in the corner of the front room, defiantly grasping all her presents, unwilling to let the other children play with them. I sensed the presence of several parents witnessing this selfish display. I was embarrassed because I was a professor in the field of human relations, and I felt that these people expected more of me and my children.

The atmosphere in the room was charged, as the other children crowded around my daughter with their hands out, asking to play with the presents they had just given her; and, of course, my daughter adamantly refused to share anything. I said to myself, "Certainly I should teach my daughter to share. The value of sharing is one of the most basic things we believe in." So I proceeded through the following process.

My first method was simply *to request*: "Honey, would you please share with your friends the toys they've given you?"

A flat, "No."

My second method was *to reason*: "Honey, if you learn to share your toys with them when they are at your home, then when you go to their homes they will share their toys with you."

Again, "No!"

I was becoming a little more embarrassed, as it was evident I was having no influence. The third method was *to bribe*: "Honey, if you will share, I've got a special surprise for you. I'll give you a piece of gum."

"I don't want a piece of gum!" she exploded.

Now I was becoming exasperated. My fourth method was *to threaten*: "Unless you share, you will be in real trouble!"

"I don't care. These are my things. I don't have to share!"

Last method was *to force*. I merely took some of the toys and gave them to the other kids. "Here, kids, play with them."

Perhaps my daughter needed the experience of possessing the things before she could give them—unless we possess something, we can never really give it. But at that moment I valued the opinion of those parents more than the growth and development of my child and our relationship. I made an initial judgment that I was right— she should share—and that she was wrong in not doing so. Based on that judgment, I proceeded to manipulate her until I ultimately forced her.

She was at *day two*, and I imposed a *day five* expectation, simply because on my own scale I was at *day two* emotionally. I was unable or unwilling to give patience or understanding, but I expected her to give! If I had been more mature, I might have allowed her to choose to share or not to share. Perhaps after reasoning with her, I could have attempted to turn the attention of the children to an interesting game, thus taking all of the emotional pressure off my child. I've since learned that once my children gain a sense of real possession, they share naturally, freely, and spontaneously.

There are times to teach and train and times not to teach. When relationships are strained and charged with emotion, attempts to teach or train are often perceived as a form of judgment and rejection. A better approach is to be alone with the person and to discuss the principle privately. But again, this requires patience and internal control—in short, emotional maturity.

Borrowing Strength Builds Weakness

In addition to parents, many employers, leaders, and others in positions of authority may be competent, knowledgeable, and skillful (at *day six*) but are emotionally and spiritually immature (at *day two*). They, too, may attempt to compensate for this deficiency, or gap, by borrowing strength from their position or their authority.

How do immature people react to pressure? How does the boss react when subordinates don't do things his way? The teacher when the students challenge her viewpoint?

How would an immature parent treat a teenage daughter when she interrupts with her problems? How does this parent discipline a bothersome younger child? How does this person handle a difference with a spouse on an emotionally explosive matter? How does the person handle challenges at work?

An emotionally immature person will tend to *borrow strength* from position, size, strength, experience, intellect, or emotions to make up for a character imbalance. And what are the consequences? Eventually this person will build weakness in three places:

First, he builds weakness in himself. Borrowing strength from position or authority reinforces his own dependence upon external factors to get things done in the future.

Second, he builds weakness in the other people. Others learn to act or react in terms of fear or conformity, thus stunting their own reasoning, freedom, growth, and internal discipline.

Third, he builds weakness in the relationship. It becomes strained. Fear replaces cooperation. Each person involved becomes a little more arbitrary, a little more agitated, a little more defensive.

To win an argument or a contest, an emotionally immature person may use his strengths and abilities to back people into a corner. Even though he wins the argument, he loses. Everyone loses. His very strength becomes his weakness.

In fact, whenever we borrow strength from our possessions, positions, credentials, appearance, memberships, status symbols, or achievements, what happens to us when these things change or are no longer there?

Obviously we remain stuck with the weaknesses we have developed in ourselves, in our relationships, and in others. In fact, people who have the habit of borrowing strength will eventually lose influence with those they most want to impress. Their children may feel belittled and crushed, with little sense of worth, identity, or individuality. Their co-workers may become rebellious and strike back in their own way, often at the very things that are treasured the most.

From what sources, then, can we borrow strength without building weakness? Only from sources that build the internal capacity to deal with whatever the situation calls for. For instance, a surgeon borrows strength from his developed skill and knowledge, a runner from his disciplined body, strong legs, and powerful lungs.

In other words, we must ask, "What does the situation demand? What strength, what skill, what knowledge, what attitude?" Obviously the possessions, the appearances, or the credentials of the surgeon or the athlete are only symbols of what is needed and are therefore worthless without the substance.

IMPLICATIONS FOR PERSONAL GROWTH

I see six significant implications of the "six-day" development process:

- *Growth is a natural process*—you reap as you sow: algebra before calculus; crawling before walking.
- *We all are at different "days"* (levels of growth) in the physical, social, emotional, intellectual, and spiritual areas. If I am at a different level from you, perhaps the things I need to work on and overcome you have already conquered, and vice versa. Your *day four* may be my *day two*.
- *Comparisons are dangerous*. Comparisons breed insecurity, yet we commonly make them among our children, co-workers, and other acquaintances. If our sense of worth and personal security comes from such comparisons, how insecure and anxious we will be, feeling superior one minute and inferior the next. Opinions, customs, and fashions are fickle, always changing. There is no security in changing things. Internal security simply does not come externally. Borrowing strength from any source that does not build and internally strengthen the borrower will internally weaken him. Moreover, comparing and borrowing breeds complacency and vanity on the one hand and discouragement and self-dislike on the other. It encourages people to seek short cuts, to be ruled by opinion, to live by appearances, and to borrow more strength from exter-

nal sources. It's best to compare ourselves only with ourselves. We can't focus or base our happiness on another's progress; we can focus only on our own. We should compare people against their own potential and then constantly affirm that potential and their efforts toward reaching it. We should ask, "How is he doing with what he's got?" instead of comparing one person against another and meting out love or punishment on the basis of that comparison.

· *There is no short cut.* If I am at *day two* (to continue the metaphor) and desire to move to *day six*, I must go through *days three, four,* and *five*. If I pretend to be at *day six* in order to impress others, eventually I will be found out. Trying to be all things to all people results in the loss of everybody's respect, including one's own. If some people are at *day three*, it is futile and hurtful to compare and criticize them because they aren't at *day five* or *six*. There simply is no short cut.

· *To improve, we must start from where we are,* not from where we should be, or where someone else is, or even from where others may think we are. By doing one more push-up each day, I could do thirty in a month. Likewise, in any area of improvement I could also exercise a little more of what it takes, such as a little more patience, understanding, or courage, slowly increasing my capacity through daily effort and discipline.

I believe that *day one* and *day two* for most of us involve getting more control over the body—getting to bed early, arising early, exercising regularly, eating in moderation, staying at our work when necessary even though tired, and so on. Too many are trying to conquer *day four, five,* and *six* problems, such as procrastination, impatience, or pride, while still a slave to their appetites. If we can't control the body and its appetites, how can we ever control our tongue or overcome our passions and the emotions of anger, envy, jealousy, or hatred? Many aspire to the fruits of *days five* and *six* (love, spirituality, wisdom in decision making) and yet are unwilling to obey the laws of *day one* (mastering of appetites and passions).

· *Introspection gives us an accurate understanding of our weaknesses and the power to overcome them.* Many of us simply don't know where to start. We don't always know what things come before other things. Someone else's pattern and process may differ from ours. What is someone else's *day five* may be our *day two*. We may be at *day four* one time and at *day one* another time—even on the same matter! At times we will need to do some work at each level simultaneously.

But the key to our growth and development is always to begin where we are, at our *day one*.

Chapter 7

SEVEN DEADLY SINS

MAHATMA GANDHI said that seven things will destroy us. Notice that all of them have to do with social and political conditions. Note also that the antidote of each of these "deadly sins" is an explicit external standard or something that is based on natural principles and laws, not on social values.

· *Wealth without work.* This refers to the practice of getting something for nothing—manipulating markets and assets so you don't have to work or produce added value, just manipulate people and things. Today there are professions built around making wealth without working, making much money without paying taxes, benefiting from free government programs without carrying a fair share of the financial burdens, and enjoying all the perks of citizenship of country and membership of corporation without assuming any of the risk or responsibility.

How many of the fraudulent schemes that went on in the 1980s, often called the decade of greed, were basically get-rich-quick schemes or speculations promising practitioners, "You don't even have to work for it"? That is why I would be very concerned if one of my children went into speculative enterprises or if they learned how to make a lot of money fast without having to pay the price by adding value on a day-to-day basis.

Some network marketing and pyramidal organizations worry me because many people get rich quick by building a structure under them that feeds them without work. They are rationalized to the hilt; nevertheless the overwhelming emotional motive is often greed: "You can get rich without much work. You may have to work initially, but soon you can have wealth without work." New social mores and norms are cultivated that cause distortions in their judgment.

Justice and judgment are inevitably inseparable, suggesting that to the degree you move away from the laws of nature, your judgment will be adversely affected. You get distorted notions. You start telling rational lies to explain why things work or why they don't. You move away from the law of "the farm" into social/political environments.

When we read of organizations in trouble, we often hear the sad confessions of executives who tell of moving away from natural laws and principles for a period of time and begin overbuilding, overborrowing, and overspeculating, not really reading the stream or getting objective feedback, just hearing a lot of self-talk internally. Now they have a high debt to pay. They may have to work hard just to survive—without hope of being healthy for five years or more. It's back to the basics, hand to the plow. And many of these executives, in earlier days, were critical of the conservative founders of the corporations who stayed close to the fundamentals and preferred to stay small and free of debt.

· *Pleasure without conscience*. The chief query of the immature, greedy, selfish, and sensuous has always been, "What's in it for me? Will this please me? Will it ease me?" Lately many people seem to want these pleasures without conscience or sense of responsibility, even abandoning or utterly neglecting spouses and children in the name of doing *their thing*. But independence is not the most mature state of being—it's only a middle position on the way to interdependence, the most advanced and mature state. To learn to give and take, to live selflessly, to be sensitive, to be considerate, is our challenge. Otherwise there is no sense of social responsibility or accountability in our pleasurable activities.

The ultimate costs of pleasures without conscience are high as measured in terms of time and money, in terms of reputation and in terms of wounding the hearts and minds of other people who are adversely affected by those who just want to indulge and gratify themselves in the short term. It's dangerous to be pulled or lulled away from natural law without conscience. Conscience is essentially the repository of timeless truths and principles—the internal monitor of natural law.

A prominent, widely published psychologist worked to align people with their moral conscience in what was called "integrity therapy." He once told me that he was a manic-depressive. "I knew I was getting suicidal," he said. "Therefore, I committed myself to a mental institution. I tried to work out of it, neutralize it, until I reached the point where I could leave the hospital. I don't do clinical work now because it is too stressful. I mostly do research. And through my own struggle, I discovered that integrity therapy was the only way to go. I gave up my mistress, confessed to my wife, and had peace for the first time in my life."

Pleasure without conscience is one of the key temptations for today's executives. Sometimes on airplanes I'll scan the magazines directed at executives, noting the advertisements. Many of these ads, perhaps two-thirds of them, invite executives to indulge themselves without conscience because they "deserve it" or have "earned it" or "want it," and why not "give in" and "let it all hang out"? The seductive message is, "You've arrived. You are now a law unto yourself. You don't need a conscience to govern you anymore." And in some ads you see sixty-year-old men with attractive thirty-year-old women, the "significant others" who accompany some executives to conventions. Whatever happened to spouses? What happened to the social mores that make cheating on spouses illegitimate behavior?

• **Knowledge without character**. As dangerous as a little knowledge is, even more dangerous is much knowledge without a strong, principled character. Purely intellectual development without commensurate internal character development makes as much sense as putting a high-powered sports car in the hands of a teenager who is high on drugs. Yet all too often in the academic world, that's exactly what we do by not focusing on the character development of young people.

One of the reasons I'm excited about taking the Seven Habits into the schools is that it is character education. Some people don't like character education because, they say, "that's *your* value system." But you can get a common set of values that everyone agrees on. It is not that difficult to decide, for example, that kindness, fairness, dignity, contribution, and integrity are worth keeping. No one will fight you on those. So let's start with values that are unarguable and infuse them in our education system and in our corporate training and development programs. Let's achieve a better balance between the development of character and intellect.

The people who are transforming education today are doing it by building consensus around a common set of principles, values, and priorities and debunking the high degree of specialization, departmentalization, and partisan politics.

· *Commerce (business) without morality (ethics)*. In his book *Moral Sentiments*, which preceded *Wealth of Nations*, Adam Smith explained how foundational to the success of our systems is the moral foundation: how we treat each other, the spirit of benevolence, of service, of contribution. If we ignore the moral foundation and allow economic systems to operate without moral foundation and without continued education, we will soon create an amoral, if not immoral, society and business. Economic and political systems are ultimately based on a moral foundation.

To Adam Smith, *every* business transaction is a moral challenge to see that both parties come out fairly. Fairness and benevolence in business are the underpinnings of the free enterprise system called capitalism. Our economic system comes out of a constitutional democracy where minority rights are to be attended to as well. The spirit of the Golden Rule or of win-win is a spirit of morality, of mutual benefit, of fairness for all concerned. Paraphrasing one of the mottos of the Rotary Club, "Is it fair and does it serve the interests of all the stakeholders?" That's just a moral sense of stewardship toward all of the stakeholders.

I like that Smith says *every* economic transaction. People get in trouble when they say that *most* of their economic transactions are moral. That means there is something going on that is covert, hidden, secret. People keep a hidden agenda, a secret life, and they justify and rationalize their activities. They tell themselves rational lies so they don't have to adhere to natural laws. If you can get enough rationalization in a society, you can have social mores or political wills that are totally divorced from natural laws and principles.

I once met a man who for five years served as the "ethics director" for a major aerospace company. He finally resigned the post in protest and considered leaving the company, even though he would lose a big salary and benefit package. He said that the executive team had their own separate set of business ethics and that they were deep into rationalization and justification. Wealth and power were big on their agendas, and they made no excuse for it anymore. They were divorced from reality even inside their own organization. They talked about serving the customer while absolutely mugging their own employees.

• *Science without humanity*. If science becomes all technique and technology, it quickly degenerates into man against humanity. Technologies come from the paradigms of science. And if there's very little understanding of the higher human purposes that the technology is striving to serve, we becomes victims of our own technocracy. We see otherwise highly educated people climbing the scientific ladder of success, even though it's often missing the rung called humanity and leaning against the wrong wall.

The majority of the scientists who ever lived are living today, and they have brought about a scientific and technological explosion in the world. But if all they do is superimpose technology on the same old problems, nothing basic changes. We may see an evolution, an occasional "revolution" in science, but without humanity we see precious little real human advancement. All the old inequities and injustices are still with us.

About the only thing that hasn't evolved are these natural laws and principles—the true north on the compass. Science and technology have changed the face of most everything else. But the fundamental things still apply, as time goes by.

• *Religion without sacrifice*. Without sacrifice we may become active in a church but remain inactive in its gospel. In other words, we go for the social facade of religion and the piety of religious practices. There is no real walking with people or going the second mile or trying to deal with our social problems that may eventually undo our economic system. It takes sacrifice to serve the needs of other people—the sacrifice of our own pride and prejudice, among other things.

If a church or religion is seen as just another hierarchical system, its members won't have a sense of service or inner worship. Instead they will be into outward observances and all the visible accoutrements of religion. But they are neither God-centered nor principle-centered.

The principles of three of the Seven Habits pertain to how we deal with other people, how we serve them, how we sacrifice for them, how we contribute. Habits 4, 5, and 6—win-win interdependency, empathy, and synergy—require tremendous sacrifice. I've come to believe that they require a broken heart and a contrite spirit—and that, for some, is the ultimate sacrifice. For example, I once observed a marriage where there were frequent arguments. One thought came to me: "These two people must have a broken heart and a contrite spirit toward each other or this union will never last." You can't have a oneness, a unity, without humility. Pride and selfishness will destroy the union between man and god, between man and woman, between man and man, between self and self.

The great servant leaders have that humility, the hallmark of inner religion. I know a few CEOs who are humble servant leaders—who sacrifice their pride and share their power—and I can say that their influence both inside and outside their companies is multiplied because of it. Sadly, many people want "religion," or at least the appearance of it, without any sacrifice. They want more spirituality but would never miss a meal in meaningful fasting or do one act of anonymous service to achieve it.

· *Politics without principle.* If there is no principle, there is no true north, nothing you can depend upon. The focus on the personality ethic is the instant creation of an image that sells well in the social and economic marketplace.

You see politicians spending millions of dollars to create an image, even though it's superficial, lacking substance, in order to get votes and gain office. And when it works, it leads to a political system operating independently of the natural laws that should govern—that are built into the Declaration of Independence: "We hold these Truths to be self-evident, that all Men are created equal, that they are endowed by their Creator with certain unalienable Rights, that among these are Life, Liberty, and the Pursuit of Happiness. . . ."

In other words, they are describing self-evident, external, observable, natural, unarguable, self-evident laws: "We hold these Truths to be *self-evident.*" The key to a healthy society is to get the social will, the value system, aligned with correct principles. You then have the compass needle pointing to true north—true north representing the external or the natural law—and the indicator says that is what we are building our value system on: they are aligned.

But if you get a sick social will behind the political will that is independent of principle, you could have a very sick organization or society with distorted values. For instance, the professed mission and shared values of criminals who rape, rob, and plunder might sound very much like many corporate mission statements, using such words as "teamwork," "cooperation," "loyalty," "profitability," "innovation," and "creativity." The problem is that their value system is not based on a natural law.

Figuratively, inside many corporations with lofty mission statements, many people are being mugged in broad daylight in front of witnesses. Or they are being robbed of self-esteem, money, or position without due process. And if there is no social will behind the principles of due process, and if you can't get due process, you have to go to the jury of your peers and engage in counterculture sabotage.

In the movie *The Ten Commandments*, Moses says to the pharaoh, "We are to be governed by God's law, not by you." In effect he's saying, "We will not be governed by a person unless that person embodies the law." In the best societies and organizations, natural laws and principles govern—that's the Constitution—and even the top people must bow to the principle. No one is above it.

The Seven Habits will help you avoid these Seven Deadly Sins. And if you don't buy into the Seven Habits, try the Ten Commandments.

Chapter 8

MORAL COMPASSING

W HEN MANAGING in the wilderness of the changing times, a map is of limited worth. What's needed is a moral compass.

When I was in New York recently, I witnessed a mugging skillfully executed by a street gang. I'm sure that the members of this gang have their street maps, their common values—the highest value being "Don't fink or squeal on each other, be true and loyal to each other"—but this value, as it's interpreted and practiced by this gang, does not represent "true north," the magnetic principle of respect for people and property.

They lacked an internal moral compass. Principles are like a compass. A compass has a true north that is *objective and external*, that reflects natural laws or *principles*, as opposed to values that are subjective and internal. Because the compass represents the verities of life, we must develop our value system with deep respect for "true north" principles.

As Cecil B. De Mille said: "It is impossible for us to break the law. We can only break ourselves against the law."

Principles are proven, enduring guidelines for human conduct. Certain principles govern human effectiveness. The six major world religions all teach the same basic core beliefs—such principles as

"You reap what you sow" and "Actions are more important than words." I find global consensus around what "true north" principles are. These are not difficult to detect. They are objective, basic, unarguable: "You can't have trust without being trustworthy" and "You can't talk yourself out of a problem you behave yourself into."

There is little disagreement in what the constitutional principles of a company should be when enough people get together. I find a universal belief in fairness, kindness, dignity, charity, integrity, honesty, quality, service, and patience.

Consider the absurdity of trying to live a life or run a business based on the opposites. I doubt that anyone would seriously consider unfairness, deceit, baseness, uselessness, mediocrity, or degradation as a solid foundation for lasting happiness and success.

People may argue about how these principles are to be defined, interpreted, and applied in real-life situations, but they generally agree about their intrinsic merit. They may not live in total harmony with them, but they believe in them. And they want to be managed by them. They want to be evaluated by "laws" in the social and economic dimensions that are just as real, just as unchanging and unarguable, as laws such as gravity are in the physical dimension.

In any serious study of history—be it national or corporate—the reality and verity of such principles become obvious. These principles surface time and again, and the degree to which people in a society recognize and live in harmony with them moves them toward either survival and stability or disintegration and destruction.

In a talk show interview, I was once asked if Hitler was principle-centered. "No," I said, "but he was value-driven. One of his governing values was to unify Germany. But he violated compass principles and suffered the natural consequences. And the consequences were momentous—the dislocation of the entire world for years."

In dealing with self-evident, natural laws, we can choose either to manage in harmony with them or to challenge them by working some other way. Just as the laws are fixed, so too are the consequences.

In my seminars I ask audiences, "When you think of your personal values, how do you think?" Typically people focus on what they want. I then ask them, "When you think of principles, how do you think?" They are more oriented toward objective law, listening to conscience, tapping into verities.

Principles are not values. The German Nazis, like the street gang members, shared values, but these violated basic principles. Values are maps. Principles are territories. And the maps are not the territories; they are only subjective attempts to describe or represent the territory.

The more closely our maps are aligned with correct principles—with the realties of the territory, with things as they are—the more accurate and useful they will be. Correct maps will impact our effectiveness far more than our efforts to change attitudes and behaviors. However, when the territory is constantly changing, any map is soon obsolete.

A COMPASS FOR THE TIMES

In today's world, what's needed is a compass. A compass consists of a magnetic needle swinging freely and pointing to magnetic north. It's also a mariner's instrument for directing or ascertaining the course of ships at sea, as well as an instrument for drawing circles and taking measurements. The word *compass* may also refer to the reach, extent, limit, or boundary of a space or time; a course, circuit, or range; an intent, purpose, or design; an understanding or comprehension. All of these connotations enrich the meaning of the metaphor.

Why is a compass better than a map in today's business world? I see several compelling reasons why the compass is so invaluable to corporate leaders:

- The compass orients people to the coordinates and indicates a course or direction even in forests, deserts, seas, and open, unsettled terrain.
- As the territory changes, the map becomes obsolete; in times of rapid change, a map may be dated and inaccurate by the time it's printed.
- Inaccurate maps are sources of great frustration for people who are trying to find their way or navigate territory.
- Many executives are pioneering, managing in uncharted waters or wilderness, and no existing map accurately describes the territory.
- To get anywhere very fast, we need refined processes and clear channels of production and distribution (freeways), and to find or create freeways in the wilderness, we need a compass.
- The map provides description, but the compass provides more vision and direction.

· An accurate map is a good management tool, but a compass is a leadership and an empowerment tool.

People who have been using maps for many years to find their way and maintain a sense of perspective and direction should realize that their maps may be useless in the current maze and wilderness of management. My recommendation is that you exchange your map for a compass and train yourself and your people how to navigate by a compass calibrated to a set of fixed, true north principles and natural laws.

Why? Because with an inaccurate map, you would be lost in a city. What if someone said "Work harder"? Now you're lost twice as fast. Now someone says, "Think positively." Now you don't care about being lost. The problem has nothing to do with industry or with attitude. It has everything to do with an inaccurate map. Your paradigm or the level of your thinking represents your map of reality, your map of the territory.

The basic problem at the bottom of most ineffective cultures is the map in the head of the people who helped create that condition. It is an incomplete map, one based on quick-fix solutions and short-term thinking toward quarterly, bottom-line results, and it is based on a scarcity mentality.

The solution is to change from management by maps (values) to leadership by compass (natural principles). A political environment inevitably points to the style of top people—that's supposed to be true north. But the style is based upon volatile moods, arbitrary decisions, raw emotion, and ego trips. Sometimes true north is called an "information system" or a "reward system" and that governs behavior. What grows is what gets watered. Principle-centered leadership requires that people "work on farms" on the basis of natural, agricultural principles and that they build those principles into the center of their lives, their relationships, their agreements, their management processes, and their mission statements.

STRATEGIC ORIENTATION

Map-versus-compass orientation is an important strategic issue, as reflected in this statement by Masaharu Matsushita, president of Japan's giant consumer electronic company: "We are going to win and the industrial West is going to lose because the reasons for your failure are within yourselves: for you, the essence of management is to get the ideas out of the heads of the bosses into the hands of labor."

The important thing here is the stated reason for our "failure." We are locked in to certain mind-sets or paradigms, locked in to management by maps, locked in to an old model of leadership where the experts at the top decide the objectives, methods, and means.

This old strategic planning model is obsolete. It's a road map. It calls for people at the top to exercise their experience, expertise, wisdom, and judgment and set ten-year strategic plans—only to find that the plans are worthless within eighteen months. In the new environment, with speed to market timetables of eighteen months instead of five years, plans become obsolete fast.

Peter Drucker has said: "Plans are worthless, but planning is invaluable." And if our planning is centered on an overall purpose or vision and on a commitment to set of principles, then the people who are closest to the action in the wilderness can use that compass and their own expertise and judgment to make decisions and take actions. In effect, each person may have his or her own compass; each may be empowered to decide objectives and make plans that reflect the realities of the new market.

Principles are not practices. Practices are specific activities or actions that work in one circumstance but not necessarily in another. If you manage by practices and lead by policies, your people don't have to be the experts; they don't have to exercise judgment, because all of the judgment and wisdom is provided them in the form of rules and regulations.

If you focus on principles, you empower everyone who understands those principles to act without constant monitoring, evaluating, correcting, or controlling. Principles have universal application. And when these are internalized into habits, they empower people to create a wide variety of practices to deal with different situations.

Leading by principles, as opposed to practices, requires a different kind of training, perhaps even more training, but the payoff is more expertise, creativity, and shared responsibility at all levels of the organization.

If you train people in the *practices* of customer service, you will get a degree of customer service, but the service will break down whenever customers present a special case or problem because in doing so they short-circuit standard operating procedure.

Before people will act consistently on the *principle* of customer service, they need to adopt a new mind-set. In most cases they need to be trained—using cases, role plays, simulations, and some on-the-job coaching—to be sure they understand the principle and how it is applied on the job.

WITH THE COMPASS, WE CAN WIN

"A compass in every pocket" is better than "A chicken in every pot" or a car in every garage. With moral compassing we can win even against tough competition. My view is that the Japanese subordinate the individual to the group to the extent that they don't tap into the creative and resourceful capacities of people—one indication being that they have had only 4 Nobel Prize winners compared with 186 in the United States. The highest leadership principle is win-win interdependency, where you are both high on individual and high on team.

But once people start to realize that this "compass" is going to be the basis for evaluation, including leadership style of the people at the top, they tend to feel threatened.

The president of a major corporation once asked me to meet with him and his management team. He said that they were all too concerned with preserving their own management style. He said that the corporate mission statement had no impact on their style. These executives felt the mission was for the people "out there" who were subject to the law, but they were above the law.

The idea of moral compassing is unsettling to people who think they are above the law, because the Constitution, based on principles, is the law—it governs everybody, including the president. It places responsibility on individuals to examine their lives and determine if they are willing to live by it. All are accountable to the laws and principles.

I'm familiar with several poignant examples of major U.S. corporations telling their consultants, "We can't continue to do market feasibility studies and strategic studies independent of our culture and people." These executives understand what Michael Porter has said: "A implementation with B strategy is better than A strategy with B implementation."

We must deal with people/culture issues to improve the implementation of strategy and to achieve corporate integrity. We must be willing to go through a constitutional convention, if not a revolutionary war, to get the issues out on the table, deal with them, and get deep involvement, resulting in wise decisions. That won't happen without some blood, sweat, and tears.

Ultimately the successful implementation of any strategy hinges on the integrity people have to the governing principles and on their ability to apply those principles in any situation, using their own moral compass.

Chapter 9

PRINCIPLE-CENTERED POWER

REAL LEADERSHIP POWER comes from an honorable character and from the exercise of certain power tools and principles. Yet most discussions of leadership focus on genetic "great man" theories, personality "trait" theories, or behavioral "style" theories. These theories have had more explanatory than predictive value. They may explain why a particular leader emerged and survived, but they neither help us predict future leaders nor help us cultivate the capacity to lead.

A more fruitful approach is to look at followers, rather than leaders, and to assess leadership by asking why followers follow.

THREE TYPES OF POWER

The reasons followers follow are varied and complex, but they can be examined from three different perspectives, each of which has different motivational and psychological roots.

At one level, followers follow out of fear—they are afraid of what might happen to them if they don't do what they are asked to do. This may be called *coercive power*. The leader in this case has created a fear in the follower that either something bad is going to happen to them or something good will be taken away from them if they do not comply. So out of fear of potentially adverse consequences, they acquiesce and "get along by going along" or by giving "lip service loyalty," at least initially. But their commitment is superficial and their energies can quickly turn to sabotage and destruction when "no one is looking" or when the threat is no longer present. A well-publicized example involves the disgruntled airline clerk who, feeling he had been unjustly manipulated, deftly wiped out the flight schedules stored in computer memories the night he quit. The cost of forced compliance? Well over a million dollars and thousands of work hours lost, with enormous negative backlash from unhappy passengers.

A second level of responding suggests that followers follow because of the benefits that come to them if they do. This may be called *utility power* because the power in the relationship is based on the useful exchange of goods and services. The followers have something the leader wants (time, money, energy, personal resources, interest, talent, support, and so on), and the leader has something they want (information, money, promotions, inclusion, camaraderie, security, opportunity, and the like). These followers operate with the belief that the leader can and will do something for them if they maintain their part of the bargain by doing something for the leader. Much of what happens in the normal operation of organizations, from billion-dollar corporations to daily family living, is fueled by utility power.

A third level of responding is different in kind and degree from the other two. It is based on the power some people have with others because others tend to believe in them and in what they are trying to accomplish. They are trusted. They are respected. They are honored. And they are followed because others want to follow them, want to believe in them and their cause, want to do what the leader wants. This is not blind faith, mindless obedience, or robotic servitude; this is knowledgeable, wholehearted, uninhibited commitment. This is *legitimate power*.

Nearly everyone has experienced this type of power at some time in their lives, as a follower, in their relationship with a teacher, employer, family member, or friend who has profoundly and significantly affected their life. It may have been someone who gave them an opportunity to succeed or excel, or encouraged them when things looked bleak, or just was available when needed. Whatever they did, they did because they believed in us, and we reciprocate with respect, loyalty, commitment, and a willingness to follow, almost without condition or restriction.

Each of these types of power has a different foundation, and each leads to different results.

THE IMPACT OF POWER

Coercive power is based on fear in both the leader and the follower. Leaders tend to lean on coercive power when they are afraid they won't get compliance. It is the "big stick" approach. It is an approach that few publicly support but may use, either because it seems justified in the face of other, bigger threats hovering over the leader or it is the expedient thing to do and seems to work at the time. But its effectiveness is an illusion.

The leader who controls others through fear will find that the control is reactive and temporary. It is gone when the leader or the leader's representative or controlling system is gone. It often mobilizes the creative energies of followers to unite and resist in new, as yet uncontrolled ways. Coercive power imposes a psychological and emotional burden on both leaders and followers. It encourages suspicion, deceit, dishonesty, and, in the long run, dissolution. As Aleksandr Solzhenitsyn, the Russian poet and philosopher, has observed, "You only have power over people as long as you don't take everything away from them. But when you've robbed a man of everything, he's no longer in your power—he's free again."

Most organizations are held together by utility power. Utility power is based on a sense of equity and fairness. As long as followers feel they are receiving fairly for what they are giving, the relationship will be sustained. The compliance that is based on utility power tends to look more like influence than control. The agency of the followers is respected and regarded, but from the perspective of "caveat emptor." Leaders are followed because it is functional for the followers. It gives them access to what the leader controls, through position or expertness or charisma. The nature of followership when based on utility power is still reactive, but the reaction tends to be positive rather than negative.

It is being increasingly acknowledged that relationships based on utility power often lead to individualism rather than teamwork and group effectiveness, as each individual is reinforced for paying attention to his own perspective and desires. Individual players may change as wants and needs fluctuate. Shifting demographics of the work force indicate that long-term loyalty, by leaders or followers, is the exception. Individuals come and go, from CEOs (as in the case of Apple Computer's shift from Jobs to Sculley) to clerks (notice the rotating carousel of faces at the local convenience store), with little repercussion in the marketplace—in a real sense we are all customers who go where we can get what we want the way we want. Sources as divergent as Frank Sinatra and Burger King proclaim we can have it "our way."

In addition, a form of situational ethics is fostered, in which individuals are continually deciding, in the absence of shared organizational values, what is best and right and fair. At its worst utility power mirrors the elements of justice prominent in a litigious society, with courts of law forcing fairness in takeovers, divorces, and bankruptcies. At its best utility power reflects a willingness to stay in a relationship, whether business or personal, as long as it has a payoff for both parties.

Legitimate power is rare. It is the mark of quality, distinction, and excellence in all relationships. It is based on honor, with the leader honoring the follower and the follower choosing to contribute because the leader is also honored. The hallmark of legitimate power is sustained, proactive influence. Power is sustained because it is not dependent on whether or not something desirable or undesirable happens to the follower. To be proactive is to continually make choices based on deeply held values. And legitimate power is created when the values of the followers and the values of the leader overlap. Legitimate power is not forced, it is invited, as the personal agendas of both leader and follower are encompassed by a larger purpose. Legitimate power occurs when the cause or purpose or goal is believed in as deeply by the followers as by the leaders. Hans Selye, the author of *Stress Without Distress*, commented, "Leaders are leaders only as long as they have the respect and loyalty of their followers."

Control is apparent with legitimate power, but the control is not external; it is self-control. Power is created when individuals perceive that their leaders are honorable, so they trust them, are inspired by them, believe deeply in the goals communicated by them, and desire to be led. Because of their sense of purpose and vision, their character, their essential nature, and what they represent, leaders can build legitimate power in their relationships with their followers. With legitimate power, ethical behavior is encouraged because loyalty is based on principles as they are manifested in persons. Ethics is ultimately grounded in a commitment to doing right things, and legitimate power elicits a willingness to risk doing right things, because they are valued, they are modeled by the leader, and they are sanctioned by the vision clarified by the leader.

THE LEADERSHIP CHOICE

Whenever a problem or opportunity arises that requires the involvement of other people, the leader must make a choice. The essential leadership choice is to decide on a power base—coercion, utility, or legitimacy. The choice will be limited by the character of the leader (who she really is and what she has become by past choices) and by her interactive skills, capacity, and history. It is relatively easy, when push comes to shove and the pressures are on, to lean on position or status or credentials or affiliations or size to force someone else to follow. And in the absence of well-developed interactive skills, or the capacity to remain true to deeply held values under pressure or a history of integrity and trust with others, it is almost impossible not to resort to force when a leader is in the middle of a crisis.

The possibilities available to the leader who must make the leadership choice can be multiplied. For example, expertise can be developed. Promotions to new position of status and power can be pursued. Information and resources can be accumulated. And the potential impact of utility power can be enhanced by maximizing proximity to followers, by lowering thresholds for engaging the leader, by simplifying mechanisms (formal policies and procedures) for creating functional relationships, and by making it easier and less costly for followers to form functional relationships. These are tactical actions that will lead to increased utility options for the leader.

For the leader who wishes to increase legitimate power, a long-term commitment is required. Trust in relationships, which is the foundation of legitimate power, cannot be fabricated ad hoc. Sincerity cannot be faked for long. Eventually leaders reveal themselves. And what a leader is, beyond what the leader can do to or for followers, ultimately determines the depth of legitimate power he has.

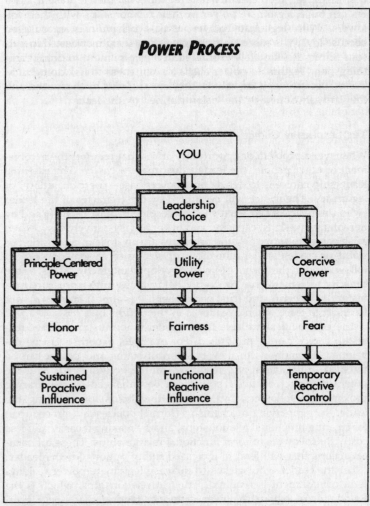

POWER PROCESS

TEN POWER TOOLS

The more a leader is honored, respected, and genuinely regarded by others, the more legitimate power he will have with others. Depending on how leaders deal with others (which includes both real and perceived intent, interactive capacity, and interactive history), the honor followers extend to them will increase or decrease and the legitimate power in the relationship will increase or decrease. To be honorable is to have power.

Here are ten suggestions for processes and principles that will increase a leader's honor and power with others.

- *Persuasion*, which includes sharing reasons and rationale, making a strong case for your position or desire while maintaining genuine respect for followers' ideas and perspective; tell why as well as what; commit to stay in the communication process until mutually beneficial and satisfying outcomes are reached.
- *Patience*, with the process and the person. In spite of the failings, shortcomings, and inconveniences created by followers, and your own impatience and anticipation for achieving your goals, maintain a long-term perspective and stay committed to your goals in the face of short-term obstacles and resistance.
- *Gentleness*, not harshness, hardness, or forcefulness, when dealing with vulnerabilities, disclosures, and feelings followers might express.
- *Teachableness*, which means operating with the assumption that you do not have all the answers, all the insights, and valuing the different viewpoints, judgments, and experiences followers may have.
- *Acceptance*, withholding judgment, giving the benefit of the doubt, requiring no evidence or specific performance as a condition for sustaining high self-worth, making them your agenda.
- *Kindness*, sensitive, caring, thoughtful, remembering the little things (which are the big things) in relationships.
- *Openness*, acquiring accurate information and perspectives about followers as they can become while being worthy of respect for what they are now, regardless of what they own, control, or do, giving full consideration to their intentions, desires, values, and goals rather than focusing exclusively on their behavior.

- *Compassionate confrontation*, acknowledging error, mistakes, and the need for followers to make "course corrections" in a context of genuine care, concern, and warmth, making it safe for followers to risk.
- *Consistency*, so that your leadership style is not a manipulative technique that you bring into play when you don't get your way, are faced with crisis or challenge, or are feeling trapped; rather, this becomes a set of values, a personal code, a manifestation of your character, a reflection of who you are and who you are becoming.
- *Integrity*, honestly matching words and feelings with thoughts and actions, with no desire other than for the good of others, without malice or desire to deceive, take advantage, manipulate, or control; constantly reviewing your intent as you strive for congruence.

To some, these principles and the ideals they represent are readily attributable to notable leaders of distinction such as Mahatma Gandhi, but they are harder to find in the much more common experiences of everyday living. In response to this concern, Gandhi replied, "I claim to be no more than an average man with less than average ability. I am not a visionary. I claim to be a practical idealist. Nor can I claim any special merit for what I have been able to achieve with laborious research. I have not the shadow of a doubt that any man or woman can achieve what I have, if he or she would make the same effort and cultivate the same hope and faith."

Leaders who activate the principle of legitimate power through the leadership choice may find they are more careful of what they ask of others but have more confidence in doing so. As their understanding of the relationship between power and leadership increases, their ability to lead others and to have influence with others without forcing them will grow. And they may experience an unusual peace of mind that comes with being a wiser, more effective leader.

This article was prepared with Blaine N. Lee, Ph.D., vice president of the Covey Leadership Center and associate director of The Center for Principle-Centered Leadership.

Chapter 10

CLEARING COMMUNICATION LINES

AT THE ROOT of most communication problems are perception or credibility problems. None of us see the world as it is but as we are, as our frames of reference, or "maps," define the territory. And our experience-induced perceptions greatly influence our feelings, beliefs, and behavior.

PERCEPTION AND CREDIBILITY

Perception and credibility problems may ultimately result in complicated knots, what we often call "personality conflicts" or "communication breakdowns." Credibility problems are far more difficult to resolve, primarily because each of the people involved thinks he sees the world as it is rather than as he is. Unaware of the distortion in his own perception, his attitude is this: "If you disagree with me, in my eyes you are automatically wrong, simply because I am sure that I'm right."

Whenever we are "so right" as to make everyone who sees and thinks differently feel wrong, their best protection from further injury from us is to label us, to peg us, to put us behind mental and emotional bars for an indeterminate jail sentence, and we will not be released until we pay "the uttermost farthing." Most credibility problems can be resolved if one or both of the parties involved will realize that at the root is a perception problem.

ATTITUDES AND BEHAVIORS

Certain attitudes and behaviors are essential to clearing communication lines.

Attitudes

- I assume good faith; I do not question your sincerity or your sanity.
- I care about our relationship and want to resolve this difference in perception. Please help me to see it from your point of view.
- I am open to influence and am prepared to change.

Behaviors

- Listen to understand.
- Speak to be understood.
- Start dialogue from a common point of reference or point of agreement, and move slowly into areas of disagreement.

When these three attitudes and behaviors are acquired, almost any perception or credibility problem can be solved.

Often, once a person understands this, he will change his manner of speech. Instead of saying "This is the way it is," he will say "This is how I see it." Instead of saying "Here it is," he will say "In my view . . ." or "In my opinion . . ." or "As I see it. . . ." Such language admits other people to the human race by telling them "You matter, too. Like mine, your views and feelings are legitimate and respectable."

When others judge us or disagree with us, our reply will be similar to the following in tone, if not in content: "Good, you see it differently. I would like to understand how you see it." When we disagree with another, instead of saying "I'm right and you're wrong," we will say "I see it differently. Let me share with you how I see it."

WORDS AND RELATIONSHIPS

I'll never forget a friend of mind who was heartsick over his relationship with his teenage son. "When I come into the room where he is reading or watching TV, he gets up and goes out—that's how bad the relationship is," he reported.

I encouraged him to try first to understand his son rather than to get his son to understand him and his advice. He answered, "I already understand him. What he needs is to learn respect for his parents and to show appreciation for all we're trying to do for him."

"If you want your son to really open up, you must work on the assumption that you don't understand him and perhaps never fully will, but that you want to and will try."

Eventually the father agreed to work on this assumption, as he'd tried about everything else. I assured him he would have to prepare himself for the communication, because it would test his patience and self-control.

The next evening about eight P.M. the father approached the son and said, "Son, I'm not happy with our relationship, and I'd like to see what we can do to improve it. Perhaps I haven't taken the time to really understand you."

"Boy, I'll say you haven't! You've never understood me!" the son flashed back.

Inside the father burned, and it was about all he could do to keep from retorting, "Why, you ungrateful little brat! Don't you think I don't understand you! Why, I've gone through the mill. I know the whole story!"

But he restrained this impulse and said, "Well, son, perhaps I haven't, but I'd like to. Can you help me? For instance, take that argument we had last week over the car. Can you tell me how you saw it?"

The son, still angry, gave his defensive explanation. The father again restrained his tendency to rush in with his own self-justifying explanation and continued to listen for understanding. He was glad he'd made up his mind to do this before the test came.

As he listened, something marvelous began to happen. His son started to soften. Soon he dropped his defenses and began to open up with some of his real problems and deeper feelings.

The father was so overwhelmed by what was happening between

them that he could hardly contain himself. He opened up also and shared some of his deep feelings and concerns as well as understandings he had regarding what had happened in the past. For the first time in years they weren't attacking and defending but were genuinely trying to understand each other. What happiness it was for both!

Around ten-thirty P.M. the mother came in and suggested it was time for bed. The father said they were communicating "for the first time" and wanted to continue. They visited until after midnight and discussed many things of importance to both of them. When the father told me of this experience a few days later, he tearfully said, "I feel like I've found my son again and he's found his dad." He was truly grateful he had gone into the experience determined inside first to understand before trying to be understood.

The crucial dimension in communication is the relationship. Many troublesome knots develop in communication lines because of poor interpersonal relations. When relationships are strained, we must be very careful about the words we use or we risk giving offense, causing a scene, or being misunderstood. When relationships are poor, people become suspicious and distrustful, making a man "an offender for a word" instead of attempting to interpret the meaning and intent of his words.

On the other hand, when the relationship is unified and harmonious, we can almost communicate without words. Where there is high trust and good feeling, we don't have to "watch our words" at all. We can smile or not and still communicate meaning and achieve understanding. When the relationship is not well established, a chapter of words won't be sufficient to communicate meaning because meanings are not found in words—they are found in people.

The key to effective communication is the one-on-one relationship. The moment we enter into this special relationship with another person, we begin to change the very nature of our communication with them. We begin to build trust and confidence in each other. In this context consider the value of a private visit with each employee, a private lunch with a business associate, a private chat with a client or customer—a time when your attention is focused upon that person, upon his or her interests, concerns, needs, hopes, fears, and doubts.

There is a compelling mountain scene poster with this invitation at the bottom: "Let the mountain have you for a day." Let's change the slogan to "Let your customer have you for an hour" or "Let your spouse have you for an evening." Try to be completely present with the other person and to transcend your own personal interests, concerns, fears, and needs. Be fully with your manager, client, or spouse. Allow them to express their interests and goals, and subordinate your own feelings to theirs.

MAP AND TERRITORY

Building harmonious relationships and achieving mutual understanding can be difficult. We all live in two worlds—the private, subjective world inside our heads and the real, objective world outside. We could call the former personal "maps" and the latter the "territory."

None of us has an absolutely complete and perfect map of the territory or of the real, objective world. While scientists constantly attempt to make better and better maps, only the creator of the territory has the complete, perfect map. All true scientists hesitate to speak of their latest theory as fact, merely as the best explanation developed to that point.

From time to time we have experiences that change our frame of reference or the map through which we view the territory, the objective world. When this happens our behavior often changes to reflect the new frame of reference; in fact, the fastest way to change a person's behavior is to change his map or frame of reference by calling him a different name, giving him a different role or responsibility, or placing him in a different situation.

SKILL AND SECURITY

We might look at the communication skill as we would at an iceberg—at two levels. The small, visible part of the iceberg is the skill level of communication. The great mass of the iceberg, silent and unseen beneath the surface, represents the deeper level—the attitudinal, motivational level. Let's call it one's security base. To make any significant long-term improvement in our communication abilities requires us to work at both levels, skill and security.

Effective communication requires skills, and skill development takes practice. A person cannot improve his tennis game merely by reading tennis books or watching great tennis players. He must get out on the court and practice what he has read or seen, progressing slowly through different levels of proficiency.

To improve our interpersonal skills, we should follow the same natural process. But, sadly, because of the stigma attached to being a "beginner," many pretend to have interpersonal skills they simply do not possess. Moreover, some are unwilling to undertake the learning process or to adopt the attitude of wanting to improve their skills of empathy. Nevertheless, the only way we can move from where we are now to where we would like to be is to accept where we are now.

I heard a story once that illustrates this idea. A certain young man went to his doctor, complaining of a great deal of boredom in his life, a feeling of restlessness, almost as if he'd been anesthetized. In essence he said, "I'm going through the motions, but I really don't care. Everything is so routine and so mechanical that there's nothing exciting in life anymore."

After examining him, the doctor wrote him out a clean bill of health physically. However, he could sense, more than he could physically diagnose, a problem deep within the man, a problem within his spiritual dimension.

"I'd like to give you some prescriptions and ask you to follow them for a day," the doctor told his patient. "First, where is your favorite place?"

"I don't know," the patient responded quickly.

"As a child, where was it? What did you really like doing?"

"I loved the beach."

The doctor then said, "Take these three prescriptions and go to the beach. One you will take at nine o'clock, one at noon, and the last one at three. You must agree that you'll follow the prescription and not read the next one until the proper time. Fair enough?"

"I've never heard of anything like this before," the patient replied skeptically.

"Well, I think it will really help you."

So the restless young man took the prescriptions and went out to the beach. He was there by nine o'clock, accompanied by no one, as instructed. There was no radio, no phone, no company. He was alone with the beach and his prescription, which he read immediately. It contained two words: "Listen carefully."

"I can't believe this," he exclaimed. "Three hours of this!" Within one minute he was bored. Having heard the seagulls circling above and the surf hitting against some nearby rocks, he wondered what he could do for three hours. "But I committed myself," he said. "I'll stay with it. After all, it's only for one day."

He began to think deeply on the idea of listening carefully. He started to listen with his ears, and soon he could hear sounds he'd never identified before. He could hear two surfs. He could hear different kinds of birds. He could hear the sand crabs. He could hear whisperings under whisperings. Soon a whole new and fascinating world opened up to him. It calmed his entire system; he became meditative, relaxed, peaceful. Almost euphoric when noon came, he was genuinely disappointed that he had to pull out the second prescription, but he stayed true to his commitment.

Three words this time: "Try reaching back." Baffled at first by the cryptic message, the man then began to reflect on his childhood as he played on the beach. One experience after another floated through his mind. He remembered clam bakes with his family. He remembered watching his brother, who was killed in World War II, running up the beach, joyfully exulting that school was out. A deep feeling of nostalgia enveloped him, stirring up many positive feelings and memories. He was deeply engrossed in his memories when three o'clock came. Again he was loath to read the next prescription because of the warmth and enjoyment he was feeling.

But still he pulled out the last prescription: "Examine your motives." This was the hardest; it was the heart of the matter, and he knew it instantly. He began looking inside introspectively. He went through every facet of his life—all types of situations with all kinds of people. He made a very painful discovery: selfishness was his dominant trend. Never transcending himself, never identifying with a larger purpose, a worthier cause, he was always asking, "What's in it for me?"

He had discovered the root of his ennui, his boredom, his lackluster life, his mechanical, ritualistic attitudes toward everything. When six o'clock came, he had been thoroughly peaceful, he had remembered, and he had looked deeply within himself. By following the three prescriptions, he had made some resolves about the course of his life from that moment on, and he had begun to change.

To listen deeply and genuinely to another on jugular issues takes an enormous amount of internal personal security. It exposes our vulnerabilities. We may be changed. And if down deep we are feeling fairly insecure, we can't afford to risk being changed. We need to sense predictability and certainty. That is the anatomy of prejudice or prejudgment: we judge beforehand so that we don't have to deal with the possibility of a new thing happening. The specter of change frightens most people.

If we are changed or influenced as a result of empathic listening, we need to be able to say, "That's okay—it makes no real difference," because down deep we are changeless. At the core is a set of values and feelings that represent the real self, a sense of intrinsic worth that is independent of how others treat us. This is our inviolate self, our true identity.

LOGIC AND EMOTION

Effective, two-way communication demands that we capture both content and intent and learn to speak the languages of logic and emotion.

The language of logic and the language of sentiment are simply two different languages, and of the two the language of sentiment or emotion is far more motivational and powerful. This is why it is so important to listen primarily with our eyes and heart and secondarily with our ears. We must seek to understand the intent of the communication without prejudging or rejecting the content. We can do this by giving time, being patient, seeking first to understand, and openly expressing feelings.

To be effective in presenting your point of view, start by demonstrating a clear understanding of the alternative points of view. Articulate them better than their advocates can. Effective presentations begin with preassessment.

SYMPATHY AND EMPATHY

Giving full attention, being completely present, striving to transcend one's autobiography, and seeking to see things from another's point of view takes courage, patience, and inner sources of security. It means being open to new learning and to change. It means moving into the minds and hearts of others to see the world as they see it. It does not mean that you feel as they feel. That is sympathy. Rather, it means that you understand how they feel based on how they see the world. That is empathy.

An attitude of empathy is enormously attractive because it keeps you open, and others feel that you are learning, that you are influenceable. Remember that the key to your having influence with them is their perceiving that they have influence with you. When we finally learn to listen, seeking first to understand, we will learn more about communication. We will learn about the absolute futility of using the mind to dominate the heart. We will learn that there are two languages—the language of logic and the language of emotion—and that people behave more on the basis of how they feel than on how they think. We will learn that unless there are good feelings between people, they will find it almost impossible to reason together because of emotional barriers. We will learn that fear is a knot of the heart and that to untie this knot we must improve our relationship.

Communication, after all, is not so much a matter of intellect as it is of trust and acceptance of others, of their ideas and feelings, acceptance of the fact that they're different and that from their point of view they are right.

FALSE STARTS

Most personal and organizational communications are governed by social values. Strong social norms often make us protective and defensive because we believe that *those guys* over there are out to get *us guys*. Many cultures—families and business firms—are hampered by social and political quagmires, governed by who you know, by image building, by making the right impressions, by meeting the right people at the right time, by the mercurial moods of the people at the top, or by an adversarial spirit.

I ask you: What percent of the time and energy in your family or business is spent in some kind of defensive or protective communication? What percent of the energy is spent in things that do not contribute to serving your spouse, your children, or your customers—wasteful things like internal squabbling, interdepartmental rivalries, politicking, and interpersonal conflicts? Most people admit that 20 to 40 percent of their time and energy is spent in these destructive ways.

As we admit to such waste, we often undertake improvement initiatives. These often start in spectacular, even dramatic ways. But soon they bog down. New initiatives die in swamp conditions where there is much politicking, defensive communication, protective communication, interpersonal rivalry, interdepartmental contests, positioning, and manipulating. No sooner is the new initiative announced than massive resistance is marshaled against it. The culture has fed so long upon itself that it attempts to cannibalize new initiatives.

New initiatives often focus on how to improve communication processes and to train people in the skills of listening and explaining clearly their points of view. Other initiatives focus on problem solving skills and how to develop effective work teams. These well-intentioned training efforts try to create a spirit of cooperation. But the culture is so politicized, so based on defending positions and coercive power, carrot-and-stick motivations, that people resist these initiatives. The culture becomes cynical. The next new initiative is perceived as another fruitless, dramatic, desperate, frantic effort to make good things happen. Gradually the culture gets fatigued and demoralized. Survival, salary, and security issues become dominant. Many adjust by finding their primary satisfactions off the job because there's no more intrinsic satisfaction on the job. They keep the job basically to fund other activities that they find more satisfying.

Until we cultivate principle-centered leadership inside our organizations, our efforts to improve communications will have little permanent value. The foundation lies with people and relationships. When we ignore the foundation, our improvement initiatives will fail or falter. Effective communication is built on the cement of trust. And trust is based on trustworthiness, not politics.

Chapter 11

THIRTY METHODS OF INFLUENCE

WE ALL WANT to have positive influence with certain people in our personal and professional lives. Our motive may be to win new business, keep customers, maintain friendships, change behaviors, or improve marriage and family relationships.

But how do we do it? How do we powerfully and ethically influence the lives of other people? I submit that there are three basic categories of influence: 1) to model by example (others *see*); 2) to build caring relationships (others *feel*); and 3) to mentor by instruction (others *hear*).

The following thirty methods of influence fall into these three categories.

EXAMPLE: WHO YOU ARE AND HOW YOU ACT

1. *Refrain from saying the unkind or negative thing*, particularly when you are provoked or fatigued. In these circumstances, to not say the unkind or critical thing is a supreme form of self-mastery. Courage is the quality of every quality at its highest testing point. If we have no model of restraint to follow, we will likely take out our frustration on our fellow workers. We may need to find new models, new examples

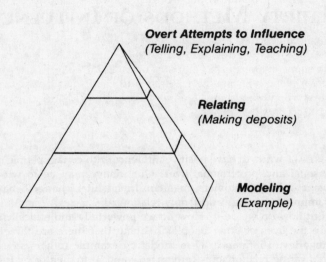

PYRAMID OF INFLUENCE

Overt Attempts to Influence
(Telling, Explaining, Teaching)

Relating
(Making deposits)

Modeling
(Example)

to follow, and learn to win our own battles privately, to get our motives straight, to gain perspective and control, and to back away from impulsively speaking or striking out.

2. *Exercise patience with others.* In times of stress, our impatience surfaces. We may say things we don't really mean or intend to say—all out of proportion to reality. Or we may become sullen, communicating through emotion and attitude rather than words, eloquent messages of criticism, judgment, and rejection. We then harvest hurt feelings and strained relationships. Patience is the practical expression of faith, hope, wisdom, and love. It is a very active emotion. It is not indifference, sullen endurance, or resignation. Patience is emotional diligence. It accepts the reality of step-by-step processes and natural growth cycles. Life provides abundant chances to practice patience—to stretch the emotional fiber—from waiting for a late person or plane to listening quietly to your child's feelings and experiences when other things are pressing.

3. *Distinguish between the person and the behavior or performance.* While we may disapprove of bad behavior and poor performance, we first need to communicate and help build a sense of intrinsic worth and self-esteem totally apart from comparisons and judgments. Doing this will powerfully inspire superior effort. The power to distinguish between person and performance and to communicate intrinsic worth flows naturally out of our own sense of intrinsic worth.

4. *Perform anonymous service.* Whenever we do good for others anonymously, our sense of intrinsic worth and self-respect increases. Moreover, we gain insight into the worth of others by serving them without expectation of publicity or reward. Selfless service has always been one of the most powerful methods of influence.

5. *Choose the proactive response.* Why do so few of us "do" as well as we "know"? Because we neglect a connecting link between what we know and what we do—we don't choose our response. Choosing requires us to gain perspective and then to decide our own actions and reactions. Choosing means to accept responsibility for our attitudes and actions, to refuse to blame others or circumstances. It involves a real internal struggle, ultimately, between competing motives or conflicting concepts. Unless we exercise our power to choose wisely, our actions will be determined by conditions. Our ultimate

freedom is the right and power to decide how anybody or anything outside ourselves will affect us.

6. *Keep the promises you make to others.* By making and keeping our resolves and promises, we win influence with others. To be and do better, we must make promises (resolutions, commitments, oaths, and covenants), but we should never make a promise we will not keep. Using self-knowledge, we can be very selective about the promises we make. Our ability to make and keep promises is one measure of faith in ourselves and of our integrity.

7. *Focus on the circle of influence.* As we focus on doing something positive about the things we can control, we expand our circle of influence. Direct control problems are solved by changing our habits of doing and thinking. Indirect control problems require us to change our methods of influence. For instance, we complain from time to time that "if only the boss could understand my program or my problem. . . ." But few of us take the time to prepare the kind of presentation that the boss would listen to and respect, in his language, with his problems in mind. With no control problems, we can control our reaction to problems, deciding within ourselves how anything or anybody will affect us. As William James said: "We can change our circumstances by a mere change of our attitude."

8. *Live the law of love.* We encourage obedience to the laws of life when we live the laws of love. People are extremely tender inside, particularly those who act as if they are tough and self-sufficient. And if we'll listen to them with the third ear, the heart, they'll tell us so. We can gain even greater influence with them by showing love, particularly unconditional love, as this gives people a sense of intrinsic worth and security unrelated to conforming behavior or comparisons with others. Many borrow their security and strength from external appearances, status symbols, positions, achievements, and associations. But borrowing strength inevitably builds weakness. We all distrust superficial human relations techniques and manipulative success formulas that are separated from sincere love.

RELATIONSHIP: DO YOU UNDERSTAND AND CARE?

9. *Assume the best of others.* Assuming good faith produces good fruit. By acting on the assumption others want and mean to do their

best, as they see it, you can exert a powerful influence and bring out the best in them. Our efforts to classify and categorize, judge, and measure often emerge from our own insecurities and frustrations in dealing with complex, changing realities. Each person has many dimensions and potentials, some in evidence, most dormant. And they tend to respond to how we treat them and what we believe about them. Some may let us down or take advantage of our trust, considering us naive or gullible. But most will come through, simply because we believe in them. Don't bottleneck the many for fear of a few! Whenever we assume good faith, born of good motives and inner security, we appeal to the good in others.

10. *Seek first to understand.* Seek first to understand, then to be understood. When we're communicating with another, we need to give full attention, to be completely present. Then we need to empathize—to see from the other's point of view, to "walk in his moccasins" for a while. This takes courage, and patience, and inner sources of security. But until people feel that you understand them, they will not be open to your influence.

11. *Reward open, honest expressions or questions.* Too often we punish honest, open expressions or questions. We upbraid, judge, belittle, embarrass. Others learn to cover up, to protect themselves, to not ask. The greatest single barrier to rich, honest communication is the tendency to criticize and judge.

12. *Give an understanding response.* Using the understanding response (reflecting back feeling), three good things happen: 1) you gain increased understanding and clarity of feelings and problems; 2) you gain new courage and growth in responsible independence; and 3) you build real confidence in the relationship. This response has its greatest value when a person wants to talk about a situation laden with emotions and feelings. But this response is more attitude than technique. It will fail if you try to manipulate; it will work if you deeply want to understand.

13. *If offended, take the initiative.* If someone offends you unknowingly and continues to do so, take the initiative to clear it up. Consider two tragic consequences of not taking the initiative: first, the offended one often broods about the offense until the situation is blown out of proportion; second, the offended one then behaves defensively to avoid further hurt. When taking the initiative, do it in

good spirits, not in a spirit of vindication and anger. Also, describe your feelings—when and how the offense took place—rather than judging or labeling the other person. This preserves the dignity and self-respect of the other person, who then can respond and learn without feeling threatened. Our feelings, opinions, and perceptions are not facts. To act on that awareness takes thought control and fosters humility.

14. *Admit your mistakes, apologize, ask for forgiveness.* When we are party to seriously strained relations, we may need to admit that we are at least partly to blame. When one is deeply hurt, he draws back, closes up, and puts us behind prison bars in his own mind. Improving our behavior alone won't release us from this prison. Often the only way out is to admit our mistakes, apologize, and ask forgiveness, making no excuses, explanations, or defenses.

15. *Let arguments fly out open windows.* Give no answer to contentious arguments or irresponsible accusations. Let such things "fly out open windows" until they spend themselves. If you try to answer or reason back, you merely gratify and ignite pent-up hostility and anger. When you go quietly about your business, the other has to struggle with the natural consequences of irresponsible expression. Don't be drawn into any poisonous, contentious orbit, or you'll find yourself bitten and afflicted similarly. Then the other person's weaknesses will become your own, and all this will sow a seed bed of future misunderstandings, accusations, and wrangling. The power to let arguments fly out open windows flows out of an inward peace that frees you from the compulsive need to answer and justify. The source of this peace is living responsibly, obediently to conscience.

16. *Go one on one.* An executive might be very involved and dedicated to his or her work, to church and community projects, and to many people's lives, yet not have a deep, meaningful relationship with his or her own spouse. It takes more nobility of character, more humility, more patience, to develop such a relationship with one's spouse than it would take to give continued dedicated service to the many. We often justify neglecting the one to take care of the many because we receive many expressions of esteem and gratitude. Yet we know that we need to set aside time and give ourselves completely to one special person. With our children, we may need to

schedule one-on-one visits—a time when we can give them our full attention and listen to them without censoring, lecturing, or comparing.

17. *Renew your commitment to things you have in common.* Continually renew your basic commitment to the things that unite you with your friends, family, and fellow workers. Their deepest loyalties and strongest feelings attach to these things rather than to the problems or issues around which differences often emerge. Differences are not ignored; they are subordinated. The issue or one's point is never as important as the relationship.

18. *Be influenced by them first.* We have influence with others to the degree they feel they have influence with us. As the saying goes, "I don't care how much you know until I know how much you care." When another feels you genuinely care about him and that you understand his unique problems and feelings, he also feels he has influenced you. He will then become amazingly open. We take the prescription because it is based on the diagnosis.

19. *Accept the person and the situation.* The first step in changing or improving another is to accept him as he is. Nothing reinforces defensive behavior more than judgment, comparison, or rejection. A feeling of acceptance and worth frees a person from the need to defend and helps release the natural growth tendency to improve. Acceptance is not condoning a weakness or agreeing with an opinion. Rather, it is affirming the intrinsic worth of another by acknowledging that he does feel or think a particular way.

Instruction: What You Tell Me

20. *Prepare your mind and heart before you prepare your speech.* What we say may be less important than how we say it. So, before your children return from school full of their own needs, stop and get control. Plumb your resources. Set your mind and heart. Choose pleasantness and cheerfulness. Choose to give full attention to their needs. Or sit a moment in the car before coming in from work and do the same. Ask yourself, "How can I bless my wife (or husband) and children tonight?" Plumb your resources. Choosing to be your best self will arrest fatigue and renew your best resolves.

21. *Avoid fight or flight—talk through differences.* Many people either fight or flee when they disagree. Fighting takes many forms, ranging from violence and open expressions of anger and hate to subtle sarcasm, sharp answers, clever comebacks, belittling humor, judgments, and reactions. Fleeing also takes various forms. One is simply to withdraw, feeling sorry for oneself. Such sulking often feeds the fires of revenge and future retaliation. People also flee by growing cold and indifferent, by escaping involvement and responsibility.

22. *Recognize and take time to teach.* With differences come supreme teaching moments. But there's a time to teach and a time not to teach. It's time to teach when 1) people are not threatened (efforts to teach when people feel threatened will only increase resentment, so wait for or create a new situation in which the person feels more secure and receptive); 2) you're not angry or frustrated, when you have feelings of affection, respect, and inward security; and 3) when the other person needs help and support (to rush in with success formulas when someone is emotionally low or fatigued or under a lot of pressure is comparable to trying to teach a drowning man to swim). Remember: We are teaching one thing or another all of the time, because we are constantly radiating what we are.

23. *Agree on the limits, rules, expectations, and consequences.* These must be clearly established, agreed upon, understood, and enforced. Personal security is largely born of a sense of justice—knowing what is expected, what the limits, rules, and consequences are. Life can be thrown out of kilter with uncertain expectations, shifting limits, or arbitrary rules: one day this, the next day that. No wonder many grow up learning to depend only on their own ability to manipulate people and life. When life becomes a game to be manipulated, the only sin is getting caught.

24. *Don't give up, and don't give in.* It is unkind to shield people from the consequences of their own behavior. In doing so, we teach them they are inadequate and weak. When we give in to irresponsible behavior by excusing it or sympathizing with it, we condone and foster spoiled, law-unto-self behavior. And if we give up—by ignoring people or tearing into them—we undermine their motivation to try. The discipline of *Don't give up, and don't give in,* tempered with love, comes from responsible, disciplined living. Otherwise we

take the course of least resistance—giving in when we care or giving up when we don't.

25. *Be there at the crossroads.* None of us want the people we care most about to make decisions that have important long-range consequences on the basis of short-range emotional perspectives and moods, personal insecurity, and self-doubt. How can we influence them? First, think before you react. Don't be controlled by your own short-range emotional moods and do something that injures whatever relationship and influence you now have. Second, understand that people tend to act in terms of how they feel instead of what they know. Motivation is more a function of the heart than the head. When we sense that our reason and logic aren't communicating with their sentiment and emotion, we should try to understand their language as we would a foreign tongue, without condemning it or rejecting them. This effort communicates respect and acceptance, lowers defenses, diminishes the need to fight, and restores the desire to do what is right.

26. *Speak the languages of logic and emotion.* The language of logic and the language of emotion are as different as English and French. When we realize we don't have a common language, we may need to communicate in one of four other ways: 1) Give time, for when we cheerfully give time, we transfer its worth to another; 2) Be patient, as patience also communicates worth and says "I'll go at your speed; I'm happy to wait for you; you're worth it"; 3) Seek to understand, because an honest effort to understand eliminates the need to fight and to defend; and 4) Openly express our feelings and be congruent with our nonverbal expressions.

27. *Delegate effectively.* Effective delegation takes emotional courage as we allow, to one degree or another, others to make mistakes on our time, money, and good name. This courage consists of patience, self-control, faith in the potential of others, and respect for individual differences. Effective delegation must be two-way: responsibility given, responsibility received. There are three phases. First, the initial agreement. People have a clear understanding of what is expected and what the resources, authority, latitude, and guidelines are. Second, sustaining the delegatees. The supervisor becomes a source of help, the advocate, not the feared adversary. He provides resources, removes obstacles, sustains actions and decisions, gives

vision, provides training, and shares feedback. Third, the account-ability process. This is largely one of self-evaluation, since delegatees are supervised by results, by actual performance.

28. *Involve people in meaningful projects.* Meaningful projects have a healing influence on people. However, what is meaningful to a manager may be meaningless to a subordinate. Projects take on meaning when people are involved in the planning and thinking processes. We all need to be engaged in a good cause. Without such projects, life loses its meaning; in fact, the life span is short for people who retire, looking for a tensionless state. Life is sustained by tension between where we are now and where we want to be—some goal worth struggling for.

29. *Train them in the law of the harvest.* We teach the "agricultural principles" of preparing the soil, seeding, cultivating, watering, weeding, and harvesting. We focus on natural processes. We align the systems, especially compensation, to reflect and reinforce the idea that we reap what we sow.

30. *Let natural consequences teach responsible behavior.* One of the kindest things we can do is to let the natural or logical consequences of people's actions teach them responsible behavior. They may not like it or us, but popularity is a fickle standard by which to measure character development. Insisting on justice demands more true love, not less. We care enough for their growth and security to suffer their displeasure.

OVERCOMING THREE BIG MISTAKES

In our attempts to influence others, we commonly make three mistakes, all related either to ignoring or short-cutting these three categories of influence.

Mistake #1: Advise before understand. Before we try to tell others what to do, we need to establish an understanding relationship. The key to your influence with me is your understanding of me. Unless you understand me and my unique situation and feelings, you won't know how to advise or counsel me. Unless you're influenced by my uniqueness, I'm not going to be influenced by your advice. Cure: Empathy—seek first to understand, then to be understood.

Mistake #2: Attempt to build/rebuild relationships without changing conduct or attitude. We try to build or rebuild a relationship without making any fundamental change in our conduct or attitude. If our example is pockmarked with inconsistency and insincerity, no amount of "win friends" technique will work. As Emerson so aptly put it, "What you are shouts so loudly in my ears I can't hear what you say." Cure: Show consistency and sincerity.

Mistake #3: Assume that good example and relationship are sufficient. We assume that a good example and a good relationship are sufficient, that we don't need to teach people explicitly. Just as vision without love contains no motivation, so also love without vision contains no goals, no guidelines, no standards, no lifting power. Cure: Teach and talk about vision, mission, roles, goals, guidelines, and standards.

In the last analysis, what we are communicates far more eloquently and persuasively than what we say or even what we do.

Chapter 12

EIGHT WAYS TO ENRICH MARRIAGE AND FAMILY RELATIONSHIPS

PROFESSIONAL SUCCESSES can't compensate for failures in marriage and family relationships; life's ledger will reflect the imbalance, if not the debt.

Relationships with spouses and with children, as with other relationships, tend toward entropy—toward disorder and dissolution. One of the most vicious and wasteful cycles in life is the cycle of marriage and divorce—of short-term romances and affairs—with all the frightful consequences to children, both those born and those aborted.

To keep marriage and family relationships healthy over time is no small task. Having a principle-centered husband-wife team at the head certainly helps. Applying the following eight principle-based practices will revitalize and enrich your family relationships.

1. Retain a long-term perspective. Without a long-term perspective on marriage and family, we will simply not endure or sustain the inevitable rigors, struggles, and challenges. With a long-term perspective, where there is a will, there is a way.

Short-term perspectives and thought processes bog us down and leave us trying to lift ourselves by our own bootstraps. To one possessing a short-term perspective, a relationship problem in the marriage or family is just another frustrating obstacle on a fast-track self-fulfillment path.

Do you have a short- or long-term perspective in your marriage and family? To find out, you might try the following experiment. Take a piece of paper and write at the top on the left side, "Short-Term Perspective," and at the top on the right side, "Long-Term Perspective." In the middle list the relevant issues, concerns, or questions you have about marriage and family. For instance, you might list such issues as the role of the husband/father and wife/mother, financial management matters, child discipline, in-law relations, birth control, moral or religious practices, life-style, problem-solving strategies, and so on. Examine each issue or concern, starting with the short term and then moving to the long term.

This exercise will give you deep insights into your relationships with your spouse and children. I encourage you to build bridges between the ideal and the real to avoid living in two isolated and artificial compartments: 1) the abstract, ethereal, idealistic, spiritual side and 2) the mundane, gritty, everyday life side. Integration builds integrity.

2. *Rescript your marriage and family life.* As children we are most dependent, vulnerable, and most needful of love, acceptance, and belonging. Our childhood experiences shape our lives. Our parents and others are roles models; we identify with them, good or bad. In effect they give us a life script. These scripts become our parts, our roles. They are more emotionally absorbed than they are consciously chosen. They rise out of our deep vulnerabilities, our deep dependency upon others, and our needs for acceptance and love, for belonging, for a sense of importance and worth, for a feeling that we matter. This is why role modeling is the most basic responsibility of parents. They are handing life's scripts to their children, scripts that in all likelihood will be acted out for much of the rest of the children's lives.

People identify with what they see and what they feel far more than with what they hear. Scripting is about 90 percent example and relationship and 10 percent telling. Thus our day-to-day modeling is far and away our highest form of influence! We must not hold forth eloquently on high moral principles and then plow back into the deep, where we spend most of our lives as grouches, as critics, as unfeeling, unloving people.

We are powerfully influenced by our scripts, but we can learn to rewrite our scripts. We can identify with new models and have new relationships. Better scripts won't come merely from reading correct principles in good books, but from identifying with and relating to the persons who live them. Correct principles cannot compensate for incorrect modeling, for bad examples. It's so much easier to teach correct principles to my students than it is to know and love them; so much easier to give brilliant advice than to empathize and be open so that they can know and love me; so much easier to live independently than to live interdependently; so much easier to be a judge than a light, a critic than a model.

Many of the problems people face in marriage rise out of conflicting role expectations or script conflicts. For instance, the husband may think it is the wife's role to take care of the garden—his mother did. And the wife may think that it is her husband's role, since her father did. A small problem becomes a large one because conflicting scripts compound every problem and magnify every difference. Study your own marriage and family problems to see if they, too, are not rooted in conflicting role expectations and compounded by conflicting scripts.

3. *Reconsider your roles.* Spouses and parents play three roles: producer, manager, and leader. The producer does the things necessary to achieve desired results: the child cleans his or her room; the father takes out the garbage; the mother puts the baby to bed. A producer may use tools to increase results.

A parent who is production-oriented may be one who cares only about a clean house or well-kept yard. He or she does most of the work and then criticizes the children for not doing their part. The children, of course, are insufficiently trained and prepared to do their part.

Many "producer" parents don't know how to delegate, so they end up doing the work themselves and killing themselves off. They go to bed every night exhausted, irritable, critical, and disappointed that others are not being more helpful. They tend to think the solution to most problems is to put their hand to the plow and get the job done. That is why their operations stay small or why their businesses go under. They simply do not know how to delegate so that others are internally motivated and follow through on expectations. When they attempt to delegate, they often end up saying "It takes me more time to explain it and to train this person than to do it myself." So they give up and go back to producing, and they end up bone weary, self-pitying, and martyred. They are forever overburdened, rushed, fatigued, and disappointed. They overreact to mistakes and move in quickly to correct them. They hover over and check up constantly, thus undermining the motivation of the children and fulfilling the prophecy "I knew it; I knew they wouldn't come through."

In the "manager" role, the parent may delegate various jobs around the home and the yard to the children. This delegation gives the parent leverage: the parent with one unit of input may produce a hundred units of productivity. The "manager" parent compensates for the weakness of the child producer. The manager understands the need for structure and systems—particularly training, communication, information, and compensation systems—and the need for standard procedures and practices based on correct principles. Much of the production may then be done on automatic pilot. However, for this very reason the manager parent tends to be inflexible, bureaucratic, methods-oriented, and systems-minded. Over time, managers tend to focus on efficiency, not effectiveness—on doing things right instead of doing the right things.

The nature of marriage and family life is interdependency. Without management in the family, the wheel is being reinvented every day; there are no established systems and procedures; everyone is exhausted from production; there is a role conflict and ambiguity; and when the work isn't done, people blame each other for the failure. Before parents can be good managers, they need a high level of independence, internal security, and self-reliance; otherwise they will not willingly choose to communicate, to cooperate, to work with and through others, to be flexible, and to adapt to the human situation and the needs of others.

In the leadership role, you can bring about change. But changes upset and disturb people, stirring up fears, uncertainties, and insecurities. Lubricate change by genuinely empathizing with the resisting concerns, helping others feel free to express their concerns and to be involved in creating new, acceptable solutions. Short of such leadership, the resistances will only solidify and lead to a kind of fossil-ized, rigid bureaucracy in the family or a cold accommodation in the marriage.

There are many well-managed families lacking leadership, pro-ceeding correctly but in the wrong direction or full of excellent sys-tems and checklists for everybody but with no heart, no warmth, no feeling. Children tend to move away from these situations as soon as possible and may not return, except out of a sense of family duty. This phenomenon is also seen in intergenerational family relation-ships: families either get together often out of mutual interest and love, or they get together only occasionally, somewhat begrudg-ingly, out of a sense of duty to a particular person. In the latter case, as soon as that person is dead, family members go their separate ways, live in different cities, and feel closer to neighbors or old friends than they do to brothers or sisters or cousins or aunts and uncles.

If the mother is constantly in a producer role, the father in a man-ager role, and no one in the leader role, the children will do little to help, except grudgingly. The leader's role is to provide direction through modeling and vision, to motivate through love and inspira-tion, to build a complementary team based on mutual respect, to be effectiveness-minded and focused on results rather than on meth-ods, systems, and procedures.

These three interdependent roles—the producer, the manager, and the leader—are vital in marriage and family life. In the early stages of marriage, both partners must play all three roles, perhaps with more emphasis on one than another. As children come along and are capable of carrying more responsibility, the manager and leader roles will tend to become increasingly important. Eventually the leader role becomes the most important for the parent or grand-parent.

4. *Reset your goals.* In our efforts to get what we want in marriage and family life, there is one powerful lesson of transcendent impor-tance: we must preserve and enhance the assets and resources that enable us to be productive. I call these two goals "P" and "PC." P stands for the production of desired results, PC for production ca-pability, which means the preservation and enhancement of the results-producing assets or resources.

For example, if a parent has neglected PC work with a teenage son, the trust level will be low, making the communication closed and mechanical. The son simply will not be open to the father's counsel on matters where experience and wisdom are needed. The father may have much wisdom and desire to counsel his son, but the son will not be open to it because of the low trust. The P work, the production of the desired results, will now suffer terribly, because the PC work has not been done. And the son may end up making decisions on a short-range emotional perspective, resulting in many negative long-range consequences.

When PC work has been ignored, a parent may need to "go the second mile" to recover a relationship. There are many other ways of going the second mile, of making emotional deposits. What may be a deposit to one person may be a withdrawal for another. "One man's meat is another man's poison." When we live the primary laws of love (PC activity), we encourage obedience to the primary laws of life (P results). There is no short cut.

In developing marriage or family relationships, short-cut techniques, artificial rewards, psych-up strategies, and duplicitous, hypocritical living may hide character flaws temporarily, but those flaws will be exposed in the next storm of life. Marriage is a courtship requiring continual deposits in the form of gentleness, kindness, consideration, small courtesies, pleasant words, and unconditional love.

Any time we neglect PC in the name of P, we may temporarily get a little more P, but eventually it will decline. If we use manipulative and intimidating techniques, we may get what we want in the short run, but eventually the trust level and communication processes deteriorate, resulting in a cynical culture. In this climate, marriage relationships deteriorate. Instead of a rich understanding, where a couple can communicate almost without words, even make mistakes and still be understood, the situation becomes one of mere accommodation, wherein they simply attempt to live independent lifestyles in a fairly respectful and tolerant way. It may further deteriorate to one of hostility and defensiveness, where a person is made an "offender for a word" and it's simply too risky to think out loud. These marriages may end up in open warfare in the courts or in a cold war at home, sustained only by children, sex, social pressure, or image projection.

In a sense, selfishness, a root cause of marital discord and divorce, is a symptom for heavy focus on P, or what we want—the results we desire. For instance, a husband who is selfish and inconsiderate for a period of time, cajoles and manipulates and intimidates to get what he wants, but eventually, because of a lack of PC, the relationship deteriorates.

The same is true with parents in relation to their children. If parents focus on what they want and threaten and intimidate, yell and scream, wield the carrot and the stick, or go the other way and indulge the kids or simply leave them alone, relationships will deteriorate; discipline will be nonexistent; vision, standards, and expectations will be unclear, ambiguous, and confused.

When the children are young and susceptible to threats and manipulation, parents often get what they want in spite of their methods. But by the time the child becomes a teenager, a parent's threats no longer have the same immediate force to bring about desired results. Unless there is a high trust level and a lot of mutual respect, they have virtually no control over their children. There is simply no reserve funds in the emotional bank account. A lack of PC work done in the formative years leads to an overdrawn emotional bank account in the teen years, a breakdown of relationship, and a lack of influence.

Emotional bank accounts are very fragile, yet very resilient at the same time. If we have a large emotional bank account, say, $200,000 of emotional reserve with others, we can make small withdrawals of $5,000 and $10,000 from time to time, and they will understand and accommodate us. For instance, we may need to make a very unpopular, authoritarian decision because of certain time pressures without even involving others or explaining it to them. If we have a $200,000 bank account and make a $10,000 withdrawal in this manner, we would still have $190,000 left. Perhaps the next day we would take the time to explain what we did and why we did it, thus redepositing the $10,000.

A PC orientation flows directly out of the character and integrity and sincerity of a person, rather than as a manipulative tactic only to get P. If we are insincere and use PC as a manipulative technology, it undoubtedly will be revealed for what it is, the net effect again being a huge withdrawal. But if we make small, sincere deposits consistently over time, we will build a huge reserve. We can make these small deposits in the form of patience, courtesies, empathy, kindnesses, services, sacrifices, honesty, and sincere apologies for past mistakes, overreactions, ego trips, and other forms of withdrawal.

5. *Realign family systems.* Four systems are needed to make a family work. For instance, if you do not have 1) *goals and plans,* on what basis can you establish 2) *stewardships and a discipline program,* or what would be the standards in 3) *teaching and training* or in 4) *communicating and problem-solving?*

If your family lacks a teaching and training program, how will you develop the skills of communication and problem-solving or the willingness to take responsibilities or do jobs or to submit to a discipline system? If you don't have a system for communication and problem-solving, when will you clarify values and select goals and make plans to achieve them? When will you do your teaching and training and set up stewardships and carry out agreed-upon disciplines? And if you don't have a system of stewardship and discipline, how will the work get done to meet goals, implement plans, develop skills, or teach and train?

All four systems are necessary. Many parents unwisely focus on one or two of these systems, thinking that success in one will compensate for failures in other systems. People tend to do what they are good at doing and what they like doing. Asking them to move outside their "comfort zone" can be very threatening and upsetting to them. But if someone will provide leadership and help lubricate the processes of growth and change—help them understand why they need all four systems and encourage them to develop the new attitudes and skills that may lie outside their present scripts or their present modes of thinking and doing—their "new birth" processes will not be aborted because of the labor pains.

6. *Refine three vital skills.* Time management, communication, and problem-solving are skills needed in every phase of marriage and family life. Fortunately improvement in these three skills lies within our own control. We can't do very much about other people's behavior, but we can do a great deal about our own, particularly in how we manage our time, how we communicate with others, and how we solve the problems and challenges of life.

Time management is really a misnomer, because we all have exactly the same amount of time, although some accomplish several times as much as others do with their time. Self-management is a better term, because it implies that we manage ourselves in the time allotted us. Most people manage their lives by crises; they are driven by external events, circumstances, and problems. They become problem-minded, and the only priority setting they do is between one problem and another. Effective time managers are opportunity-minded. They don't deny or ignore problems, but they try to prevent them. They occasionally have to deal with acute problems or crises, but in the main they prevent them from reaching this level of concern through careful analysis into the nature of the problems and through long-range planning.

The essence of time management is to set priorities and then to organize and execute around them. Setting priorities requires us to think carefully and clearly about values, about ultimate concerns. These then have to be translated into long- and short-term goals and plans and translated once more into schedules or time slots. Then, unless something more important—not something more urgent—comes along, we must discipline ourselves to do as we planned.

Communication is a prerequisite to problem-solving and one of the most fundamental skills in life. Communication could be defined as mutual understanding. The main problem in communication is the "translation" problem: translating what we mean into what we say and translating what we say into what we mean. The first challenge, therefore, is to learn to say what we mean; the second challenge is to learn to listen so that we understand what others mean. The key to "accurate translation" or effective two-way communication is high trust. You can communicate with someone you trust almost without words. You can even make mistakes in your verbal communication and still find that they get your meaning. But when the trust level is low, you will find that it really makes little difference how hard you try to communicate or how good you are in technique or how clear your language is. When trust is high, communication is easy, effortless, instantaneous, and accurate. When trust is low, communication is extremely difficult, exhausting, and ineffective. The key to communication is trust, and the key to trust is trustworthiness. Living a life of integrity is the best guarantee of maintaining the climate of effective communication. As with all natural processes, there are no short cuts, no quick fixes.

Problem-solving. The real test of our communication skill comes in interactive problem-solving in real-life marriage and family situations. The classic approach to problem-solving deals with four questions: 1) Where are we? 2) Where do we want to go? 3) How do we get there? 4) How will we know we have arrived?

The first question—Where are we?—focuses on the importance of gathering and diagnosing reality data. The second question—Where do we want to go?—deals with clarifying values and selecting goals. The third question—How do we get there?—involves generating and evaluating alternatives, making a decision, and planning the action steps to implement it. The fourth question—How will we know we have arrived?—involves setting up criteria or standards to measure or observe or discern progress toward our objectives or goals.

When problems are emotionally charged, as they often are in marriage and family situations, most people make assumptions about the first two questions—Where are we? and Where do we want to go?—and then begin to argue and fight over the third question—How do we get there from here? This only compounds the problem and increases people's emotional investment in what they want, cultivating the scarcity mentality. They then begin to define winning as defeating someone, to think in terms of dichotomies (either/or approaches), and to go for win/lose solutions. When both parties have this attitude, then lose/lose is almost inevitable. One of the parties may feel overpowered or intimidated and take up a lose/win position, but this will result only in temporary resolution of the problem, with far more serious problems downstream.

What we want is a win/win solution wherein both parties feel good and feel committed to the decision and action plan. To achieve this takes more than time; it takes patience, self-control, and courage balanced with consideration. In short, it takes considerable maturity and the exercise of our higher faculties.

7. *Regain internal security.* Most people derive their security from external sources—that is, from the environment, possessions, or the opinions of others, including one's spouse. The problem with any external source is dependency on those sources, which means that our lives become buffeted and made uncertain and insecure by whatever happens to those sources.

We need to cultivate interdependency from sources that are constant and faithful regardless of circumstances. The ability to rescript our lives and to stay with these new scripts requires a great deal of courage. Courage arises out of an internal sense of personal worth, personal value, and personal security. Consider seven sources that are independent of circumstance or opinion.

True north principles. The most fundamental source and the root of all the rest, one that can absolutely be relied on in any given set of circumstances, is our adherence to a set of changeless principles. This means constantly educating and obeying our conscience. The more we do these things, the greater will be our happiness and growth in marriage and the more we will be given wisdom and guidance and power in solving or transcending the various problems and challenges we encounter.

Rich private life. Cultivate the habit of private meditation, contemplation, prayer, and study of the scriptures or other inspirational literature. Many people are bored when they are by themselves, because their lives have been a merry-go-round of activity, almost always with other people. Cultivate the ability to be alone and to think deeply, to "do nothing," to enjoy silence and solitude. Reflect, write, listen, plan, visualize, ponder, relax. A rich private life nourishes our sense of personal worth and security.

Appreciate nature. If you become deeply immersed in the beauties of nature—especially the mountains or the seashore and particularly early in the morning or in the evening—you will experience magnificent creation, and nature will feed its quiet beauty and strength into your soul. It is almost like being given a fresh tank of oxygen. Nature is one of the best scripting sources and teaches many beautiful principles and processes.

Think of a vacation you have had where you were close to the nature and experienced quiet times in beautiful settings such as canyons, lakes, rivers, streams, seashores, or high mountains. What were you like? Were you not more contemplative, more inwardly peaceful and tranquil? Now, think of another vacation filled with fun but also with schedules and rush and travel and socials, time spent at carnivals, circuses, amusement parks, or whatever. What were you like when you returned from that vacation? Were you not exhausted, spent, frazzled, and still in need of a real vacation?

Sharpen the saw. Cultivate the habit of sharpening the saw physically, mentally, and spiritually every day. Cultivate the habit of regular stretching, aerobic, and toning exercise at least every other day. Weekend exercise isn't enough; in fact, it may hurt more than help if we overdo it. As we grow older, our bodies don't have the flexibility and resiliency to deal with those weekend stresses. Regular, vigorous exercise is vital to radiant health and unquestionably influences not just the quantity of our years but the quality of life in those years. We must never get so busy sawing that we don't take time to sharpen the saw.

Give service. Anonymous service is particularly important. The philosophy that we will find our life when we lose it in service is a totally true paradox. If our intent is to serve, to bless others, without self-concern, a by-product of our service comes within—a kind of psychological, emotional, spiritual reward in the form of internal security and peace. Such a reward comes in the second mile.

Show integrity. When we are true to the light we have been given, when we keep our word consistently, when we are striving continually to harmonize our habit system with our value system, then our life is integrated. Our honor becomes greater than our moods, and we can have confidence in ourselves because we know ourselves. We know that we will be true and faithful under temptation. Integrity is the foundation of all true goodness and greatness. The internal security that emerges from it eliminates the need to live for impression, to exaggerate for effort, to drop names or places, to borrow strength from credentials or possessions or fashions or affiliations or associations or status symbols. We have no need for cynicism or sarcasm or cutting humor. Our sense of humor becomes spontaneous, healthy, and proportionate to the situation.

That other person. The final source of security is another person who loves us and believes in us even when we don't believe in ourselves. In a sense, this source is external to oneself and imperfect. But I mention it because there are those people who are true and faithful and so inwardly anchored and rooted that we can depend upon them—not in the ultimate sense, but in the more proximate sense. They know us; they care about us; their love is unconditional; and they will stay with us when everyone else deserts us, particularly when we desert ourselves.

Most mothers and many fathers have unconditional love toward their children. Maybe it's what the mother goes through to bring the child into the world that gives her such an unconditional love and a continuing belief in the basic goodness and potential of her son or daughter. Those who are principle-centered also possess the same capacity.

Such individuals can make all the difference in our lives. Think of your own life. Did you ever have a teacher, a leader, a neighbor, a friend, a coach, or an adviser who believed in you when you didn't believe in yourself? One who stayed with you regardless? Not someone who was soft and permissive with you, someone who gave in to you, but someone who would neither give in to you nor give up on you.

To me, the thrilling challenge is the awareness of how we can be such a person to other people.

8. Develop a family mission statement. One of the most powerfully unifying experiences that a family can have is in creating a family mission statement. Too many families are managed on the basis of instant gratification, not on sound principles and rich emotional bank accounts. Then, when stress and pressure mount, people start yelling, overreacting, or being cynical, critical, or silent. Children see it and think this is the way you solve problems—either fight or flight. And the cycles can be passed on for generations. This is why I recommend creating a family mission statement. By drafting a family constitution, you are getting to the root of the problem. If you want to get anywhere long-term, identify core values and goals and get the systems aligned with these values and goals. Work on the foundation. Make it secure. The core of any family is what is changeless, what is always going to be there. This can be represented in a family mission statement. Ask yourself, "What do we value? What is our family all about? What do we stand for? What is our essential mission, our reason for being?"

As important as the end product is—a piece of paper that captures the family mission—even more important is what happens in the process of creating it. If the family mission statement is really to serve as a constitution—something that guides, governs, and inspires—*every* member of the family must be involved. The mission statement must embody principles that are valued by every member. Let the mission evolve over many weeks and months. Create opportunities where feelings can be expressed openly, with no judgment, where real effort is made to deeply understand what is important to each child. Allow plenty of unforced time, and be very patient.

I am reminded of our own family's first effort to create a mission statement. My football-playing son's first shot at it was this: "We are one hell of a family, and we kick butt!" We had great experiences together over several months. We learned a great deal about each other, and in the end we were united around a mission in which we are committed to supporting each other. I would like to share with you our mission statement. I hesitate in doing so because I wouldn't want you to use it as a model for yours. It is only an example:

"The mission of our family is to create a nurturing place of order, truth, love, happiness, and relaxation, and to provide opportunities for each person to become responsibly independent and effectively interdependent, in order to achieve worthwhile purposes."

I have seen the powerful influence this statement has had on each member of our family. I see our children making significant decisions in their lives based on their internalized desire and commitment to achieving worthwhile purposes and contributing to society. I commend you to this powerfully unifying process.

Chapter 13

MAKING CHAMPIONS OF YOUR CHILDREN

SANDRA AND I have nine children, and we consider all of them champions. Of course, neither they nor we have arrived; daily we pray for wisdom, strength, forgiveness, and the power to do better.

We have tried in various ways with each of our children to make them champions. The following ten keys, incidentally, also apply to making champions of the people you employ, manage, or lead.

· *First, we work to build our children's self-esteem.* From the day they are born we affirm them a great deal, believing in them and giving them lots of positive feedback. We express confidence in them and in their potential. We try not to compare them with each other or with other people.

I have always believed that how people feel about themselves inside is the real key to using their talent and releasing their potential. And how they feel about themselves is largely a function of how they are seen and treated by others, particularly their parents.

When our children were young—preschool age—we tried to build their self-esteem by spending a lot of time with them, listening to them, playing with them, and affirming them. For example, I still spend a tremendous amount of time with our youngest child, Joshua, and I thoroughly enjoy it. When I return from a trip—even if I'm gone only one day—we celebrate by going to a neighborhood store for a treat. As soon as we're in the car together, he'll nuzzle up to me and say, "Oh, we're here together again, just you and me." And then I start saying, "Ah, oh. . . ." By the time we get to the store, we're just filled with each other. And then at night he says, "Will you tell me a story again tonight, Dad?" I say, "Oh, of course, son." So he gets right next to me, and I tell him stories.

• *Second, we encourage primary greatness*. We teach them that there are two kinds of greatness: primary greatness—which is the principle-centered character—and secondary greatness, which is the greatness that the world acknowledges. That's been a constant theme. We try to inspire them to go for primary greatness first and not to compensate for character weakness by substituting or borrowing strength from secondary sources (popularity, reputation, possessions, natural talents, and so on).

For example, our son Sean showed primary greatness scores of times while on his mission to South Africa—constantly denying himself, disciplining himself, loving others, affirming everyone he worked with, and finally extending his mission to influence more people. He learned, often the hard way, that the critical issues of life revolve around God's opinion and glory or man's opinion and glory.

Sean has also shown primary greatness in his courage to make tough decisions in the face of tremendous pressure. As a starting quarterback on the BYU football team, he learned to read the defense and change the play when he felt inwardly that the play sent in was not going to work. He developed poise, patience, and skill to read coverage and throw to the open receiver. When he sensed that the team was getting low, he'd return to the huddle high and exude an attitude of "We're going to score—we're going to make something happen." When he was sacked, he'd hop back up, pat the tackler on the back, and say, "Good hit." He tried to get close to a player who was discouraged and had lost faith in himself.

While he wants to play well and win games, his primary goal in college is to prepare for life and for graduate school. Right now he's not thinking in terms of a long-term football career, knowing that a serious injury can change everything anyway.

· *Third, we encourage them to develop their own interests.* For instance, when Joshua saw the movie *Karate Kid,* he wanted to take karate lessons. I immediately signed him up, knowing full well that he'd likely get turned on by something else in two weeks and gradually lose interest in karate. But I want him to try something when he's excited about it. I try to affirm him in his choice of activities. For example, recently we were throwing the football in the hallway and he said, "Notice how good I am at football." He doesn't doubt his ability to do many different things well.

When we detect real talent in our children, we encourage them to develop it. For example, I could see Sean's athletic ability long before he participated in competitive athletics. When he was in grade school, I could sense the flexibility, coordination, quickness, and balance in his body. I'd encourage him by suggesting, "Why don't you compete? Why don't you enter the races?" But he was always a little hesitant for fear that if he tried, he might fail, and it would be better not to try than to experience failure. One day he finally consented to compete in some races at school. He won all of them, and once he got a sense of what he could do, he started competing in several sports.

· *Fourth, we try to create an enjoyable family culture.* We want our children to get more fun and satisfaction from the family than from the school or from their peers or from any other outside influence. Basically, we don't want them to have anything to rebel against; we want the family culture to be fun and affirming and to have many opportunities associated with it. There should be no feeling of limitation, no feeling that you can't do something. We cultivate the attitude "You can do things, even great things, if you plan ahead and work for it."

We try to have regular dates, at least one a month, with each child and do something that is special to that child. We also have frequent one-on-one personal visits or interviews with them. We also have a lot of fun with birthdays. We call them "birthweeks" and dedicate the whole week to that person. Goings and comings are highlighted. We also have home evenings and family devotionals. We try to keep these positive and encourage everyone to express why they love or appreciate each other.

· *Fifth, we plan ahead.* We plan several major family events at least six months in advance. Our son Stephen and his wife, Jeri, said that a major hesitancy of moving first to Dallas, where he worked for IBM, and then to Boston, where he attended Harvard Business School, was that they didn't want to miss the fun things we had planned together as a family.

I think many parents fail to make champions of their children by not planning fun family events—events that become traditional. Part of the fun of any activity is in planning it; in fact, there's often as much satisfaction in the anticipation as there is in the realization of the event. Money is often an excuse, a cop out, for not planning or doing anything. What you do doesn't have to be expensive to be fun. What's important is that you have fun family times, that your children participate in planning them, that you all get excited anticipating them, that everybody feels part of them and thinks they were fun when they look back on them.

Of course, the extended family is a very important part of this planning. Our children keep close to their cousins and are concerned about their welfare and success. We often involve four generations in our family activities, and we all take great interest in each other. We don't want to miss family things, even the teenagers. That attitude is important to building champions because it gives children identity, builds their self-esteem, provides them with a caring support system, and offers them service opportunities.

 • *Sixth, we try to set an example of excellence.* We all try to excel in what we do so that excellence becomes an unspoken, unwritten norm. We have never had to tell our kids to study and do their homework, perhaps because they constantly sense the value of reading and learning. It's part of the family culture as well as the expectation at school. We'll help them with homework if they ask, but we try to empower them to be independent of us.

For example, once we gathered as a family to discuss the use of television in our home. Much reading and research had convinced me that we Americans in general, and my family in particular, were spending too much time in front of a TV and letting our minds atrophy. I knew exactly what would happen, however, if I presented this information to my family in the form of an arbitrary limitation on TV viewing: screaming, complaining, and harsh withdrawal symptoms.

Instead we met together in a family council and discussed some of the data about what is happening to families because of TV and what values are being espoused in many shows. I explained how some people regard TV as an open cesspool in their homes or a plug-in drug that can have a powerful, though subtle, influence. To emphasize my point, I even shared Alexander Pope's well-known statement concerning vice:

> Vice is a monster of so frightful mien,
> As to be hated needs but to be seen;
> Yet seen too oft, familiar with her face,
> We first endure, then pity, then embrace.

Our discussion ended with a decision to try to limit ourselves to about one hour of TV a day—good entertainment and education. Obviously we've not always reached that goal; but when we have, the results have been spectacular. Homework has been done more completely and more conscientiously. Reading, thinking, analyzing, and creating have replaced viewing.

• *Seventh, we teach them to visualize to help them realize their own potential.* When Sean was playing quarterback in high school, for example, I had many one-on-one visualization experiences with him, particularly on nights before games.

Visualization is based on the principle that all things are created twice: first mentally and then physically. Most training in athletics is physical. Coaches may talk about mental toughness and concentration, but very few have any sort of consistent system for mental rehearsal or visualization. However, world-class athletes are almost all visualizers; they literally experience their victories in their minds long before they experience them in fact.

When I started working with Sean in this area, I taught him how to relax and then described in vivid detail different situations in a football game. Sean would see himself performing ideally in each situation.

Such mental preparation has its payoffs. In a state championship game, for example, his team (Provo High School) fell behind by two touchdowns, and the momentum was with the other team. Provo was way back near their own end zone after having been thrown for a loss. I "saw" Sean make up his mind. "I'm not just going to take assignments. I'll consider the plays sent in, but we're going to have to make this thing happen." I could both see and feel it, and the team could feel it. That's when the momentum shifted. It all started in his head. They drove all the way down the field and scored a touchdown, and then another one, and another one, and won the game. I think they won largely because Sean and others had already handled such situations time and time again in their minds.

As he prepared for each football season at BYU, he spent some time every day in visualization. He's also watched films of former great BYU quarterbacks—Robbi Bosco, Steve Young, Jim McMahan, Marc Wilson, and Gifford Nielson—and they became on-the-field mentors and models.

• *Eighth, we adopt their friends*. For instance, we adopted several of Sean's football teammates. We video-taped all of the games and invited everyone to our home after each game to see those films. This helped create a kind of family/team culture.

Individual champions are often part of championship teams. That's why we invest so much in the teams and clubs, schools and classes, our children belong to. When family, friends, school, and church are all aligned, it makes a powerful training system. Any time something gets out of alignment—when there's a problem with a peer, for example—we just adopt the peer. It's better than trying to get them to drop the peer.

• *Ninth, we teach them to have faith, to believe and trust others, and to affirm, build, bless, and serve others*. Sean learned on his mission that empathy is the key to influence—that you've got to be very sensitive to the feelings and perceptions of others. If you're going to build champions, you've got to take an interest in people, especially the downcast and outcast. The key to the ninety-nine is the one.

In football, Sean takes an active interest in people no one will take an interest in, such as walk-on freshmen—and it's genuine interest; it's not feigned. He's convinced that the main reason people don't reach their potential is because they doubt themselves. He affirms them. People become great if you treat them in terms of their potential. The key to success with people is to believe in them, to affirm them.

• *Tenth, we provide support, resources, and feedback*. We exchange letters and phone calls with all of our children to affirm each other.

Such constant affirmations have a cumulative effect. They become a strong emotional support to people.

We also rely on each other for honest feedback, as good feedback is essential to growth. Sean has always welcomed it. For instance, he said to his football coaches, "I want you to know I want feedback. You're not going to offend me. Just tell me whatever you feel at any time." He's constantly willing to learn from those who have the knowledge and the skill. He's very open and teachable, even when some of the lessons are extremely tough to take.

Building champions requires constant effort. We strive endlessly and find the need to return to basics often.

MANAGERIAL
and
ORGANIZATIONAL
DEVELOPMENT

INTRODUCTION

Very early in my life, at age twenty, I was assigned to manage the work of scores of others and to train men and women more than twice my age in the principles and skills of effective management and leadership. It was a humbling, frightening experience.

Like me, many people—once on their own—soon find themselves in some sort of "management" position. Often these responsibilities come before we are ready for them. But we learn by doing and by making mistakes, and over time we gain some degree of competence and confidence.

In this section I focus on issues and challenges that face all managers—supervision, delegation, participation, expectations, and performance agreements. I also address issues relevant to organizational leadership. When we become leaders of organizations, we encounter a whole new set of problems. Some of these are chronic, others are acute. Many are as common to Fortune 500 companies as they are to families, small businesses, and volunteer groups: certain conditions of organizational effectiveness apply across the board.

Although I deal mostly with the corporate issues of structure, strategy, streams, and systems, I maintain a strong individual character component in our PS model of principle-centered leadership. No leader can afford to forget that personal and organizational integrity are closely intertwined. Nor can any leader afford to lose sight of the mission and shared vision—the constitution of the corporation.

Resolving Management Dilemmas

Principle-centered leadership will also help you resolve the classic managerial and organizational dilemmas:

- How can we have a culture characterized by change, flexibility, and continuous improvement and still maintain a sense of stability and security?
- How do we get our people, the culture, aligned with the strategy so that everyone in the organization is as committed to the strategy as those who formulated it?
- How do we unleash the creativity, resourcefulness, talent, and energy of the vast majority of the present work force, whose jobs neither require nor reward such use?
- How do we clearly see that the dilemma of whether to play tough hardball to produce a bottom line or to play softball to "be nice" to people is based on a false dichotomy?
- How do we serve and eat the lunch of champions (feedback) and then the dinner of champions (course correction) within the context of the breakfast of champions (vision)?
- How do we turn a mission statement into a constitution—the supreme guiding force of the entire organization—instead of a bunch of nebulous, meaningless, cynicism-inducing platitudes?
- How do we create a culture where management treats employees as customers and uses them as local experts?
- How do we create team spirit and harmony among departments and people who have for years been attacking, criticizing, contending for scarce resources, playing political games, and working from hidden agendas?

Again, as you read the chapters in this section, you will gain an understanding of the basic principles of effective organizational leadership, and you will be empowered to resolve these and other tough management questions by yourself.

TWO MASTER PRINCIPLES

Principle-centered leadership is practiced from the inside out on personal, interpersonal, managerial, and organizational levels. Each level is "necessary but insufficient." We have to work at all four levels on the basis of certain principles. In this section I will focus on the master principles of management and leadership:

• *Empowerment* at the *management level*. If you have no or low trust, how are you going to manage people? If you think your people lack character or competence, how would you manage them? When you don't have trust, you have to control people. But if you have high trust, how do you manage people? You don't supervise them—they supervise themselves. You become a source of help. You set up a performance agreement so they understand what's expected. You overlap their needs with the needs of the organization. You have accountability, but they participate in the evaluation of their performance based on the terms of the agreement. People are empowered to judge themselves because their knowledge transcends any measurement system. If you have a low-trust culture, you have to use measurement because people will tell you what they think you want to hear.

• *Alignment* at the *organizational level*. What would your organization look like in a low-trust culture with a control style of management? Very hierarchal. What is the span of control? Very small, because you can only control so many people. You resort to "gofer" delegation; you prescribe and manage methods. Your information system gathers immediate information on results so you can take decisive corrective actions. You use the carrot-and-stick motivation system. Such primitive systems may enable you to survive against soft competition, but you are easy prey for tough competitors.

If you have high trust, how is your organization structured? Very flat, extremely flexible. What's the span of control? Extremely large. Why? People are supervising themselves. They are doing their jobs cheerfully without being reminded because you have built an emotional bank account with them. You've got commitment, and they are empowered. Why? Because you have built the culture around a common vision on the basis of certain bedrock principles, and you are striving constantly to align strategy, style, structure, and systems with your professed mission (your constitution) and with the realities out there in the environment (the streams).

My challenge to you is this: When you find something out of alignment, work on it developmentally at all four levels from the inside out on the basis of the four master principles.

Chapter 14

ABUNDANCE MANAGERS

EXECUTIVES who are expert at handling "hot potatoes" keep cool by concentrating more on creating markets for their products and less on protecting their "turf," promoting their "thing," and getting their "piece of the pie."

Two potato farmers from Idaho made it big in business by cultivating an abundance mentality. J. R. Simplot and Nephi Grigg both built successful frozen-food companies (J. R. Simplot Company and Ore-Ida Foods) on the idea that one can create a market, not just steal shares from others.

Simplot, the major spud supplier to McDonald's, and Grigg, who founded Ore-Ida and later sold it to Heinz, found that creating new wealth doesn't always mean taking it away from other players in the market. Like other legends of their time, Ray Kroc and J. Willard Marriott, Simplot and Grigg built their own markets for their products.

They did it with an *abundance mentality*—a bone-deep belief that "there are enough natural and human resources to realize my dream" and that "my success does not necessarily mean failure for others, just as their success does not preclude my own."

Over the past twenty-five years of working with organizations and with individuals, I have observed that the abundance mentality often makes the difference between excellence and mediocrity, particularly because it eliminates small thinking and adversarial relations.

There is so much negative energy in organizations and in our society. People think of taking the legal approach to problem-solving, often at the first blush of a problem. Many are looking out for number one, anxious to get their "piece of the pie" and protect their "turf." Such self-centered activity springs from a belief that resources are limited. I call it the *scarcity mentality*.

The normal distribution curve, embedded deep in the bowels of both academia and business, tends to spawn the scarcity mentality because of the perceived "zero sum" situation. If people somehow avoid being "scripted" into a scarcity mentality by their schooling, they may acquire it from an athletic or social experience.

People with a scarcity mentality tend to see everything in terms of "win-lose." They believe "There is only so much; and if someone else has it, that means there will be less for me." They have a very hard time, for instance, being genuinely happy for the successes of other people—particularly if these people are from their own company, household, or neighborhood—because in some way they may feel that something is being taken from them.

If you see life as a "zero sum" game, you tend to think in adversarial or competitive ways, since anyone else's "win" implies your loss. And if you were brought up on conditional love and constant comparisons, you adopt a scarcity script, thinking in dichotomies—either haves or have-nots, either "I'm okay, you're not okay" or "I'm not okay, you're okay."

In my life, I've gone through many cycles of abundance and scarcity thinking. When I have an abundance mentality, I am trusting, open, giving, willing to live and let live, and able to value differences. I realize that strength lies in differences. I define unity not as sameness, but as complementary oneness, where one's weakness is compensated by the strength of another.

People with an abundance mentality employ the negotiation principle of win/win and the communication principle of seeking first to understand before seeking to be understood. Their psychic satisfactions don't come from winning or beating others or from being compared with others, either positively or negatively. They are not possessive. They don't force and push natural processes by requiring other people to tell them where they stand all the time. They don't get their security from someone else's opinion.

An abundance mentality springs from an *internal security*, not from external rankings, comparisons, opinions, possessions, or associations. People who derive their security from such sources become dependent on them. Their lives are affected by whatever happens to the sources of their security. Scarcity thinkers believe that resources are scarce. So if their associate gets a big promotion or if their friend receives some great recognition or has some major achievement, their security or identity is threatened. They might compliment the person, but inwardly they are eating their heart out. They feel as if something is being taken from them because their security lies in being compared favorably with other people, not in their integrity to natural laws and principles.

The more principle-centered we become, the more we develop an abundance mentality, the more we love to share power and profit and recognition, and the more we are genuinely happy for the successes, well-being, achievements, recognition, and good fortune of other people. We believe that their success adds to—rather than detracts from—our lives.

SEVEN CHARACTERISTICS OF ABUNDANCE MANAGERS

What characteristics distinguish abundance thinkers such as Simplot, Grigg, Kroc, and Marriott from scarcity thinkers? Consider the following seven.

• *They return often to the right sources.* In *The Seven Habits of Highly Effective People*, I suggest that the most fundamental source, and the root of all the rest, is the principle source. If our lives are centered on other sources—spouse, work, money, possession, pleasure, leader, friend, enemy, self—distortions and dependencies develop.

Abundance thinkers drink deeply from sources of internal security—sources that keep them gentle, open, trusting, and genuinely happy for the successes of other people . . . that renew and re-create them . . . that nurture and nourish abundance feelings, enabling them to grow and develop and giving them comfort, insight, inspiration, guidance, protection, direction, and peace of mind. They look forward to returning to these springs. To go for any length of time—even a few hours—and not seek this refreshment would cause them genuine withdrawal pains, similar in the physical sense to going without food and water.

• *They seek solitude and enjoy nature.* People with an abundance mentality reserve time for solitude. People with a scarcity mentality are often bored when they are alone because of the merry-go-round nature of their lives. Cultivate the ability to be alone and to think deeply, to enjoy silence and solitude. Reflect, write, listen, plan, prepare, visualize, ponder, relax.

Nature can teach us many valuable lessons and replenish our spiritual reserves. Serene natural settings make us more contemplative and peaceful and better prepared to return to the fast pace of our careers.

• *They sharpen the saw regularly.* Cultivate the habit of "sharpening your saw" every day by exercising mind and body.

For mental exercise, I suggest cultivating the habit of reading widely and deeply. Take an executive development course now and then to add discipline and accountability. When we continue our education, our economic security is not as dependent upon our jobs, our boss's opinion, or human institutions as it is upon our ability to produce. The great unseen job market is called "unsolved problems," and there are always many vacancies for those who exercise initiative and learn how to create value for themselves by showing how they essentially represent solutions to these problems.

In the book *Executive Jobs Unlimited,* Carl Boll basically suggests that people who fail to sharpen the saw regularly find not only that their saw becomes dull, but also that they become obsolete and increasingly dependent upon playing it safe. They become protective, politically or security minded, and start wearing the "golden handcuffs."

• *They serve others anonymously.* By returning often to nurturing sources of internal security, they restore their willingness and ability to serve others effectively. They take particular delight in anonymous service, feeling that service is the rent we pay for the privilege of living in this world. If our intent is to serve others without self-concern, we are inwardly rewarded with increased internal security and an abundance mentality.

• *They maintain a long-term intimate relationship with another person.* This is a person (or persons)—usually a spouse or close friend—who loves us and believes in us even when we don't believe in ourselves. But they are not permissive; they neither give in nor give up. Such people can make all the difference in our lives.

Often people who have an abundance mentality serve this role in relationship to many other people. Whenever they sense someone is at the crossroads, they go the second mile in communicating their belief in that person.

• *They forgive themselves and others.* They don't condemn themselves for every foolish mistake or social blunder. They forgive others for their trespasses. They don't brood about yesterday or daydream about tomorrow. They live sensibly in the present, carefully plan the future, and flexibly adapt to changing circumstances. Their self-honesty is revealed by their sense of humor, their willingness to admit and then forget mistakes, and their ability to cheerfully do the things ahead that lie within their power.

• *They are problem-solvers.* They are part of the solution. They learn to separate the people from the problem being discussed. They focus on people's interests and concerns rather than fight over positions. Gradually others discover their sincerity and become part of a creative problem-solving process, and the synergistic solutions coming out of these interactions are usually far better than those originally proposed because they are not compromise solutions.

THE LAW OF THE FARM

Procrastinating and cramming don't work on a farm. The cows must be milked daily. Others things must be done in season, according to natural cycles. Natural consequences follow violations, in spite of good intentions. We're subject to natural laws and governing principles—the laws of the farm and harvest.

The only thing that endures over time is the law of the farm. According to natural laws and principles, I must prepare the ground, put in the seed, cultivate, weed, and water if I expect to reap a harvest. So also in a marriage, or in helping a teenager through a difficult identity crisis—there is no quick fix, no instantaneous success formula where you can just move in by getting psyched up at some positive mental attitude rally with a bunch of new success formulas.

The law of the harvest governs. Natural laws, principles, operate regardless. So get these agricultural principles at the center of your life and your relationships. As you do, your mind-set will change from a scarcity to an abundance mentality.

In the context of the "potato farmer," the abundance mentality ultimately means "more pounds with less peel." And in plain "John Wayne" English, that's the bottom line.

Chapter 15

SEVEN CHRONIC PROBLEMS

Every day we're bombarded with advertisements promising fast, easy, and free results or relief. What we often forget is that most "wonder drugs" work only on acute symptoms, not on chronic problems.

What is an acute illness? It is one that causes us immediate pain. Chronic illness is the persistent, continuing disease that underlies the acute pain.

Most people are into solving acute illnesses and problems. They want the sharp pain to be relieved now. They want broken relationships to be instantly repaired. They find, however, that the more they seek quick fixes and attempt to apply some gimmick, some technique, that seems to work for someone else, or that seems to have instant appeal, the worse the chronic problem becomes.

For instance, if I am chronically fatigued—that is, if my reserve capacities are depleted; if my working style has put me into a situation of management by crisis; if I am always overexerting or pressing myself to do far more than I should do; if my emotional life is a function of other people's opinions of me to the point that I am always trying to become all things to all people; or if I am just stressed out—I could develop a chronic case of mononucleosis or some other disease. This would become manifest in certain symptoms, and I might try to treat these symptoms with some medicine that promised a quick solution.

But the promise is deceptive. There is no quick fix to chronic problems. To solve these, we must apply natural processes. The only way we can reap the harvest in the fall is to plant in the spring and to water, weed, cultivate, and fertilize during the long summer. We seem to understand that fact of life when working in a natural system; however, when it comes to social systems we often practice quick fixes. For example, how many of us crammed in school? How many of us got good grades, even graduate degrees, by cramming? Inwardly we know we didn't get the best education possible because we didn't pay the price day in and day out. Rather, when we were hurting in one area, we worked on that immediate hurt. Then, when another crisis broke out, we ran to that.

That life-style breaks people down and burns them out, and then their capacity to relate well with others, particularly under stress and pressure, is reduced to a minimum. Their life becomes a function of what is happening to them. They become victimized by it all.

SURGERY MAY BE REQUIRED

Many individuals and organizations suffer from some serious chronic problems, and the long-term solutions often require surgery.

I once visited a friend who is the head of surgery at a hospital. He allowed me to observe about twenty different operations. I also assisted him in replacing blood vessels. I held the instrument that kept the chest wall open while he replaced three vessels. I felt those vessels; they were stiff and brittle because they were filled with plaque, a cholesterol substance.

"Why don't you just clean them out?" I asked.

He said, "For a while you can reverse the process, but over time, the plaque, the cholesterol, becomes the very content of the wall."

I then asked, "Now that you have corrected these three places, is the man clear?"

He said, "No, it's through his whole system. He has a chronic vascular problem, a heart disease problem. I can see that he exercises because some of the supplementary circulatory system has been developed, but he hasn't changed other aspects of his lifestyle. He's got a chronic problem. I'm only working on the three most acute things that might cause a heart attack or stroke because of the lack of oxygen flow to those parts of the body."

The one thing people don't want to change is their life-style, but they generally must change if they want to deal with the chronic nature of their most serious problems.

CHRONIC PROBLEMS IN ORGANIZATIONS

Individuals constitute organizations. Even though we try to exercise more discipline in our professional lives, our personal tendencies are carried with us into our organizations. There we continue to look for a quick fix around the symptoms, the acute painful symptoms, rather than deal with the chronic habit patterns built into day-to-day operations.

Chronic individual problems become chronic organizational problems as a "critical mass" of people bring these problems with them through the gates each day and as social values encourage instant gratification and quick solutions to deep and difficult problems.

Although this is particularly true in America, I would say, from my international experience, that to some degree, the following seven problems are universal—they apply to many other cultures' organizations, even to departments and individuals within organizations.

Problem 1—*No shared vision and values: either the organization has no mission statement or there is no deep understanding of and commitment to the mission at all levels of the organization.*

Most executives don't realize what's involved in creating a mission statement that truly represents deeply shared values and vision at all levels of the organization. It takes patience, a long-term perspective, and meaningful involvement—and few organizations rank high in those virtues. Many organizations have a mission statement, but typically people aren't committed to it because they aren't involved in developing it; consequently it's not part of the culture. Culture, by definition, assumes shared vision and values, as represented by a mission statement put together and understood and implemented by all levels of the organization.

My experience suggests that if you don't have a corporate constitution and govern everything else by that constitution, you will likely have the other six chronic problems in your organization, in spades.

To be most effective, your mission statement should deal with all four basic human needs: economic or money need; social or relationship need; psychological or growth need; and spiritual or contribution need. Most mission statements do not deal with all four needs. Many leave off the psychological or the need for human growth and development. Some lack wording on win-win relationships, equity in economic compensation, and the commitment to a set of principles or values and to service and contribution to the community, suppliers, and customers, as well as owners and employees.

This first chronic problem is like an unseen iceberg. If the company has a "mission" of sorts, the problem is not clearly evident—executives may not see that the mission is not deeply shared. But the lack of shared vision and values is the seed bed of almost all other problems.

Problem 2—*No strategic path: either the strategy is not well developed or it ineffectively expresses the mission statement and/or fails to meet the wants and needs and realities of the stream.*

In recent years the best strategic thinking has changed from a "road map" to a "compass" model because we are in a wilderness—the stream, the environment, is so unpredictable that road maps are worthless. People need compasses that are fixed on constitutions (the mission statement with its set of principles and values) so they can flexibly adapt to the environment.

The old strategic planning model was called *ends* (where we are going), *ways* (how we are going to get there), and *means* (how we organize the resource). The new model calls for people to use a compass and a set of principles and values and to create ways to achieve the ends. The natural tendency of most organizations is to forecast by extrapolating trends and to call it strategic planning. The leaders of these organizations never really ask, "Where do we want to be in five years?" or "What kind of an organization do we want to have?" Instead they become very reactive to the environment, to the stream they operate in. So, while the strategic plan reflects the stream, it doesn't reflect the vision. Other organizations become so mission- or vision-driven that their strategy does not reflect the stream.

Good strategic planning reflects both vision and stream. Make sure your strategic path leads from your mission statement and reflects its vision and values and also reflects the environmental realities, the stream, so that you are not producing obsolete products and services. It's tough to create and maintain that balance. It takes tremendous judgment and wisdom. It takes a social radar with regard to the stream. It also takes a deep commitment and conscience with regard to the value system. If you don't have a deeply embedded and shared value system at the center of your organization, you will likely lack internal security, so you will seek it from the outside. You then vacillate and become subject to all the fickle forces at play on the outside.

Problem 3—*Poor alignment: bad alignment between structure and shared values, between vision and systems; the structure and systems of the organization poorly serve and reinforce the strategic paths.*

The alignment problem is prevalent everywhere. Ask yourself: "Is our mission statement a constitution? Is it the supreme law of the land? Does every person who comes into the organization make a commitment of allegiance to that constitution? Is every program, every system, even our organizational structure, subject to the constitution?" If your answer is "No"—and it usually is—you have an alignment problem.

If you don't have a shared value system, you don't have an inner source of security. So where do you get the security? In rigid structure and systems. Why? Because it gives you predictability, a sense that the sun will come up tomorrow. By having rigid structure and systems in place, you have a sense of predictability. But you have very little flexibility to adapt to the stream—and that can kill you in a hurry, as many American companies and industries can attest.

Many American companies are being managed on a span of control of one to six, one to seven, maybe even one to ten. All of a sudden they have competition out there with a span of control of one to fifty or more—and a totally different cost structure. They know that unless they restructure, they can't possibly compete; yet some companies keep the same old structure, simply because "That's the way things are done around here." Other organizations are downsizing because the stream is forcing them to simplify the structure and systems. And that is causing great consternation; people are fearful. They are looking for a new structure while they are still dependent on the old.

Many executives say they value capitalism, but they reward feudalism. They say they value democracy, but they reward autocracy. They say they value openness and *glasnost*, but they behave in ways that value closeness, hidden agendas, and politicking.

The acute symptoms of this chronic problem are interpersonal conflicts and poor interdepartmental relations (turf wars). And the "quick fix" is to come up with cosmetic solutions—a new temporary training program on communication skills—but the trust is shot, so it means nothing. The next cosmetic solution might be to rearrange the compensation system in an attempt to get some temporary motivation. But then people feel ripped off because management is messing around with their rice bowl and they no longer know what is going to happen tomorrow. The new compensation system may force them to increase productivity through competition, even if their governing values are teamwork and cooperation.

Problem 4—*Wrong style: the management philosophy is either incongruent with shared vision and values or the style inconsistently embodies the vision and values of the mission statement.*

In a sense, this chronic problem is even more fundamental than the other three—because most people get their style from their upbringing, from early mentors, either in their family or in their schools or business. Our early mentoring has an enormous impact on our style because our emotional and psychological need for acceptance is very strong when we are highly dependent. Whether we like it or not, an authoritarian father, even an abusive father, may be our only link to survival, so his style becomes our style.

When we encounter a style that is very different from our own —an abrasive, abusive, or confrontational style, for example—we may be shocked. For example, my eight-year-old son, Joshua, was shocked to hear in the news of a boy his same age who was abandoned by his parents. He was shocked for two days. He asked, "How could that happen?" He couldn't even see that to be an option—because the action was so foreign to him.

When people find themselves in a new stream with a new value system that is inconsistent with their particular style—be it authoritarian, permissive, or democratic—they must have a new birth. They must get so deeply involved in the new value system that they get reprogrammed by it. It must become the new constitution to their own personal life.

The style of staff people is strongly influenced by the style of senior executive mentors, and most people are mentored toward management, not toward leadership. Consequently they think efficiency; they think things. They don't think people; they don't think principles—because they weren't mentored that way.

With so much diversity and mobility in our society, it's often a challenge to make your style congruent with the vision and values of your organization. You may need to adapt your style to some degree. That's why principle-centered leadership is so vital. If you're principle-centered, you can be very flexible, very fluid, on the surface of your life, as long as the style is congruent with those principles.

Some may wonder if it's possible for senior managers, old dogs, to learn a new style or trick. Some may contend that our styles—whether we are vocalists, comedians, or managers—are so deeply imprinted that by the time we turn ten, twenty, or thirty, they're etched in stone. I think that although it is very difficult to adapt or change our style, it's not impossible. Our leadership style can be "situational," but before we're able to make a change, we may require new mentors and models.

One of the ongoing debates is whether leaders are made or born. I believe most are reborn, through some kind of mentoring—learning and applying correct principles. That's why great leaders serve as mentors and help bring about a whole new generation, a total transformation. But the personal price of doing it is tremendous; you may have to pay a "fourfold"—that is, you may have to sacrifice and suffer enormously to make significant changes.

An organization can tolerate many different styles as long as people are anchored in the same governing principles. Still, it's wise to try to find an environment that is compatible with your style. Your style will fit better in some organizations than in others. You need real wisdom to decide where you best fit and whether your style is congruent with the organizational style, recognizing how hard it is to change.

Problem 5—*Poor skills: style does not match skills, or managers lack the skills they need to use an appropriate vision.*

Sometimes I find that people want to shift to a different style but they simply lack the skills. They don't know, for example, how to set up a complete delegation; how to use empathy to get the other person's point of view; how to use synergy to create a third alternative; or how to work up a win-win performance agreement. Now, lacking knowledge and skills is not a deep chronic problem, because through education and training we may solve those problems.

For instance, beginning skiers soon develop a certain style, skill level, and comfort zone on the slopes; however, they lack the skills to effectively negotiate the hill under certain conditions. Their style and skills may be suited to only one kind of snow, terrain, or weather condition; they would not be prepared for whatever comes. Even if they have the desire, motivation, and physical ability, they still need improved skills to negotiate effectively.

By developing their skills, people may also develop their desire, even change their style. For example, when people get a new time management tool and the skill training to go with it, they often make some major changes in their lives. Or when people start to learn and apply the skills of empathy, they may find that the development of these skills enhances their style. In fact, Carl Rogers, the father of the human potential movement, claimed that if you really want to help people change, empathize with them. Gradually they gain new insights and start to realize new potential; in a sense, the very process starts to change them.

Problem 6—*Low trust: staff has low trust, a depleted emotional bank account, and that low trust results in closed communication, little problem-solving and poor cooperation and teamwork.*

Trust determines the quality of the relationship between people. And in a sense, trust is a chicken-and-egg problem. If you attempt to work on building trust at the exclusion of other chronic and acute problems, you will only exacerbate your situation. For example, one of the best ways to build trust is to work on the mission statement and to work on alignment issues. But if you try to do this while keeping a closed management style, your people will always be walking on eggs without much trust in your words.

Low trust spoils communication in spite of skill training. For example, in low-trust cultures managers usually come up with performance agreements, job descriptions, and mission statements that people don't buy into. And when they don't buy into them, they don't use them as a constitution; instead they try to set up policy and procedure manuals to preserve their jobs and build their pyramids.

The trust level—the sense that "I can trust you" or "You're a trustworthy person" or "You're a person who will admit to a mistake" or "You're approachable" or "You're open and teachable" or "If you make a promise, you keep it"—is a gut-level sense that really undergirds the rest. If you're fundamentally duplicitous, you can't solve the low-trust problem; you can't talk yourself out of problems you behave yourself into.

Trustworthiness is more than integrity; it also connotes competence. In other words, you may be an honest doctor, but before I trust you, I want to know that you're competent as well. We sometimes focus too much on integrity and not enough on personal competence and professional performance. Honest people who are incompetent in their area of professed expertise are not trustworthy.

Problem 7—*No self-integrity: values do not equal habits; there is no correlation between what I value and believe and what I do.*

If a person lacks integrity, how is he going to build an emotional bank account? How is he going to be trustworthy? How is he going to adapt his style to match the demands of the new stream? How will he create a culture where there is genuine trust?

And if a company lacks integrity, how is it going to satisfy its customers? How is it going to keep its best employees? How is it going to stay in business?

A person who fails to live by his value system probably doesn't have a mission statement. Without a clear statement of values, our habits will be all over the place. Of course, we may have a mission statement but fail to live by it. We are then hypocritical or duplicitous.

Corporate duplicity is much the same, only compounded, since a corporation is made up of individuals. That's why, when we detect one or more of the seven chronic problems in an organization—and when the senior executives want to blame everybody and everything else for those problems—we have them look in the mirror to identify one of the primary sources. They need not look at anyone else or ask any question except one: "Do I have integrity myself?"

PROBLEMS ARE CURABLE

These seven chronic problems are curable. They are also common—the competition likely has as many cancers as you do. Success in business is a relative thing; it is not measured against an ideal such as excellence, it is measured against the competition. And since most organizations have these problems to some degree, people learn to live with chronic problems all their professional lives. They may even have long tenures, unless the pain gets too acute.

I'm confident that enlightened leaders can cure these seven chronic problems, not just treat the symptoms, and create better societies. But to do that they've got to change hearts, build trust, revise the structure and systems. Most leaders are trying to do that to some degree. They are trying to create a profitable, informed, skilled, productive, cooperative, quality organization. And they are beginning to value people, the top line, as much as they value the profits, the bottom line.

Chapter 16

SHIFTING YOUR MANAGEMENT PARADIGM

Victor Hugo once said, "There is nothing so powerful as an idea whose time has come."

When the book *In Search of Excellence* took America by storm, it was a clear indication that the time had come for the idea and the ideal of excellence. Well, it's now high time for many individuals and companies to make a quantum leap in performance, a healthy change of habits, a major shift in patterns; otherwise it's business as usual— and that's simply not cutting it anymore.

But the question now is "How?" How do we become more effective? I have found that if you want to make slow, incremental improvement, change your attitude or behavior. But if you want to improve in major ways—I mean dramatic, revolutionary, transforming ways—if you want to make quantum improvements, either as an individual or as an organization, change your frame of reference. Change how you see the world, how you think about people, how you view management and leadership. Change your *paradigm*, your scheme for understanding and explaining certain aspects of reality. The great breakthroughs are breaks with old ways of thinking. As the paradigm shifts, it opens up a whole new area of insight, knowledge, and understanding, resulting in a quantum difference in performance. Consider the following three examples from history.

• Throughout the ages, hundreds of thousands have died of disease and infection. In war, for every man killed in battle, dozens more lost their lives to disease and infection. Likewise, in childbirth thousands of mothers and newborn babies have lost their lives. The problem was that medical doctors were slow to accept the paradigm-shifting notion that fermentation, putrefaction, infection, and disease could be caused by bacteria too small to see. It wasn't until Louis Pasteur in France and Ignaz Philipp Semmelweis in Hungary and others changed the paradigm in the minds of physicians that medical science made any significant progress against disease and infection.

• It was a paradigm shift that gave birth to this land of freedom. When Thomas Jefferson wrote in the Declaration of Independence that government derives its just powers from the consent of the governed, he and those who signed that document set up a new pattern of government. There would be no divine right to rule on this land, no imposed overlords. The only public officials would be those chosen by the voice of the people. Out of that paradigm has come the freest people and the most prosperous country in the history of the world.

• Using the wrong paradigm has crippled entire nations. In 1588 Spain was the most powerful nation in Europe. Its coffers were full of gold from the New World, and her ships were the mightiest vessels on the seven seas. But the English weren't intimidated, and when the remains of Spain's proud armada limped back into port, it was obvious that the paradigm had shifted. The nimble ships and resourceful, innovative English captains were the new rulers of the waves.

In our day, we have seen similar shifts in the business world and from some of the same causes. Some of the world's mightiest corporations have put their trust in their cash reserves, capital assets, technologies, strategies, and buildings, only to witness, as did the Spaniards, smaller companies with a different paradigm—one better suited to the current marketplace—humble them in their battle for customers.

Think of the paradigm shifts in your own life. If you are married, remember what it was like to be single. What happened to your paradigm of life when you married? If you have served in the military, remember when your name and role were changed as you progressed from private to officer. You see an entirely new world. You view your responsibilities differently. You look at life through a new paradigm—a new map—resulting in fundamental, dramatic, revolutionary changes. If you are a grandparent, remember when your first grandchild came? You were called by a new name and perceived in a new role.

Having a new name and role, a new paradigm, your behavior and your attitudes shift dramatically. In fact, the fastest way to change a person's paradigm is to change their name or their role.

Remember what it was like when you first became a manager? Didn't you begin to see everything differently? And that was a revolutionary change. The same problems we complained about before, we saw differently as we assumed the responsibility to resolve them.

Crises, too, can bring about paradigm shifts, as we are forced to determine our priorities in life. For example, when Anwar Sadat was president of Egypt, he swore in front of millions of people on television, "I will never shake the hand of an Israeli as long as they occupy one inch of Arab soil. Never, never, never." And the crowds would chant, "Never, never, never."

But in his heart Sadat knew that he was living in a perilous, interdependent world. Fortunately he had previously learned how to work with his own mind and heart to bring about a paradigm shift inside himself. He'd learned it as a young man while he was imprisoned in a solitary cell in Cairo Central Prison. He learned how to get into a meditative state of mind, to look at the program in his head against the reality of the day, and to bring about within himself a paradigm shift to see the whole situation differently. And this eventually led him to that unprecedented bold peace initiative at Jerusalem and to the peace process that eventually resulted in the Camp David Accord.

I submit that if we focus our attention on techniques, on specific practices, on "to do" lists, on present pressures, we might make some small improvements. But if we want to move ahead in a major way, we need to shift our paradigm and see the situation in a totally new way.

FOUR MANAGEMENT PARADIGMS

I'd like to offer four basic management paradigms and suggest that while each of them has merit, three of them are fundamentally flawed because they are based on false assumptions about the nature of people.

FOUR PARADIGMS

NEED	METAPHOR	PARADIGM	PRINCIPLE
Physical/Economic	Stomach	Scientific Authoritarian	Fairness
Social/Emotional	Heart	Human Relations (benevolent authoritarian)	Kindness
Psychological	Mind	Human Resource	Use and Development of Talent
Spiritual	Spirit (whole person)	Principle-Centered Leadership	Meaning

• *First, the scientific management paradigm.* Using this paradigm, we see people primarily as stomachs (economic beings). If that's my view of my people, my task as a manager is to motivate them through the great jackass method, the carrot and the stick—the carrot in front to entice and intrigue them, lead them to their benefits, and the stick behind. Notice that I am in control. I am the authority. I am the elite one. I know what is best. I will direct you where to go, and I will do it through the carrot and stick. Of course, I must be fair with the economic rewards and the benefit package. But it's all designed to meet the needs of one's stomach.

The assumption about human nature associated with this para-

digm is the *economic man* assumption. This means that we are motivated primarily by our quest for economic security. The manager
who operates on this assumption would wield the carrot and the
stick. If the assumption were correct, people would respond consistently from the motivation to make a living for themselves or provide
a livelihood for their families.

The management style would be authoritarian. An authoritarian
manager makes the decisions and gives the commands, and workers
conform and cooperate, perform and contribute, as requested to receive the economic rewards of pay and other benefits. Many organizations and managers work on this assumption. From time to time
they may give lip service to an enlarged view of man's nature, but
fundamentally they see themselves as manipulating an economic
reward package in order to get the behavior they want.

• *Second, the human relations paradigm.* We acknowledge that people
are not only stomachs, but also hearts (social beings). We see that
people have feelings. Hence we treat people not only with fairness,
but with kindness, courtesy, civility, and decency. But it may only
mean a shift from being an authoritarian to being a benevolent authoritarian because we still are the elite few who know what's best.
The power still lies with us, but we are kind to people as well as fair.

The assumption associated with this paradigm is the *socioeconomic
man* assumption. We recognize that in addition to having economic
needs, people also have social needs: to be treated well, to be liked
and respected, and to belong. This view of human nature is the basis
for the human relations movement.

This assumption still leaves management in charge, still making
the decisions and giving the commands, but at least human relations
managers try to create a harmonious team or company spirit and
provide opportunities for people who work together to get to know
each other and enjoy each other in social and recreational situations.
Managers who operate on this assumption may become permissive,
soft, and indulgent because they have high needs for belonging and
being popular and hate to impose any firm standards or expectations
on others. Many managers have fallen into this false dichotomy.
They think, "We are either tough or soft, strong or weak. If we don't
take charge, others will take charge of us." And since authoritarianism will almost always achieve more than permissiveness, managers
who buy in to the socioeconomic assumption will resolve that di-

lemma or dichotomy by adopting a management style of benevolent authoritarianism.

The benevolent autocrat is like a kindly father who knows what's best for his children and takes care of them as long as they comply with his wishes and desires. And when they don't, he perceives this rebellion as a form of disloyalty or ingratitude. "After all I have done for them, look at what they do to me."

• *Third, the human resource paradigm.* Here we work not only with fairness and kindness, but also with efficiency. We care about contribution. We see that people have minds in addition to stomachs and hearts. In other words, people are cognitive, thinking beings. With this larger understanding of man's nature, we begin to make better use of their talent, creativity, resourcefulness, ingenuity, and imagination. We begin to delegate more, realizing that people will do what's necessary if they're committed to a particular goal. We begin to see people as the main resource: not capital assets, not physical properties, but people—their hearts and minds. We begin to explore ways to create an optimal environment, a culture that taps their talents and releases their creative energy. We recognize that people want to make meaningful contributions. They want their talents identified, developed, used, and recognized.

At this stage we see that people are also psychological beings. This means that in addition to needing economic security and social belonging, people need to grow and develop and to contribute effectively and creatively to the accomplishment of worthwhile objectives. Managers with this paradigm would see people as bundles of latent talent and capacity. Their goal would be to identify and develop this capacity to accomplish the objectives of the organization. When people are seen as economic, social, and psychological beings with strong needs and desires to grow and develop and have their talents used in creative and constructive ways, managers try to create an environment in which people can contribute their full range of talents to the accomplishment of organizational goals.

• *Fourth, principle-centered leadership.* Now we work with fairness, kindness, efficiency, and effectiveness. We work with the whole person. We see that people are not just resources or assets, not just economic, social, and psychological beings. They are also spiritual beings; they want *meaning*, a sense of doing something that matters. People do not want to work for a cause with little meaning, even though it taps their mental capacities to their fullest. There must be purposes that lift them, ennoble them, and bring them to their highest selves.

Using this paradigm, we manage people by a set of proven principles. These principles are the natural laws and governing social values that have characterized every great society, every responsible civilization, over the centuries. They surface in the form of values, ideas, ideals, norms, and teachings that uplift, ennoble, fulfill, empower, and inspire.

Principle-centered managers see that people have more creative energy, resourcefulness, and initiative than their jobs presently allow or require. People are crying, "Believe in me." IBM's bedrock is their belief in the dignity and potential of the individual. Once you have the principle-centered paradigm, you will produce the evidence to support your new perceptions of people. People live up to the expectations of them.

People spend their creativity on their own goals and dreams—and much of that energy is lost to the organization. Negative synergy is an enormous waste of human talent. The formula for positive synergy is involvement + patience = commitment. The employee behind the desk should be treated like the customer in front of the desk. There is nothing under heaven that can buy voluntary commitment. You can buy a man's hands and back, but not his heart and mind.

Tom Peters suggests that as the center of power shifts away from the elite authoritarian group—however benevolent it may be—every person in the organization will feel more empowered.

It's nothing less than a 180-degree shift in the way we think about managing and leading. The models and the metaphors of the past have been the manager as a cop, as a referee, as a devil's advocate, as a nay-sayer, as a pronouncer. The words that we found that seem much more appropriate in the excellent companies are the manager, the leader, as a cheerleader, as a coach, as a facilitator, as a nurturer of champions. The drum beat, and the drum beat that has been so sadly missing, was it all comes from people.

People want to contribute to the accomplishment of worthwhile objectives. They want to be part of a mission and enterprise that transcends their individual tasks. They don't want to work in a job that has little meaning, even though it may tap their mental capacities. They want purposes and principles that lift them, ennoble them, inspire them, empower them, and encourage them to their best selves.

I often ask people if they would take the job of digging a hole and filling it eight hours a day, five days a week, until they retired at age sixty-five for a salary of a million dollars a year, with an annual cost-of-living adjustment. Some think they would take such a job to improve their present economic situation, but they would be going bananas within a few years in spite of the economic rewards or their attempts to put their time and money to good use off the job. Man does not live by bread alone, unless perhaps that's all he has to live by.

This enlarged view of human nature underscores the need to make work challenging and fulfilling. Principle-centered leaders try to automate routine, boring, repetitive tasks and give people a chance to take pride in their jobs. They encourage participation in decision making as well as other important matters. In fact, the more important the decision, the more challenging the problem, the more they attempt to tap the talents of their human resources. They continually seek to expand the areas over which their people could exercise self-direction and self-control as they develop and demonstrate better insight and ability.

Most surveys in organizations show that people want to be managed by principles. They want meaning and purpose in their lives. They want their bosses to treat them as whole people. But they want the people who report to them to respond to the human relations paradigm. In other words, "I want you [up there] to ask for my opinion, but I want you [down there] to go along with my opinion like a good soldier. Be cooperative and helpful and go along."

The scientific management (stomach) paradigm says, "Pay me well." The human relations (heart) paradigm says, "Treat me well." The human resource (mind) paradigm suggests, "Use me well." The principle-centered leadership (whole person) paradigm says: "Let's talk about vision and mission, roles, and goals. I want to make a meaningful contribution."

I suggest that we cultivate the *principle-centered leadership* paradigm, which not only embraces the principles of fairness and kindness and makes better use of the talents of people for increased efficiency, but also leads to quantum leaps in personal and organizational effectiveness.

Chapter 17

ADVANTAGES OF THE PS PARADIGM

I ONCE WORKED with the executive team of a multibillion-dollar organization based in Dallas, Texas. I asked them, "Do you have a mission statement?"

Hesitantly they brought it out. It read: "To enhance the asset base of the owners." I said, "Do you put that on the wall to inspire your customers and employees?"

"Well, you know, it's kind of a private one, but we don't go for this idealistic crap. I mean, isn't that what business really is all about—to make money?"

And I said, "I'm sure that's one of the important purposes. But I'll tell you what your culture's like."

I then described their culture: interpersonal conflicts, interdepartmental rivalries, subgroups polarized around key philosophical issues, back-talking and bad-mouthing, cosmetic niceties on the surface exchanges. I next described their industry: unionized with people working on two cylinders; deep, entrenched interests between departments; special contests and promotions constantly going on to make sales quotas.

They said, "How do you know so much?"

"You just told me. You're only dealing with the economic need of people on one level on the basis of false assumptions. That's why everybody is looking elsewhere to meet their other needs and make more meaningful contributions."

"Well, what do you suggest?"

I then presented a new paradigm of management. During the presentation, they began to see the need for fundamental change in their culture, and they asked, "How long will it take to fix?"

I said, "Well, you know, it depends how bad you're hurting. If you're not hurting, it may never happen. If you're hurting either through the force of circumstances or the force of conscience, and if that pain is widely felt in the culture, you could do it—you could develop a balanced mission statement and start to align style and structure and systems with it within a year or two."

"There is one thing you don't understand about us, Stephen. We work fast. We'll whip this baby out this weekend."

What was their ultimate business, their paradigm? In their minds the ultimate business was real estate—things they could buy and sell "over a weekend." But they didn't have the culture to create true teamwork because they were working with a false paradigm of management.

To help you analyze your operations and achieve your goals, I recommend that you adopt a paradigm that more closely describes the true nature of organizations. I call it the *PS paradigm*.

One P and Seven S's

In the PS paradigm of principle-centered leadership, all components start with an "S"—except for the one "P"—and that stands for People.

• *People*. The PS paradigm is not based upon the efficiencies of organizational structure and management style and systems; rather, it is based upon the effectiveness of people. It recognizes that people are the highest value because people are the programmers—they produce everything else at the personal, interpersonal, managerial, and organizational levels. Culture is only a manifestation of how people see themselves, their co-workers, and their organizations.

• *Self*. We may have many concerns "out there" in the streams within and without our own organization, but if we want to bring

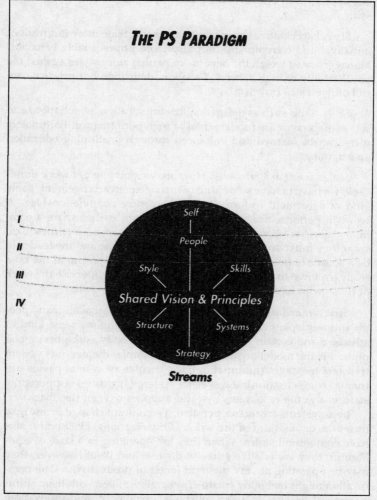

THE PS PARADIGM

Self

People

Style   Skills

Shared Vision & Principles

Structure   Systems

Strategy

Streams

I
II
III
IV

© 1991 Covey Leadership Center

about meaningful change, we must start within our circle of influence, with those things we can control directly. Again, it's the inside-out approach; in effect, change and improvement must begin with self.

• *Style*. Participative styles of management create more innovation, initiative, and commitment, but also more unpredictable behavior. Managers must weigh the benefits of participatory styles against the predictability of high control. To talk participation but practice control only creates cynicism.

• *Skills*. Skills such as delegation, communication, negotiation, and self-management are fundamental to high performance. Fortunately these can be learned and enhanced through continuing education and training.

• *Shared vision and principles*. How are we going to get work done? Well, we have to have some kind of management arrangement, some kind of agreement to formalize and organize our relationships. A win-win performance agreement, where both parties share a common vision based on common principles, liberates both parties to do what they must do: the worker to get the job done and the leader to be a source of help, a servant. Without such an agreement the boss really isn't free to be the servant because he must supervise the work of those who haven't accepted responsibility for results.

• *Structure and systems*. In organizations, we relate with many people in interdependent ways, and interaction requires some kind of structure and certain kinds of systems. The body is the best metaphor; it is the model organization. For example, the nervous system transfers messages (information); the circulatory system passes nutrients (compensation); the skeletal system (structure) supports the stature; and the respiratory systems supplies oxygen (feedback).

These systems are interdependent; a significant change in one may upset the equilibrium of the whole. Organizations, like bodies, also have equilibrium states. When they are operating in a state of equilibrium, they are relatively free of distress and pain; however, they may be operating at very different levels of productivity. One organization might be highly creative; synergistic; filled with team spirit, a sense of mission, passion, purpose, excitement, and innovation; and relatively free of painful handicaps. Another organization may be characterized by a strong adversarial or political climate, protective or defensive behaviors, low productivity, low profit. It, too, is in a state of equilibrium, but at a low level of performance.

Six systems are common to most organizations:

1. *Information*. To have an accurate, balanced, and unbiased picture of what is happening, executives need a stakeholder information system—a system that tells them what is happening inside the organization and inside the minds and hearts of all stakeholders. Good data makes for good decisions (assuming wise judgment).
2. *Compensation*. Money, recognition, responsibility, opportunity, and other perks of position and office are compensations. An effective compensation system has both financial and psychic rewards built into it. It rewards synergistic cooperation and creates a team spirit.
3. *Training and development*. In effective HRD programs, the learner is responsible for the learning; the instructor and institution are seen as helpful resources; the training is learner-controlled rather than system-controlled, meaning the learner can go at his or her own pace and choose the methods for meeting the mutually agreeable objectives; the learner is required to teach what is learned, as teaching the material to a third party greatly reinforces commitment while improving retention; and there is a close correlation between the goals of the training program and the career plans of each individual.
4. *Recruiting and selecting*. Principle-centered leaders recruit and select people carefully, matching the candidate's abilities, aptitudes, and interests with the requirements of the job. What people enjoy doing and do well is closely linked to what they do for the company. Interviewing, screening, and hiring are done in the best interests of both parties. The patterns of success evident in the work history of the individual match the pattern of success required in the company and industry. Discrepancies should be openly discussed. And, before making a decision to hire, promote, demote, or fire, effective leaders seek counsel, in confidence, from respected colleagues and supervisors.
5. *Job design*. Just as homes are designed to meet the needs and tastes of people, so also might jobs be designed to tap many of the interests and skills of people. People need a clear sense of what the job is about, how it relates to the overall mission of the company, and what their personal

contribution could be. They also need to know what resources and support systems are available, and they should enjoy some degree of autonomy in determining what methods to use to get desired results. Feedback, like the wiring in a home, should be built in from the beginning, as well as provisions for growth and new opportunity.

6. *Communication*. One-on-one visits—to work out the win-win performance agreement and the accountability process—are keys to effective organizational communications, along with staff meetings held as needed with action-oriented agendas and minutes; employee suggestion systems that reward ideas that result in savings; open-door and due-process policies and procedures; annual skip-level interviews; anonymous opinion surveys; and ad hoc committee brainstorming. Communications systems will function more effectively if they are organized around a shared vision and mission. Systems are often misaligned because they are designed by people with scarcity mentalities who have a hard time building high trust with other people. They're threatened by competency around them. They want every idea to come from them. They have a hard time giving recognition and sharing power.

• *Strategy*. The strategy should be congruent with the professed mission, with available resources, and with market conditions. Moreover, the strategy should be monitored and changed to reflect shifts in the wind, including the status of the competition.

• *Streams*. There are many streams (operational environments) inside and outside an organization. These need to be monitored periodically to make sure that strategy, shared vision, systems, and the rest are all in alignment with the external realities. Also, wise executives will read the trends and anticipate changes in the stream to avoid being capsized or left high and dry.

It all starts with people, the programmers. You have to work with the soft S's first in order to change the hard S's—as these are just the outward manifestations of the minds of people.

The key to quality products and services is a quality person. And the key to our personal quality is character and competence and the emotional bank account we have with other people. Principle-centered people get quantity through quality, results through relationships. In their marriage, family, business, and community, their guiding principle is this: "We will not talk about each other behind each other's backs to anyone. We may be constructively critical in an effort to help others, but we're not into cheap shots. If we have a disagreement with someone, we go directly to that person to clarify a position or to resolve the problem." That takes tremendous courage and a lot of character strength—and that comes out of being principle-centered and having a PS paradigm.

Four Characteristics

A paradigm is a model of nature. To improve a paradigm is to make an effort to get a clearer understanding of what nature is, and in every field of endeavor these are called theories or explanations or models. It doesn't matter how good your behavior is or how good your attitude is if your paradigm is flawed.

The PS paradigm has four characteristics that describe nature better than most paradigms.

• *First, it's holistic.* In other words, it deals with the whole package. Everything is included: you can put finance, physical structures, and technologies under structure. You can put both the working styles and skills and complementary leadership styles and skills of people under managerial. It deals with an open system, not a closed system, with anything and everything in "the stream"—the environment "inside" your organization, your industry, and the wider society.

No organization is perfectly aligned. Everyone faces a hostile environment, either inside or outside the company. Proactive, principle-centered people are not victimized by it. They move continually toward alignment and try to make sense of the milieu in which they live their lives and operate their businesses—the impact of the larger society; the economic, social, and political trends; the cultural forces; the international markets.

• *Second, it is ecological,* meaning everything is related to everything else, as in any ecosystem. In an ecosystem, not only do we deal with everything, but everything is very interrelated and interdependent. An initiative in one area affects every other area. Some management paradigms assume that an organization is a kind of disconnected, mechanical, nonorganic, nonecological environment. But all organizations are ecosystems within larger biospheres and thus part of nature. Nature doesn't have compartments in it. It is one indivisible whole. Heightened environmental awareness has made American society much more aware of natural ecosystems. We can say, "Wow, those burning oil wells and oil spills are going to affect the environment, the weather, the growing season, the quality of life far away."

In Operation Desert Storm, we witnessed a massive assault, where the Army, Navy, Marines and Air Force operated as one unit instead of separate divisions. They were all part of the same ecosystem with clearly defined roles. And they were well led. General Schwarzkopf said, "If I had a choice to do the expedient thing and win the day's battle or to do the principled thing and lose, I'd do the principled thing because in the long run it will affect other things—it will come back and get you in different ways." Quite a guy. I loved the way he expressed his mission statement. When a reporter asked him, "What would you like to have said about you in an epitaph?" he said, "A soldier who served his country with honor, who loved his troops and his family."

• *Third, it is developmental.* That means you have to do some things before you can do other things, math before algebra. Growth and progress come by way of a sequential process. Yet many traditional paradigms of management are nondevelopmental. They assume that you do not really need to go through a process: you can just move in at any level and improve the situation with a quick fix. The sequential developmental process is powerfully communicated through the metaphor of the six days of creation. Real progress starts with self and works from the inside out.

• *Fourth, this paradigm is based on proactive people, not inanimate things, plants, and animals.* Unlike the rest of nature, people are volitional, capable of choices. Granted, some people's volition and influence may be small because of the psychic scarring and traumas of their childhood or current environment. People who come from a competition orientation tend to think defensively and protectively and in terms of scarcity. Those who live in an atmosphere of affirmation and unconditional love tend to have an intrinsic sense of personal security and an abundance mentality.

Most management paradigms try to turn people into things by making them more efficient. That's why many managers see the human resource as expendable. If that view is widespread in the culture, people will try to protect themselves by developing some kind of collective power, maybe a union, and by lobbying for social legislation to mitigate the exploitative, opportunistic tendencies of aggressive management. You can be efficient with things, but you must be effective with people. If you try to be efficient with people on emotional issues, you'll end up fighting or fleeing and making a withdrawal from the emotional bank account.

The four characteristics of the PS paradigm—holistic, ecological, developmental, and people-, not things-, oriented—make it better suited for business management and principle-centered leadership.

Chapter 18

Six Conditions of Empowerment

IN EVERY FIELD of endeavor we make assumptions regarding the ultimate nature of reality. If the fundamental assumptions or premises are wrong, the conclusions will also be wrong, even when the reasoning process from those premises are right.

Sound conclusions can come only from consistent reasoning based on a correct premise or assumption.

Often people forget this simple, almost self-evident truth. An entire field of so-called objective knowledge may be based upon subjective assumptions. In our respective fields we would be wise to question and to validate as far as possible through research and literature the assumptive base upon which our particular field of knowledge is founded. For instance, psychology is based on certain assumptions about human nature. Whether they realize it or not, business leaders are practicing psychologists in the sense that their attempts to motivate people are based on their assumptions of human nature.

In his *Autobiography*, Lee Iacocca writes that in addition to all the engineering and business courses he had in college, he also took four years of psychology and abnormal psychology. "I'm not being face-tious when I say that these were probably the most valuable courses of my college career. The focus of one course [at the state hospital psychiatric ward] was nothing less than the fundamentals of human behavior: What motivates that guy?"

Most top executives today recognize the validity of principle-centered leadership. But the question becomes one of implemen-tation: How can a top executive act on the "whole person" assumption? How can the organization reflect this enlarged view of people? How can managers uproot a deeply imbedded authoritar-ian or benevolent authoritarian style? How can they rid the com-pany of excess psychic and structural "baggage" and give people the freedom and flexibility to think and act in ways consistent with this enlarged view of man?

"Lean and agile," the watchwords of General Electric Corporation, make sense in many situations. I'll never forget one particular trip to Europe with my family. After a short time of touring, we had accu-mulated so much stuff in the form of clothing, gifts, travel brochures, souvenirs, and mementos that we were bogged down by excess luggage. We decided to send two-thirds of it home with a friend several days before the end of our stay. We felt so free, so unbur-dened, so capable of following our instincts and interests. We no longer had to worry whether there would be enough room and en-ergy for all our luggage.

I'm suggesting that executives may need to rid themselves of some false assumptions about human nature and simplify their organiza-tions before they can make full use of their human resources and experience the benefits of increased effectiveness. As Lee Iacocca suggests, maybe we should study motivation before we set up struc-ture. Using the maxim of the architect—"Form follows function"—we might attempt to identify and clarify our assumptions before we develop our strategies and systems.

To motivate people to peak performance, we first must find the areas where organizational needs and goals overlap individual needs, goals, and capabilities. We can then set up win-win agree-ments. Once these are established, people could govern or supervise themselves in terms of that agreement. We would then serve as sources of help and establish helpful organizational systems within which self-directing, self-controlling individuals could work toward fulfilling the terms of the agreement. Employees would periodically give an accountability of their responsibilities by evaluating themselves against the criteria specified in the win-win agreement.

These are the first four conditions of empowerment: 1) Win-win agreement; 2) Self-supervision; 3) Helpful structure and systems; and 4) Accountability.

Essentially the win-win agreement is a psychological contract between manager and subordinate. It represents a clear mutual understanding and commitment regarding expectations in five areas: first, desired results; second, guidelines; third, resources; fourth, accountabilities; and fifth, consequences.

To better understand how to set up and manage the win-win agreement, let's review each of these five steps.

• *First, specify desired results*. Discuss what results you expect. Be specific about the quantity and quality. Set budget and schedule. Commit people to getting the results, but then let them determine the best methods and means. Set target dates or timelines for the accomplishment of your objectives. These objectives essentially represent the overlap between the organizational strategy, goals, and job design, and the personal values, goals, needs, and capabilities. The concept of win-win suggests that managers and employees clarify expectations and mutually commit themselves to getting desired results.

• *Second, set some guidelines*. Communicate whatever principles, policies, and procedures are considered essential to getting desired results. Mention as few procedures as possible to allow as much freedom and flexibility as possible. Organizational policy and procedure manuals should be brief, focusing primarily on the principles behind the policy and procedures. Then, as the circumstances change, people are not frozen—they can still function, using their own initiative and good judgment and doing what's necessary to get desired results within the value framework of the company.

Guidelines should also identify no-no's or failure paths that experience has identified as inimical to accomplishing organizational goals or maintaining organizational values. Many a management-by-objective program goes down in flames because these failure paths or no-no's are not clearly identified. People are given the feeling that they have almost unlimited flexibility and freedom to do whatever is necessary to accomplish agreed-upon results and end up reinventing the wheel, encountering certain organizational sacred cows, upsetting apple carts, getting blown out of the saddle, and becoming increasingly gunshy about ever exercising initiative again.

The general attitude of employees then becomes, "Let's forget about this MBO stuff. Just tell us what you want us to do." Their expectations are blasted, and the scar tissue on their behinds is so thick that they begin to see the job purely as a means to an economic end and seek to satisfy their higher needs in other places off the job.

When identifying the no-no's or sacred cows, also identify what level of initiative a person has regarding different responsibilities: is the person to wait until told, or ask whenever he has a question, or study it out and then make a recommendation, or do it and report immediately, or do it and report routinely? In this way expectations are clarified and limits set.

In some areas of responsibility, the initiative level would simply be to wait until told, while in other areas, higher levels could be exercised, including, "Use your own good judgment and do what you think is appropriate; let us know routinely what you're doing and what the results are."

• *Third, identify available resources.* Identify the various financial, human, technical, and organizational resources available to employees to assist them in getting desired results. Mention the structural and systemic arrangements and processes. Such systems might include information, communication, and training. You may want to identify yourself or other people as resources and indicate how these human resources could be used. You may want to set some limits on access or merely share your experience and let the person decide how to benefit most from it.

• *Fourth, define accountability.* Holding people accountable for results puts teeth into the win-win agreement. If there is no accountability, people gradually lose their sense of responsibility and start blaming circumstances or other people for poor performance. But when people participate in setting the exact standard of acceptable performance, they feel a deep sense of responsibility to get desired results.

Results can be evaluated in three ways: measurement, observation, and discernment. Specify how you will evaluate performance. Also, specify when and how progress reports are to be made and accountability sessions held. When the trust level is high, people will be much tougher on themselves than an outside evaluator or manager would ever dare be. Also, when trust is high, discernment is often more accurate than so-called objective measurement. That's because people know in their hearts much more than the measurement system can reveal about their performance.

• *Fifth, determine the consequences.* Reach an understanding of what follows when the desired results are achieved or not achieved. Positive consequences might include financial and psychic rewards, such as recognition, appreciation, advancement, new assignment, training, flexible schedule, leave of absence, enlarged scope of responsibilities, perks, or promotion. Negative consequences might range from reprimand to retraining to termination.

WORKING TOWARD SELF-MANAGEMENT

These five features of a win-win agreement basically cover what a person needs to understand before undertaking a job. We clarify the desired results, the guidelines to work within, the resources to draw upon, the means of accountability, and the consequences of on-the-job performance. But we do not deal with methods. Win-win is a human resource principle that recognizes that people are capable of self-direction and self-control and can govern themselves to do whatever is necessary within the guidelines to achieve the desired results.

When more than two individuals are involved in the win-win agreement, the psychological contract becomes a social contract. We may set up the agreement with a team or a department or an entire division. Whatever the size of the group, all the members should participate in developing the win-win agreement. This social contract then becomes even more powerful, more reinforcing, and more motivating than the psychological contract because it taps into the social nature and human need to belong to and be part of a meaningful team project or effort.

One of the strengths of this psychological or social win-win contract is that it is almost infinitely flexible and adaptable to any set of circumstances or to any level of maturity or competence. If the ability or desire to do a job is small, then you would identify fewer and smaller results; perhaps have more guidelines, including procedures; make resources more available, attractive, and visible; have more frequent accountability with tighter, clearer, more measurable criteria; have consequences follow immediately, making feedback powerfully reinforcing.

In another situation, where there is a great deal of maturity, ability, and desire to do a job, the win-win agreement would have broader, longer-range desired results with fewer guidelines, particularly regarding procedures and policy. You might make the resources available but not necessarily that visible; have less frequent accountability, using discernment as well as measurement to evaluate performance; and set longer-term consequences with particularly heavy emphasis on intrinsic psychological rewards rather than extrinsic rewards.

Once a win-win agreement is established, people can then supervise themselves in terms of that agreement.* Managers may then serve as sources of help and establish helpful organizational structures and systems upon which self-directing, self-controlling individuals can draw to fulfill the win-win agreement. Having participated in the formation of the agreement, employees feel good about giving accountability on their responsibilities periodically; basically they evaluate themselves against the specified criteria. When the win-win agreement is set up properly, they will do whatever is necessary to accomplish the desired results within the guidelines.

Helpful organizational systems greatly facilitate the fulfillment of win-win agreements. These systems might include strategic planning, company structure, job design, communication, budgeting, compensation, information, recruitment, selection, placement, training, and development. In a helpful system people receive information about their performance directly, and they use it to make necessary corrections.

If any of the so-called helpful systems are really hurtful win-lose systems, they will override the win-win agreement. This is particularly the case with the compensation system. If management talks win-win but rewards win-lose, they defeat their own system. It would be analogous to telling one flower, "Grow! Grow!" and then watering another flower.

All the systems within the organization must be totally integrated with and supportive of the win-win agreement. Win-win should be reflected in recruiting and hiring and training. It should also be evident in professional development, compensation, job design, company structure, strategic planning, and mission and goal selection, as well as in all tactical activities.

* For free examples of win-win agreements and a sample form to create your own, please call 1-800-255-0777.

WIN-WIN PERFORMANCE APPRAISALS

In a win-win agreement, people evaluate themselves. Since they have a clear, up-front understanding of what results are expected and what criteria are used to assess their performance, they are in the best position to evaluate themselves.

The old notion is that the manager evaluates the performance of his people, sometimes using a secret set of subjective criteria that he springs on them at the end of a specified work period. This, of course, is absolutely insulting to people, which is why some managers do not have good performance appraisals. Unless expectations are clarified and commitments made up front, people can expect performance appraisals to be difficult, embarrassing, and sometimes downright insulting.

The manager's attitude is helpful, not judgmental. He may identify himself as a resource in the win-win agreement. He may serve as a trainer when his people undertake new tasks or new responsibilities or as a counselor in the areas of career planning and professional development. He involves his people in establishing the win-win agreement and allows them to evaluate their own performance. If the trust level is high, the employee's evaluation will be more accurate, more complete, more honest, than the manager's evaluation ever could be, because the person knows all the conditions and the details.

If the manager becomes aware of changing trends or other conditions that are not part of the original agreement, he would reopen the agreement for rethinking, replanning, and reformulating.

THE OTHER TWO CONDITIONS

At the center of these four conditions are two other conditions: skills and character. Character is what a person is; skills are what a person can do. These are the human competencies required to establish and maintain the other four. Hence they are really preconditions to the establishment of trusting relationships, win-win agreements, helpful systems, and employee self-supervision and self-evaluation.

In a low-trust culture, it is difficult to establish a good win-win agreement or to allow self-supervision and evaluation. Instead, there would be a need for control systems and for external supervision and evaluation. Before a manager could set up the four conditions

SIX CONDITIONS OF EMPOWERMENT

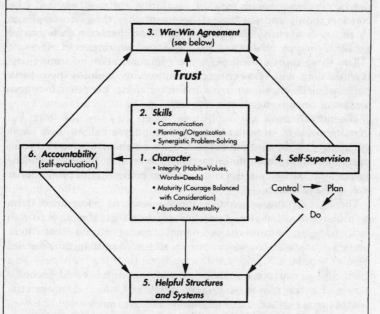

3. Win-Win Agreement
(see below)

Trust

2. Skills
- Communication
- Planning/Organization
- Synergistic Problem-Solving

6. Accountability
(self-evaluation)

1. Character
- Integrity (Habits=Values, Words=Deeds)
- Maturity (Courage Balanced with Consideration)
- Abundance Mentality

4. Self-Supervision

Control → Plan

Do

5. Helpful Structures and Systems

Win-Win Agreement—Psychological/Social Contract: clear mutual understanding and commitment re-expectations:

1. Desired Results: overlapping organizational mission/strategy/goals/job design with personal values/goals/needs—including time lines
2. Guidelines: policies, no no's, levels of initiative, and a few possible procedures
3. Resources: human, budgetary, structural, systematic
4. Accountability: standards of performance, when to give progress reports, etc.
5. Consequences: natural organizational and logical personal consequences—financial, psychological, opportunity, perks, scope of responsibility, etc.

already discussed, he would clearly need to begin making deposits into the emotional bank account and do whatever is necessary to build a trust relationship so that the win-win agreement could be established. And once the win-win agreement is in place, the other conditions will follow logically and naturally.

The character traits most critical to establishing the win-win agreement are integrity (habits are congruent with values, words with deeds, expressions with feelings), maturity (courage balanced with consideration), and the abundance mentality (there is plenty out there for everybody). A person with these character traits can be genuinely happy for the success and accomplishments of others.

The three most critical skills are communication, planning and organization, and synergistic problem-solving because these three personal skills enable an individual to establish the other four conditions of organizational effectiveness.

When individuals are duplicitous, when they say one thing but practice another, or when they bad-talk people behind their backs but sweet-talk them to their face, there is a subtle but eloquent communication that undermines trust and, inevitably, leads to win-lose agreements and arrangements requiring external supervision, control, and evaluation.

These six conditions are so interdependent that if any one of them is thrown out of balance, it will immediately affect the other five; in fact, changing just one character trait can affect all the other conditions. For instance, consider the character trait of maturity, defined here as "courage balanced with consideration." If a manager had a great deal of courage but lacked consideration, he would probably express himself clearly and aggressively but would listen poorly, without true empathy. Consequently the agreement would be win-lose. He would get his way, thinking that his way is best for everyone concerned. He would likely not encourage or allow his people to express their true feelings. He would fail to tap the internal motivation, requiring external motivation or supervision and the use of good control systems and performance appraisal procedures and compensation systems to reinforce desired behavior.

On the other hand, if a person lacks courage but is high on consideration, high in the need for acceptance and popularity, he will tend to develop a lose-win psychological contract where people do their own thing. Often these agreements lead to various forms of self-indulgence and organizational chaos. People may begin to blame others for poor performance or bad results. They may also get very demanding. Such behavior only reinforces the lose-win agreement, which eventually cannot be economically sustained and hence leads to win-lose central control as management battles to survive and maintain some semblance of order. Anarchy breeds dictatorship. As Patrick Henry put it, "If we don't govern ourselves wisely, we will be governed by despots."

Banking on the Results

To illustrate the power of the win-win agreement approach to organizational effectiveness, let me recount one experience. I was one of a group of consultants involved in an organizational improvement project with a large banking organization with hundreds of branch offices. This bank had budgeted three-quarters of a million dollars for a six-month training program for junior executives.

The idea was to take college graduates and put them through a series of rotating positions. After spending two weeks in one department, they would shift to another for a period of two weeks. After the six-month program, they would be assigned to a branch office in some kind of a junior executive position.

Top management wanted this whole program carefully analyzed and improved.

The first thing we did was press to understand what their objectives were. We wondered if there was an up-front understanding about expectations. There was not. We found that the expectations were very general, very vague, and that there was widespread disagreement among the top officers of the bank over what the objectives and priorities should be.

We continued to press them until finally they hammered out what they wanted a person to be able to do by the end of the training period, before being assigned to a junior executive position. They came up with around forty objectives for these trainees. We boiled these down to forty objectives—the desired results.

The next step was to give these objectives to the trainees. These people were excited about their jobs and about the chance to move into a junior executive position rather rapidly; they were entirely willing to identify with these objectives, internalize them, and do what was necessary to accomplish them.

They understood the objectives; they understood the criteria for evaluation. They had a complete list of resources that they could draw upon to accomplish those objectives, including reading materials and visits with departments managers and to outside educational agencies. They realized that they could be assigned to a junior executive position as soon as they could demonstrate competency in those forty areas.

This motivated them so much that they accomplished the objectives in three and a half weeks, on the average.

This performance totally astounded most of the top executives. Some of them could hardly believe it. They carefully reexamined the objectives and the criteria and reviewed the results to ensure that the criteria had been met. Many of them said that three and a half weeks simply was not enough time for these trainees to get the kind of seasoning and exposure that would give them mature judgment.

We basically said, "Fair enough. Write some tougher objectives, including the kinds of problems and challenges that would require seasoned judgment." Six more objectives were hammered out, and almost everyone agreed that if the trainees could accomplish those six things along with the other forty, they would be better prepared than most of the trainees who had gone through the six-month program.

We next shared those six additional objectives with the trainees. By this time they were allowed to supervise themselves. We witnessed a tremendous release of human energy and talent. Almost all the trainees accomplished these other six objectives in a week.

In other words, we found that the six-month program could be reduced to five weeks with even better results by setting up a win-win agreement with these young junior executives.

This has far-reaching implications in many areas of management, not just training. And some of the enlightened managers in this bank began to see them. Others were very threatened by this whole process, feeling that there was a certain amount of time that people had to put in to win their stripes. But no one could deny the results.

The win-win agreement is all about getting desired results.

THE MANAGER'S LETTER

Management consultant Peter Drucker introduced the concept of the manager's letter many years ago. It suggests that the subordinate prepare some kind of a written outline of desired results, guidelines, resources, accountabilities, and consequences and send it to his or her manager.

For years now I have worked with this concept in many different settings: in my consulting and training practice, in the establishment and management of my own business; in working with undergraduate and graduate students at Brigham Young University; and in my family life. I am absolutely convinced that if we really want high productivity and enhanced production capability, we must work with these six conditions of effectiveness.

I also know it is not easy. It takes time and patience—we can't keep pulling up the flowers to see how the roots are coming. The win-win agreement may not be set up overnight. It may take a lot of clear thinking and honest communication up-front. It also takes a lot of maturity to engage in mutual influence interactions. It requires a great deal of discipline and consistency and follow through and reinforcement. Whenever I have faltered in any one of these areas, I have negatively affected the conditions and the outcomes.

We can start in small ways and have small successes until our confidence in the overall concept increases and grows. We can then apply it to larger areas of responsibility. If your people don't care to write a letter containing the elements of a win-win agreement, perhaps you can write it and ask them if it accurately represents the agreement. If writing is threatening altogether, then don't write it. But make sure that it's a clear, good, mutual, oral understanding. Make certain also that it's flexible and open to change when changing circumstances or understandings warrant it.

Attitudes are important. The manager's basic attitude is one of "Where are we going?" or "Where do you want to go?" or "What are your goals, and how can I help you?" Then downstream the attitude is one of "How is it going, and how can I help you?"

I was introduced to this way of thinking in an organization many years ago by a manager whose entire attitude and manner was truly one of "What are you trying to accomplish, and how can I help you?" His sincerity and his faith in my potential empowered me and released enormous human commitment and effort to do what was necessary to accomplish the results, including drawing upon him as an extremely valuable resource.

I have also come to believe that whatever view we have of people is self-fulfilling; that is, we will produce the evidence to support our view. If we have an enlarged view of human nature and human potential, we will gradually find the evidence to support our view until we feel inwardly confirmed and reinforced.

Chapter 19

Managing Expectations

Each of us enters into jobs, relationships, and situations with certain implicit expectations. And one of the major causes of "people problems" in families and organizations is unclear, ambiguous, or unfulfilled expectations. Conflicting expectations regarding roles and goals cause many people pain and problems, adding stress to relationships.

Conflicting Expectations

Examples of conflicting expectations include the following.

• *Company mergers.* Look at what happened with Roger Smith at General Motors and Ross Perot at Electronic Data Systems. When these two cultures came together, the executives clashed in their attempts to deal with tough problems and mesh two different social wills. We saw, on one hand, Ross Perot advocating the rights of the common worker—trying to do away with layers of management and special executive privileges, seemingly unaware that certain features of the GM culture are intergenerational and simply can't be done away with overnight. Consultants can't mandate changes like that. It takes more education and a lot of communication. But most people in acquisitions and mergers don't get into meaningful two-way communication. They play either hard ball or soft ball, win-lose or lose-win.

• *Marriage relations.* Today, many of the once hidden issues and expectations of marriage are out in the open. But there is still much debate over the role of the man and the woman. For example, if a young man from a more traditional family approaches marriage with the implicit expectation "I'm the breadwinner, and you take care of the kids," he may be in for a rude awakening. It's evident that young and old couples alike are struggling with conflicting role expectations. Many women are unfulfilled without a professional career outside the home—a phenomenon fueled by a society that doesn't provide much appreciation, validation, and reinforcement for women as homemakers.

• *Education.* Each special-interest group sees education through its own pair of glasses, and each points to different problems and proposes different solutions. One burgeoning issue is the emerging trend toward providing character education in the schools, which is more and more needed as the traditional two-parent family breaks down.

• *Parent-child relations.* Parents often experience conflicting expectations in their relationships with their children, especially as these children enter teenage years. Parent and child have different ideas about their roles, and these ideas change as they go through various stages of growth and development.

• *Government relations.* Is the role of government to do good, or is the role of government to keep people from doing harm? If I am working with someone who believes that the government's role is to do good, we may have totally different expectations, which leads to conflict, disappointment, and cynicism.

• *Hiring and promoting.* What a new person expects of the job and the company is often very different from what his or her employer expects. During the "honeymoon" period, these expectations are soft and negotiable. It's a good time to clarify them while people are open and willing to talk things through.

If the system is unfair, it shows when people are hired or promoted. For example, if new employees are paid more, the people in place will say, "How come you pay them this when I've been working here this long and make less?" When managers violate such expectations, they must live with the consequences: trust goes down, and people start moonlighting; they come up with other agendas; they wonder what's going on; or they become almost paranoid and begin to see things in the worst possible light.

• *Interdepartmental and entrepreneurial projects.* Any time you have interface among different departments or among people from different disciplines, you can expect conflicting expectations. In fact, at the outset of any interdepartmental or entrepreneurial project, you will likely find several examples of violated expectations.

• *Customer relationships.* Seasoned managers of product and service companies know how hazardous it is to have customers who expect more than the company can possibly deliver. Therefore they monitor and manage client expectations through empathy and through customer information systems.

They try to identify people's feelings and expectations: "What are they thinking?" "What are they expecting us to do?" "What service do they expect after the sale?" "What kind of a social relationship do they expect?" If these expectations are not clarified, customers will be disappointed and disillusioned—and later lost.

• *Stakeholder conflicts.* Several entities have a stake in the success of an organization: employees, suppliers, customers, stockholders, the community, and so forth. Each group, however, has its own agenda, and these conflicting agendas often result in disabling disputes and misdirection.

THE PROBLEM: IMPLICIT EXPECTATIONS

An expectation is a human hope, the embodiment of a person's desires—what he or she wants out of a situation such as a marriage or a family or a business relationship. Each of us comes into a situation with certain implicit expectations. These come from our previous experiences, from earlier roles, from other relationships. Some of these expectations may be quite romantic, meaning they aren't based on reality. They're picked up from media or from some fantasy.

There's a difference between an expectation and reality. An expectation is an imaginary map, a "should" map rather than an "is" map. But a lot of people think that their maps are accurate, that "This is the way it is—your map is wrong."

Implicit expectations—these human wants, wishes, and desires —are the baggage we carry with us into a relationship, into a company, or into a business as customers. For example, if we go shopping, we may implicitly expect courteous and competent service. If a certain store violates those expectations, we are usually quick to change to one that is more customer-oriented and fulfills our psychological wants and needs.

Wise managers make things very explicit, spelling out "what we do and don't do" so that the client can say "Okay, we understand and feel good about that" or "We feel good about one area but would suggest another approach to serving our needs in this other area." They explicitly state what their mission is, what their resources are, and what they have chosen to do and not do with their resources.

THE SOLUTION: THE PERFORMANCE AGREEMENT

The performance agreement is the solution to the problem of conflicting expectations. It is the tool for managing expectations. It makes all expectations explicit.

The performance agreement is a clear, mutual understanding and commitment regarding expectations surrounding roles and goals. If management can get a performance agreement between people and groups of people, management has solved many of its problems.

That's because the performance agreement embodies all the expectations of all the parties involved. And if these parties trust each other and are willing to listen and speak authentically, and to synergize and learn from each other's expressions—then usually they can create a win-win performance agreement. They can create a situation where everybody has the same understanding regarding expectations.

There are three parts to a performance agreement: the two preconditions (trust and communication); the five content elements; and the reinforcement of the systems and structure of the organization.

• *Trust*. Coming in, people carry many implicit expectations and some hidden agendas. Often, real agendas and feelings are hidden because the trust level isn't high enough to share them. Trust, then, is one precondition of a good performance agreement, and the foundation of trust is the character of trustworthiness—the feeling in others that you will honor your commitments.

If trust has been eroded and respect lost, it's difficult to form win-win performance agreements because there's no foundation for it. Companies or departments within companies can still work out acceptable performance agreements, however, by starting small and letting the process of making and keeping agreements gradually develop or rebuild the trust. Construct the best performance agreement you can under the circumstances—even if it's a compromise—and then work toward a synergistic win-win deal next time around.

The performance agreement should always be open and negotiable—open by either party at any time. If the situation changes, either party can initiate the communication process and change the agreement. Although there may be certain inviolate principles, parts that would not be negotiable, much of it is open for discussion.

• *Communication*. The second precondition, then, is communication, a reality-testing process: "Oh, I didn't realize you felt that way. You mean you expected me to take the first step? I see. Now, let me tell you what I thought."

It's horizontal communication, an authentic sharing between people as prized contributors—as equals, not as superiors and subordinates: "I expected you to exercise more initiative. I was waiting on you! Now that I understand what you expect, next time I'll study it out and make recommendations."

That's the dialogue of people trying to clarify the expectations of a working relationship. Such communication is easier when the culture supports it. Unfortunately, in many companies talking formally about expectations seems almost illegitimate, yet it's a big part of the informal office talk: "What is your agenda? What are you really concerned about?"

I highly recommend the communication process outlined by Roger Fisher and William Ury in their book, *Getting to Yes*. It's a sensible process for making expectations explicit and arriving at a mutually rewarding agreement. Consider again the four basic principles:

- Separate the people from the problem.
- Focus on interests, not positions.
- Invent options for mutual gain.
- Insist on using objective criteria.

This win-win negotiation process requires the skill of empathy, seeking first to understand. People have lots of front-burner concerns they want to express, and they want first to be understood.

"Seeking first the interest of another" means finding out what his interests are, what is good for him, his growth and happiness. You can't assume you know what's best for the person. Find out through empathy, then build that into the agreement.

Clarifying expectations about roles and goals is the essence of team building. The idea is to get different groups together—salespeople with manufacturing or purchasing people, for example—and sharing expectations regarding roles and goals in an atmosphere that isn't emotionally charged.

Once people go through this interaction and make their implicit expectations explicit, it is just amazing what happens. People begin to say, "I didn't realize that. I thought you meant something else. No wonder you felt that way! I see, then, you probably interpreted what I did the next week in this way."

"Yeah, that's exactly what I thought."

It's amazingly therapeutic. People are relieved. "Gosh it's good to finally get this out on the table." By getting agendas on the table, we know where we all stand. We can then enter the negotiation process.

PRINCIPLES OF WIN-WIN PERFORMANCE

In forming win-win performance agreements, keep the following principles in mind.

- *Specify desired results, but don't supervise methods and means*— otherwise, you'll be buried in management minutiae and your span of control will be severely restricted.
- *Go heavy on guidelines, light on procedures,* so that as circumstances change, people have the flexibility to function, exercising their own initiative.
- *Mention all available resources* within the organizations as well as outside networks.

- *Involve people in setting the standards* or criteria of acceptable and exceptional performance.
- *Maintain trust and use discernment,* more than so-called objective or quantitative measurements, to assess results.
- *Reach an understanding of what positive and negative consequences might follow* achieving or failing to achieve desired results.
- *Make sure the performance agreement is reinforced by organizational structure and systems* to stand the test of time.

FROM CONTROL TO RELEASE MANAGEMENT

A win-win performance agreement is much more than a job description. Most companies already have job descriptions that define what the job is and what is expected of the person in the position. Most of that's very clear and explicit. But the performance agreement goes beyond the job description by making the implicit expectations part of a win-win contract, established through a process of synergistic communication.

Most job descriptions have very little sense of what constitutes a "win" for the employee. The only win for them is that they've got the job and make the money. The job description doesn't address other needs—psychological, spiritual, social needs. They're not being expressed at all.

Moreover, a job description is usually focused on methods and based on external control. The performance agreement moves us from external control to internal control, from a situation where someone or something in the environment controls someone to a situation where a person can say, "I understand, and I am committed because it's a win for me, too."

The performance agreement shifts the whole approach from control to release management. The reason most companies don't use release management is because they don't manage people by win-win performance agreements.

If managing expectations by performance agreements is not something that is now done in a company, individual managers can still initiate this and do it on their own. But they should be aware that they are dealing with social will, and they had better not be naive to think they can just hammer out some psychological performance agreement, because that performance agreement is interwoven with all social contracts, the unspoken culture of the organization.

A smart manager would say, "We have to be aware of the culture, of the nature of the situation, of the social will." More powerful than a psychological contract is a social contract, and culture is nothing more than a composite social contract. And what we call "shared values" is merely making implicit kinds of norms explicit—"This is how we do things around here."

Managing expectations by performance agreement is one of the things that "ought to be done around here."

Chapter 20

ORGANIZATIONAL CONTROL VERSUS SELF-SUPERVISION

Bob, vice president of a large manufacturing firm, is happy about his company's decision to make substantial cuts in middle management, thus widening the span of control and putting more authority in the hands of lower-level managers. He feels especially pleased about the potential savings in money and time and the associated "empowerment" of human resource within the company.

As one of the lower-level managers, Fred is also happy about the decision. He will no longer have to deal with excessive red tape, lengthy persuasion processes, and largely unnecessary meetings. He can take the ball and go with it.

The direction feels good; everyone anticipates healthy change and growth within the organization.

Within a week of the decision, Fred has the opportunity to handle a major problem in his new role. A customer phones to tell him that an insurance problem with inventory has come up, creating a significant strain in accepting the huge shipment that just arrived from Fred's firm. After considering the problem carefully, Fred makes what he feels is the best possible decision.

"You're a good customer; we value your business. Return the shipment and we'll get back together when your insurance concerns are resolved." Fred feels he has acted in harmony with the company emphasis on customer satisfaction and is pleased with his decision.

When Bob hears about it, he hits the roof.

"How could you possibly tell them to send it all back?" he explodes. "We've just finished a major run to send back east, and there is no place—*no place*—to put it! We don't have margin to cover return shipping costs on an order that size."

"But what about the company policy on customer satisfaction?" Fred demands. "Do we mean what we say or don't we?"

"Sure, we want our customers to be happy. But that doesn't mean we have to swallow their mistakes lock, stock, and barrel! You should have handled this another way."

Fred walks out of the office burned and gunshy, resolving never to put his neck on the line again. Bob sits at his desk, head in hands, wondering why in the world lower-level managers are so incompetent and resolving never to let Fred put his neck on the line again.

The need for effective autonomy has apparently come into head-on conflict with the need for organizational control.

THE CHRONIC CONFLICT

This scenario is played out daily on many different levels in a wide variety of organizations, including business, political, service, and even family. It reflects what many see as a conflict between the need for operational integrity and the benefits of greater self-supervision.

Organizational Control	—— CONFLICT ——	Self-Supervision

As this scenario repeats itself time and time again, it becomes a "chronic conflict" that precludes building either value, creating a downward spiral of trust that leads to cynicism, "snoopervision," tightening control, and constant tension.

The need for control—for overall integrity, direction, and continuity within the organization—is obvious. But equally obvious is the need—both for the individual and for the effectiveness of the organization—for greater individual autonomy and freedom, for decisions to be made as close as possible to the action front. The core problem is not the conflict, but rather the idea that there is a conflict—the paradigm or mental framework of dichotomous thinking that leads to "either/or" assumptions.

Effectiveness isn't a case of either organizational control or self-supervision. Both values are sound; both elements are vital to an effective organization. Rather than "or" logic, it's "and" logic—organizational control and self-supervision.

An "empowered" organization is one in which individuals have the knowledge, skill, desire, and opportunity to personally succeed in a way that leads to collective organizational success. In order to understand how the elements of this chronic conflict can be converted into conditions that nurture empowerment, we need to examine our basic paradigm of organizations.

THE MECHANICAL VERSUS THE AGRICULTURAL PARADIGM

Many people view organizations with a mechanical paradigm or mind-set. The organization is like a machine; if something is broken, it needs to be fixed. If you can find the problem, get the right part, stick it in, and turn it on, it will work.

But organizations are not mechanical; they are organic. To see organizations through the agricultural paradigm is to see them as living, growing things made up of living, growing people. Living things are not immediately "fixed" by replacing nonworking parts; they are nurtured over time to produce desired results.

Desired results in the organization are created not by the mechanic but by the gardener. The gardener knows that life is within the seed. Although it is impossible to make the seed grow, the gardener can select the best seed and then use "and" logic to create the conditions—correct soil temperature, adequate sunshine, water, fertilizer, weeding, cultivation, and time—that maximize growth.

Organizational agriculturalists work with six critical conditions to nurture empowerment in organizations. (These are the same six conditions introduced in chapter 18.)

One condition directly addresses the chronic conflict between organizational control and individual autonomy through win-win agreements—agreements that represent a "win" for the individual and a "win" for the organization as well. Such agreements are based on the "and" logic that seeks for mutual benefit and works to create a greater overlap between what the organization cares about and what the individual within the organization cares about.

	Organization	Individual
Organizational	_____	Self-
Control		Supervision

Win-win agreements, essentially, are contracts between individuals that represent a clear, up-front mutual understanding and commitment in five areas.

Desired results—not methods—identify what is to be done (goals, objectives) and when.

Guidelines specify the parameters (principles and policies) within which results are to be accomplished.

Resources identify the human, financial, technical, or organizational support available to help accomplish the results.

Accountability sets up standards of performance, time of evaluation, and methods of measuring progress.

Consequences specify—good and bad, natural and logical—what does and will happen as a result of the evaluation. They also give the reason—the "why"—for doing.

Such agreements provide necessary structure for empowerment, but win-win is more than a contract. It is a way of thinking and interacting in the organization that leads to a big win for all stakeholders, including customers and stockholders as well as employees. It is the paradigm that seeks constantly for mutually and maximally beneficial, creative, third-alternative solutions. As individuals operate on a day-to-day basis within the framework of win-win, organizational control and self-supervision are no longer seen as values in conflict. In fact, they become two additional conditions of empowerment.

"Control" does not mean some people controlling others; it means the organization is "in control"—the parts work together responsibly to create the desired results. This condition could be labeled "accountability" in the larger sense. The organization is accountable, or responsible, to the people in it for overall results. Individuals are accountable to the organization for their performance. All parts of the organization are accountable to each other for the integrity of the organization. Within the framework of accountability, work efforts are aligned with the needs of the organization, and the organization has the ability to monitor and support individual and group performance. People feel responsible for the accomplishment of relevant tasks, and the trust level is high.

Self-supervision, then, becomes the practical process in which individuals plan, execute, and control their own performance within the agreement. Win-win facilitates effective autonomy in which individuals have access to the primary elements of empowerment—knowledge, skill, desire, and opportunity. Time and money wasted on snoopervision can be reinvested in high-leverage leadership and management activities.

	Win-Win Agreements	
Organizational Control		Self-Supervision

As every gardener knows, you have to water what you want to grow. If the desired results are for individuals to work together effectively in a high-trust win-win culture, helpful systems and structures must be created that will reinforce those results. A compensation system that rewards competition among employees cannot nurture cooperation. A communication system that puts roadblocks in the way of direct line accountability limits effectiveness. Both the systems and the structures—the organizational framework and role definition—need to facilitate, not impede, the accomplishment of desired results.

	Win-Win Agreements	
Organizational Control		Self-Supervision
	Helpful Systems and Structures	

AT THE HEART OF EMPOWERMENT

These four conditions—win-win agreements, accountability, self-supervision, and helpful systems and structures—provide the framework in which empowerment becomes possible. Whether or not it becomes a reality depends on the strength of the two vital conditions that give life to the other four.

Real win-win is impossible to achieve in an atmosphere of mistrust and suspicion. No amount of lengthy negotiation can really resolve problems created by the dishonesty, deceit, lack of responsibility, or self-serving interest of the parties involved. Trust is the fruit of trustworthiness; thus, at the heart of empowerment must be basic character.

The high-trust culture in which win-win can succeed is created by people of integrity, maturity, and abundance mentality. People of integrity make and keep commitments to themselves and to others. People of maturity balance courage with consideration. They are able to express their ideas and feelings with courage balanced with consideration for the ideas and feelings of others. People of abundance mentality assume that there is plenty out there for everybody. They deeply value other people and recognize unlimited potential for third-alternative solutions. People of character are free to interact with true synergy and creativity, unrestrained by the doubt and suspicion that permeate low-trust cultures.

Closely associated with character is the other condition at the heart of empowerment—fundamental skill in the areas of communication (the ability to deeply understand others and to be understood by others), organization (the ability to plan, act, and do), and synergistic problem-solving (the ability to arrive at third-alternative solutions). Just knowing about win-win is not the same as knowing how to create it.

	Win-Win Agreements	
	Character	
Organizational Control		Self-Supervision
	Skills	
	Helpful Systems and Structures	

These six conditions nurture empowerment. Although one person cannot create effective positive change by "fixing" another's broken character or "replacing" a malfunctioning skill, there are specific things leaders can do within their circle of influence to improve the conditions that lead to empowerment in any living, growing organization.

1. Take inventory and evaluate personal and organizational effectiveness in each of the six areas.
2. Focus on creating change in personal character and skills and then expand to interdependent areas of influence.
3. Start the process of creating win-win agreements with supervisors or subordinates.
4. Work to create and strengthen supportive systems and structures within the organization.
5. Teach, exemplify, and reinforce.

These action steps are not "quick-fix" techniques; they are based on sound, time-proven principles of growth and change. Leaders who choose timeless principles as the foundation for their deep central paradigms of leadership understand that natural laws in the human dimension are just as real as those in the physical dimension. They understand that growth in the individual and in the organization follows the same process as growth in the garden, so they work to create the conditions that nurture growth.

Principle-centered leaders realize, too, that growth comes from the inside out, so they focus first on changing themselves and then on expanding to other areas of influence in the organization. As they increase their own capacity and work to integrate correct principles in a congruent, agricultural way, empowerment becomes a vital reality for effective organizations and for the people who work in them.

This chapter was prepared with A. Roger Merrill, vice president of the Covey Leadership Center and associate director of the Center for Principle-Centered Leadership.

Chapter 21

INVOLVING PEOPLE IN THE PROBLEM

INVOLVEMENT is the key to implementing change and increasing commitment. We tend to be more interested in our own ideas than in those of others. If we are not involved, we will likely resist change. But before you start involving people in the problems of your organization, you may want to learn a few new skills. Let me explain.

I once played racquetball with an older, overweight medical doctor. He told me that he had played a great deal when he was younger. Even so, because he was so out of shape, I thought he would give me very little competition and, therefore, little exercise.

I was wrong. Even though I was in far better shape and had a great desire to win, he had more shots in his repertoire—his higher level of skill compensated for his physical condition. I barely won the first game, and he totally dominated the next two games.

I kept saying to myself, "If I'm going to win, I've got to change." And I tried to change, but for some reason I couldn't. He kept making me play his game. I tried to play my game and make my shots. I tried to be more aggressive, but I simply lacked the repertoire of shots and the skills. I tried objectively to assess the situation and make some adjustments. Nothing seemed to help.

THE MANAGEMENT DILEMMA

Business managers sometimes find themselves in a similar dilemma. They sense that they ought to be doing better in the competitive market but seem powerless to make necessary changes. Bringing about changes in people and in organizations is not simple; or if it is simple, it is not easy. We are dealing with momentum, with attitudes, with skill levels, with perceptions, and with established patterns. People tend to cling to old views, old ways, old habits. And old styles and habits are hard to change.

To make or break a habit takes great commitment, and commitment comes from involvement—it acts as a catalyst in the change process.

Of course, the down side of involvement is risk. Whenever you involve people in the problem, you risk losing control. It is so much easier, simpler, and safer—and seemingly so much more efficient—to not involve others, but simply to tell them, to direct them, to advise them.

In his book, *Managing*, former ITT president Harold Geneen writes: "Most chief executives slip into authoritarian roles without realizing that the process is going on. Subtly, they change [because] it's easier and less time-consuming to be authoritarian."

Most authoritarian managers and executives are not tyrants. Most are benevolent—using the principles of *human relations* to the fullest to direct behavior and get desired results.

To manage by the principles of *human resources* is to leave safe territory. Involvement is a ticket to adventure. The executive really never knows at the outset what will happen or where he or she will end up. Is the risk worth taking?

"One of the primary, fundamental faults with American management," responds Geneen, "is that over the years it has lost its *zest for adventure,* for taking a risk, for doing something that no one has done before. The reason behind this change is the mistaken belief that professional business managers are supposed to be sure of themselves and never make a mistake."

So managers are caught between these two positions: the safer, easier, more efficient human relations position of directive, authoritative leadership and the far more risky, but infinitely more effective human resource principle of involvement.

Quality and Commitment

An effective decision has two dimensions: quality and commitment. By weighing these two dimensions and multiplying them, we can determine the effectiveness factor. For example, let's suppose that we make a quality decision—a perfect 10 on a 10-point scale; however, for some reason the commitment to that decision is low—a 2 on a 10-point scale. As a result we have a relatively ineffective decision (by multiplying 10 and 2, we get an effectiveness factor of 20).

Now let's assume that by involving others, we compromise the quality of the decision (it drops from 10 down to 7), but we increase the commitment to it (let's say from 2 to 8).

In this case we have an effectiveness factor of 56 (7 times 8). That means the decision may not be as good, but it is almost three times as effective!

Nonetheless, many young or new managers hesitate to involve people in decision making for fear of opening up other options, contaminating their own thinking, or compromising their position.

Eventually, through experience, most managers learn that the effectiveness of their decisions depends on quality and commitment, and that commitment comes through involvement. They are then willing to assume the risks and to develop the skills of involving people appropriately.

Driving and Restraining Forces

Kurt Lewin, one of the great social scientists, contributed enormously to our understanding of the change process. His force field analysis theory, developed some forty years ago, depicts the dynamics at play in a change process. (See the diagram on the next page.)

The lower line represents the present level of activity or performance. The dotted line above represents the desired level or what might be called the "objective" of the change effort. The arrows pushing down against the first line are the "restraining forces," and the arrows pushing up are the "driving forces." Sometimes the restraining forces are called "resisting forces," or "discouraging forces," and the driving force arrows are often called "encouraging forces." The present level of performance or the present behavior represents the state of equilibrium between the driving and the restraining forces.

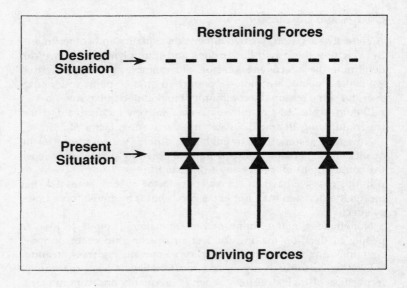

One of Lewin's earliest and most significant studies came as a result of a commission from the United States government to see what he could do to change the buying, cooking, and eating habits of American housewives during World War II. To help the war effort, government agents encouraged women to buy and use more of the visceral organs and less of the muscle cuts of beef.

They explained the facts and logically presented the driving forces—patriotism, availability, economy, and nutrition—to motivate and encourage housewives to buy, cook, and serve the visceral cuts of beef to their families. But they underestimated the restraining forces. People simply were not used to eating tongue, heart, and kidney. The women didn't know how to buy such products, how to serve them, how to cook them. They feared their families would respond negatively.

They resisted change until they started meeting together and gaining an understanding of the nature of the problem. When the housewives really got involved in the nature of the problem—the same problem that the government was facing—they gradually loosened up, "unfroze" their perceptions, broadened their thinking, and seriously considered alternatives. As these women came to understand how their change of diet could help the war effort, and as they expressed themselves fully—without fear of being censured, embarrassed, or ridiculed about their fears and doubts—many actually changed their buying and eating habits.

Lewin and the government learned an important lesson:

> *When people become involved in the problem, they become significantly and sincerely committed to coming up with solutions to the problem.*

SOLUTIONS TO PROBLEMS

I can personally attest to the power of involving people in the problem, even in family problems.

One night I was visiting with my oldest daughter about some of her feelings and concerns. After I listened for a while, she asked me if I had anything I wanted to talk about. I decided to involve her in a problem that had irritated my wife and me for some time—that of getting the children down and in bed at an hour that gave them sufficient sleep and gave us some time to ourselves.

To my amazement, she came up with some ingenious ideas. Once involved, she felt responsible, and her responsible involvement contributed greatly to the solution.

On another occasion I wanted to keep my cars in good running condition without having to invest an inordinate amount of time and money for maintenance. I went to the manager of a local service station and involved him in the problem. I expressed my trust in him and in his judgment. The moment he felt involved, he became responsible for results. He took care of my cars as if they were his own. He serviced them personally, made preventive check-ups, and gave me the best deals on purchases.

Enlightened leaders and business managers throughout the world have used this simple principle in one way or another for many years. They know that when people are meaningfully involved, they willingly commit the best that is in them. Moreover, when people identify their personal goals with the goals of an organization, they release an enormous amount of energy, creativity, and loyalty.

Again, Harold Geneen writes: "The mental attitude of the executive when he faces a decision is most important. I wanted the ITT executive to be imaginative and creative, also objective about the facts of the situation at hand. The climate control is in the hands of the chief executive. To me, the most important element in establishing a happy, prosperous atmosphere was an insistence upon open, free, and honest communication up and down the ranks of our management structure."

If we use an authoritarian or benevolent authoritarian approach to problem-solving, we slip into a kind of condescending or vertical communication pattern. If people sense that we are "talking down" to them or that our motive is to manipulate them into making a change, they will resist our efforts.

INCREASE DRIVING OR DECREASE RESTRAINING FORCES?

The question managers often ask when they learn about Force Field Analysis is, "Which is the best approach—to increase the driving forces or to decrease the restraining forces?"

Certainly the easiest and simplest approach is to increase the driving forces, because we have control over them. Traditionally this approach is used the most, even though it is less effective. What happens is that people put on a big push. That is, to use our diagram again, they add two or three more arrows of force or energy to get company performance or personal behavior up to the desired level. But they don't change the essential nature of the restraining forces. They only create new tensions at the higher level, and as soon as those are relaxed, performance springs back to the same old standard or level.

We see this happening in organizations when one new management principle after another comes and goes, when there is a big drive for cost-consciousness for a period of time—until everyone becomes so sensitive about costs that they forget about sales. Predictably, the next new drive focuses on marketing and sales. Everyone becomes more customer- and service-oriented until, little by little, they get the sales back up—only to lose control of costs once again. When the work force becomes cynical, management then sponsors more socials, parties, and bowling leagues; they get into a country club atmosphere and forget about sales and costs.

An organization that goes through such cycles, one after another, dealing with different crises, soon becomes cynical. The trust level gets very low. The communication processes deteriorate as the culture becomes polarized between "us and them." Then the next new drive or the next new technique, however beautifully packaged and powerfully endorsed by experts from the outside, has little, if any, effect. Cynicism is simply too thick. The trust level is too low, and the next new effort is seen as the next new manipulation by management to get what they want.

The question of whether to increase driving or decrease restraining forces is analogous to the question "If I'm driving a car and see the emergency brake is partly on, should I release the brake or put on more gas?" Accelerating may increase the speed, but it may also burn up the engine. Releasing the brake, on the other hand, would allow you to attain high speeds more efficiently.

Accordingly I suggest that we spend our first energy, usually about two-thirds of our energy, on reducing the restraining forces and one-third on increasing the driving forces. However, since every situation is different, we should first study the nature of the restraining forces and work on those. Many of these forces will transform into driving forces.

By getting other people involved in the problem, we release some of the natural driving forces already in people. When our external driving forces are synchronized with their internal drives and motivations, we can create a synergistic problem-solving team.

Chapter 22

USING STAKEHOLDER INFORMATION SYSTEMS

WE ONCE WORKED with a large banking organization that was losing a high percentage of its middle managers. The top executives couldn't understand why.

The only human resource information they had was anecdotal, coming primarily from exit interviews, which is an incomplete and inadequate source of information because of high emotional content and unscientific sampling. Based on these interviews, management assumed that the problem was the compensation system. So they modified the compensation system, only to find that it didn't make any difference at all.

Using our system of human resource accounting, we gathered reliable information and found that the real problem was that they were attracting entrepreneurial people and then asking them to crunch numbers in middle-management positions—there was no intrinsic satisfaction, no challenge, no excitement.

Once they got the feedback, they adapted to that reality and restructured the organization around entrepreneurial talent and around systems that rewarded the entrepreneurial spirit. Thereafter, the bank lost very few people, except ones who didn't really fit the culture. And the change unleashed an enormous amount of energy and talent throughout the organization because people were no longer blocked by old rules, regulations, procedures, and policies.

Accounting for People

Until our information system accounts for people as well as things, we will operate our organizations in the dark. Of course, some people don't mind the dark, especially those who are into "mushroom management," the primary ethic being "Keep people in the dark, pile lots of manure on them, and when they are fully ripe, cut off their heads and can them."

The ethic of the principle-centered leader is expressed well in the following plea: "From the cowardice that is afraid of new truth, from the laziness that is content with half-truth, from the arrogance that thinks it has all truth, O God of Truth deliver us."

An organization is an ecological system, and the information system must deal with the whole environment to help executives understand what's going on. Until an executive understands what's going on, his judgments and decisions will be flawed, distorted, incomplete, or inaccurate. People believe what they want to believe, and what is strongly desired is easily believed.

Since an organization is an ecological system, it needs an information system that deals with all the stakeholders. The primary information system of most companies is financial accounting; however, financial accounting deals only with measurable things, not with people problems and challenges. Things are programs; people are the programmers.

Financial accounting is the wrong tool for diagnosing people problems, monitoring stakeholders, and understanding the chronic causes and sources of problems. It focuses almost exclusively on acute problems and surface effects: revenues, costs, and so forth. Executives who rely exclusively on financial information systems will get a completely distorted picture of what is going on.

Making Sense of What's Happening

We have developed a sophisticated diagnostic tool to help executives gather and organize data and make sense of what's happening inside and outside their organizations. We call it *Human Resource Accounting* or *Stakeholder Information System*. Basically it helps executives monitor the condition of all stakeholders, using some personal and organizational profiling surveys as well as their own diagnostic and discernment skills.

For instance, a few years ago the top management of a major hotel chain knew they had problems: profits were down, productivity had dropped, morale was low. They could sense an undercurrent of dissatisfaction, but they couldn't pinpoint the cause. They had no concrete information on which to base a decision. They brought us in as consultants, hoping for a quick fix.

However, an organizational assessment survey showed that the real problem was that people were not trained; they were not sure what management expected them to do or how to do it. The survey identified several areas where the employees perceived a need for improvement: system effectiveness, leadership, organizational climate, human effectiveness, working environment, and interdepartmental relations. Executives found the data so valuable that they decided to do this survey annually.

In another instance the CEO of a company perceived himself and his company as being very people-oriented. But when we did an audit, we found that people throughout his company had no sense of career development, no clear career path, no idea of what peak performance would mean to them. As a result, a majority of his managers and executives were actively looking for work in other firms or thinking about it. As he learned of their feelings, he was able to remedy the situation before it resulted in the loss of key people. For him, the survey revealed a dangerous "blind spot."

To know what's happening with all the stakeholders of your organization, you need to monitor 1) *the people* (their perceptions, motivations, values, habits, skills, and talents); 2) *the formal organization* (the physical environment, the technology, and the strategy, structure, policies, and procedures); and 3) *the informal organization* or culture (the values and norms emerging from the interaction between people and the organization). Although this data gathering may be time-consuming, if done correctly it will give an accurate picture of what is happening inside the organization.

• *The people system.* The people system includes the self-system. The perceptions and feelings of people affect their behavior. When diagnosing the strengths and weaknesses of people, gather as much data as possible. Personnel records will tell us some things about our people, but managers should supplement these records with one-on-one visits, group meetings, open-door briefings, and suggestion systems, as well as the use of scientific instruments that give us a more objective picture of what's happening with our people. Compared with traditional accounting of physical and financial resources, human resource accounting may be considered subjective and soft, but if we accept that feelings are facts to the people who hold them, and that those facts influence their behavior in our organizations, we must acknowledge that "soft" human data can be very "hard." Organizations using effective stakeholder information systems have an enormous competitive advantage.

• *Formal organization.* When we begin to diagnose the strengths and weaknesses of the formal organization, we really get back to people, because all the background factors rest ultimately in the values, motivations, and perceptions of people. The formal organization is abstract. It may appear concrete because we can chart it and measure it, account for its sales and costs. However, organization charts, job descriptions, chains of command, lines of authority, and channels of communications are really just abstract descriptions of things. The external background factors are the economic, social, political, and cultural trends of society. People's perceptions, motivations, and values make up these trends. They tells us what's happening, and what people are thinking, and what they will likely be doing and thinking in the days to come. It's important to study the trends in our particular industry and to relate our unique strengths, our distinctive competencies, to those industrial trends.

The internal factors basically represent the traditions underlying the organization and the values of the founders, owners, and directors of the enterprise. As we examine these external and internal background factors, we can see how strategy is formed as well as organizational structure and the establishment of the many different kinds of systems, policies, and procedures that represent the muscle, nerves, and arteries of the organization.

• *Informal organization or culture.* Now, as we integrate the people, including self, with the formal organization—with the physical environment, technology, strategy, structure, and systems—we get culture, the informal organization, with its values, norms, mores, and unwritten expectations and assumptions.

When the norms of the informal organization conflict with the standards of the formal organization, we find adversarial relations between management and labor, between "us and them." In an adversarial culture, management inevitably thinks more in terms of controlling and directing human behavior than in releasing human potential toward win-win goals, where people's needs and interests overlap the needs and interests of the organization.

Culture is difficult to define and even more difficult to measure, yet we can all feel it. Often we cannot change the culture directly, but we can change the self system, our own character and skill. We can do a number of things with the formal organization to change the way we put people together, define their jobs, and design their responsibilities.

If we're wise in the way we do these things, we can gradually help create a powerful win-win culture. But if we lack sincerity and integrity and only do things to please or appease people, we may well create a culture that is more cynical, protective, and defensive than the one we were trying to improve. Just as the body creates defensive mechanisms to safeguard its own welfare, so might a culture. Although we cannot improve our health directly and immediately, we can improve it significantly by obeying a number of natural health laws over a period of time. Likewise, if we follow correct principles— fairness, human relations, human resources, and meaning—and integrate those principles into structure and systems, we can greatly influence the culture.

The more we take a slow, scientific approach in gathering and diagnosing data about what is happening inside organizations, the more hesitant we are to move in quickly and throw our weight around to shape up everybody and everything. Instead we begin to pay the price to cultivate the kind of personal maturity, character strength, and skills necessary to be a catalyst in improving our culture. We realize that we can no longer supply and supervise methods if we want to hold people responsible for results. We begin to establish win-win agreements with people, motivating them to cultivate certain desired skills and character traits and allowing them to supervise themselves under the terms of the agreement. We set up helpful structures and systems, and we require people to give an accounting regularly.

It all takes time, patience, and self-discipline. And it will take interaction with others to build teams and to identify goals that have meaning to all the people involved. The processes may be hard and painful, but in the long run these processes are not as painful or risky or time-consuming as operating in the dark, without accurate data on your most important resource—people.

How Effective Is Your System?

The main reason for assessing human resources and for setting up stakeholder information systems is to deal more effectively with people—with your employees and with your other stakeholders: suppliers, customers, investors, and so on. Decision makers need to see a balanced picture and to receive information in user-friendly ways.

Many assessment programs break down because executives don't involve the people who supply the feedback in action planning and problem-solving based on that feedback. When you get good feedback from people, you need to act on it. Often you need an outside agent or internal consultant—some catalyst to bring energy, expertise, and discipline to the problem-solving process.

The classic problem-solving process involves eight steps:

1. Gather data
2. Diagnose data
3. Select and prioritize your objectives
4. Create and analyze alternatives
5. Select one of them (make a decision)
6. Plan the action steps to carry out that decision
7. Implement the plan
8. Study the results against the objectives

Then it's back to step 1.

In contrast, human resource accounting often begins and ends with gathering data. We may do a little diagnosis, often without any training or tools. And then we hit and miss in our efforts to develop objectives based upon our diagnosis, to think through alternatives, and to make decisions and implement them.

When we do an assessment or survey, we create the expectation that the data will be used for decision-making purposes. When problem-solving around feedback is not done, people are disillusioned because their expectations are violated. Moreover, if management and the organizational structure, systems, and style continue to reinforce the financial accounting data, the culture then becomes cynical about opinion and attitude surveys.

Decision makers, too, may get turned off because they can see the negative effects. So they revert to their old style and to the safety of partial, incomplete data dealing with effects rather than with causes and the complete picture.

Financial accounting then supplants human resource accounting because the former appears to be hard, precise, scientific, systematic, objective, and definitive while the latter appears to be soft, subjective, imprecise, malleable, nebulous, messy, Pandora's box stuff. Assessment instruments can be as accurate, hard, and objective as financial accounting, but ultimately, all accounting and information systems are subjective because they are based on certain assumptions.

Anyone who understands the roots of financial accounting knows that it is highly subjective; it only has the appearance of objectivity. But put so-called objective data against "soft" and "subjective" human data, and the numbers will always win. That's why we use computer data at beauty pageants and award celebrations: to give the appearance of objectivity when, in fact, the judgments are subjective.

Objectivity simply means more opinions. When I served on the administrative council of a major university, I used to say, "We've got to look at leadership criteria in admitting students." The response was, "No, we can't. How are we going to tell parents 'Your son wasn't admitted because he doesn't have leadership potential'?" So we looked at grades and test scores because these "objective" criteria produced more predictable outcomes.

Business and industry have the same problem: how to assess people on the front end in ways that predict success. If we are long on management and short on leadership, how do we correct the imbalance? We have assessments that deal with selection and hiring, but most of these tools only raise red flags. They can't test for motivation, which is the key element in performance.

I recently read that there are seven kinds of intelligence that can be measured now. Only one of the seven—the verbal-mathematical-logical index—is used in determining IQ. But there are six others—

kinesthetic, spatial, interpersonal, intrapersonal, creative, and aesthetic—that can now be measured. And research shows that virtually every person rates very high in at least one of those seven categories.

One advantage of using an assessment (such as our Seven Habits Profile) to measure personal capability or performance is to get pretest and posttest data. For people who go through our training, the locus of control shifts from external to internal. Such training also creates a halo effect, meaning if you measure and record it, people tend to want to do better. Indeed, what you measure tends to improve.

One possible short-term disadvantage of training and assessments is that people become very proactive and, over time, form a dynamic subculture. They start seeing that there are options in life. The good news is that the net result is often a better fit between people and jobs, between personal and organizational needs. Some say, "You know, we might lose some people if we start asking questions." But if there's not a good fit, it's usually counterproductive to be there anyway. Nonetheless, if you put short-term and hard data against long-term and soft data, short-term and hard data will always win out. The health and welfare of the goose get pushed out of the picture as people go after the golden eggs.

START ASSESSING CUSTOMERS

To establish the practice of human resource accounting, you should start with a customer information system. But don't neglect the other stakeholders, including stockholders. In a world of leveraged buyouts and hostile takeovers, you're inviting trouble if you aren't assessing these stakeholders. Unless you regularly account for all of your stakeholders, your organization will likely not survive its competition.

That message is slowly beginning to register. I once spoke to some engineers, who must use their left brains to deal with techniques and technology. I told them, "Your primary problems are people. And you can't solve people problems with a thing mentality." They were shocked to hear it put that way, but they agreed.

If you emphasize short-term production, your people will only want financial information systems, even though these primarily serve owners and managers who want answers to such questions as

"What are the sales?" "What's the net?" "What's the return on the dollar invested?" "What's my dividend?" "How can I support my life-style?" "How can I get the income or growth I want?" They are often unaware that their long-term returns would be higher if there was an ecological harmony among all stakeholders.

The owners are driving financial accounting systems, and the managers are responding to ownership. Employees are a means to an end, without getting much respect—until we compete with many Japanese companies whose executives have learned how to mobilize, energize, and value people at all levels. Now we listen to employees because they're the cutting edge. They're the people who deal with the customer.

The purposes of human resource accounting are continuous quality improvement, team building, and individual progression—of course, even people who get some feedback can get mired and plateaued. One reason is that they're not getting the right feedback. They then fall back to a comfort zone and get arrogant, lazy, and cowardly. They don't want to face some realities. The mirror is too accurate. They don't want to see themselves naked. They would rather see themselves clothed with position, power, and robes of respectability. To be exposed is to be vulnerable.

It takes an exceptional chief executive to expose himself voluntarily to external scrutiny and to set up information systems that make him accountable to the other stakeholders.

One such executive is Ken Melrose, CEO of Toro. He has put a chart outside his office because he wants people to see how he's doing against certain objectives. By measuring and charting his performance, he makes himself accountable and motivates himself to improve.

If you measure it and post it, you will improve it. Doctors now use biofeedback to assess the condition of people in critical condition. I heard of one doctor who put a feedback monitor on the ceiling, right above his patients' heads, with a needle pointing to "life or death." The patients just stare at it, but it gives them good information on what's happening inside their bodies. Using that feedback, they can start to take control over seemingly involuntary body processes.

Basically that's what's happening to many American companies. They're getting feedback from the market that says "You're facing death" or "You're facing extinction and you'd better do something about it."

It's better to be humbled by the word than by the force of circumstances. However, few people will go through an assessment process if they aren't part of a program or group. Some highly self-motivated people, who have a lot of inward security, may informally seek feedback regarding their effectiveness.

The irony is that the more a person cares about what other people think, the less he can afford to care about what other people think because he's too vulnerable to it. So he avoids getting the data. How can he possibly risk finding out what you think about him? What if you reject him? What then?

The opposite is also the case. The less a person needs to care about what people think, the more he cares about what people think. Because we don't get our security from people. We get our security from within, from integrity to our value system. And if we value being effective with others, we'll adapt our styles, skills, and views. We will get our security from within and our effectiveness from without.

Companies and people who seek and use objective feedback on their performance usually have internal security. And they're more humble, more open, and more willing to learn and to adapt. Some might say they're naive, because they're soft and malleable. But if they get their security from unchanging internal sources, they can afford to be vulnerable and flexible on the surface.

In one scene of the movie *Roger and Me*, we see a woman bludgeoning a rabbit to death while talking the whole time. It is symbolic of what is happening in many corporations and in many professions. In education, medicine, accounting, insurance, publishing, and law, many people are thinking of alternatives because they've lost confidence in the same old thing. The major industries in this country are very vulnerable because they haven't really listened very much. The old structures and systems are still in place, but those venerable old walls may come tumbling down when someone walks around the city blowing a trumpet.

FOUR LEVELS OF IMPROVEMENT

To invest in stakeholder information systems, an executive must buy into the paradigm of continuous improvement at four levels: personal, interpersonal, managerial, and organizational. All four are needed. The one you neglect will have a negative, domino effect on the others, bringing down the house of cards.

If we aren't trustworthy, how can we have trust on an interpersonal level? And if we don't have trust at the interpersonal level, how are we going to empower others with a sense of stewardship for results? The control styles of management in this country come out of low trust. And low trust comes out of too much duplicity, hypocrisy, and inconsistency. People who walk into their problems can't talk their way out of them. The popular strategies of self-talk, visualization, and affirmation are necessary but insufficient. It takes a real commitment at all four levels.

You may also need to use different kinds of human resource accounting. On one end of the continuum are formal, scientific, and systematic forms; on the other end are meaningful one-on-one visits, continue-stop-start surveys, empathic listening, and emotional bank account building. Use both formal and informal systems, including suggestion systems, speak-up systems, open-door systems, resident ombudsman, and regular scientific profiling. Make it a policy that no one gets promoted unless he gets high marks on these instruments, not only from his superiors and peers, but also from his subordinates.

Your gut feeling may tell you that feedback in one area of the survey isn't all that accurate. But be careful not to throw the baby out with the bath water. Don't deny data just because you don't like it. It's tempting to say, "Those idiots over there don't know what they're talking about," and then go on your own anecdotal research.

In an open, trusting culture, you can get good data in one afternoon by using a continue-stop-start survey. The problem is that such informal surveys don't have the same legitimacy, power, or level of sophistication; therefore people may not pay as much attention to them. Data must be not only accurate but valued.

Accurate feedback should be highly valued. It's hard for someone who's divorced from the day-to-day operations of a company, as well as for someone who's totally immersed in the operations, to know what's really going on. Hence there's a need for good feedback. Otherwise you get greasy meals. You get insulated and isolated. And you don't really know what's happening. People tell you what you want to hear. And you like it. You don't want to deal with all the problems. You may even develop your own private networks for getting information. And it's usually anecdotal; the safe thing is to hear it from just a few people.

In some companies people are rewarded for participating in assessments, even if they bring bad news. It's very healthy to build "due process" into your operations and correct principles into your constitution. Unless you have a complete information system and a strong reinforcement system, your mission statement is nothing more than platitudes. Because eventually the management style will drive structure and system.

Stakeholder information systems put teeth into a mission statement, turning it into a constitution, the supreme law of the land— because you are gathering data on it, looking at it regularly, problem-solving and action planning around it, and rewarding people on the basis of it.

In the "Analogy of the Cave," Plato talks about people turning to and from the light and living with relative degrees of darkness and light, truth and error. People don't want to face the truth or the light, unless the market imposes that task on them—unless they virtually have no choice but to seek feedback and do something about it regularly. They prefer to live and work in relative darkness, in a comfort zone or a protected market niche where they can live with a 30 percent margin of error. But in world-class competition, that doesn't cut it. They may survive temporarily in their industry or their particular market, but if they want to have a long-term competitive advantage, they've got to improve.

Once you get information, you tend to use it. When you get enough people with information, you raise the consciousness and unleash energies. The higher the consciousness, the more the social, national, and political will develops. For the principle-centered leader, information then becomes power, the power of a collective will to accomplish the mission of the organization.

Chapter 23

COMPLETED STAFF WORK

WHEN WORKING with organizations that are mired in meetings and committee work, I counsel executives to use the tried and true principle known as completed staff work.

Effective human resource management begins with effective delegation, with making the best possible use of the time and talents of people. Often we delegate out of necessity: we simply have more work to do than we can do alone.

Consider the classic case of Moses and Jethro. Moses was killing himself trying to do everything for the children of Israel, to judge all matters large and small. His father-in-law, Jethro, saw all this and advised, "The thing that thou doest is not good. Thou wilt surely wear away, both thou and this people that is with thee: for this thing is too heavy for thee; thou art not able to perform it thyself alone."

Jethro then counseled Moses to do two things. First, Moses was to teach the people principles that embodied his judgments so they wouldn't have to come to him to decide every matter. They could reflect on the principles and think their problems through on their own. This is a powerful form of delegation— teaching principles and trusting the people to apply them. Second, Moses was to choose faithful followers and delegate all small matters to them, retaining to himself only matters of major importance. Both of Jethro's recommendations required Moses to take more time at first in setting things up and to take risks.

Delegation does take more time in the beginning, and many who feel they are now pushed to the hilt simply won't take this time to explain, to train, to commit. Take the manager who reasoned why he was still doing tasks his employees could do: "I can do the job faster than it takes me to explain it. Besides, I do it better." However, soon he accumulates so many things to do that he feels he has even less time to delegate or to explain and train.

Many executives get involved in the same rationalization. "Every time I delegate it, it doesn't get done; or if it does, it gets done poorly, and I have to redo it myself. So why delegate? It just takes more time." But they end up leading harassed lives, putting in fourteen-hour days, neglecting their families and their health, and undermining the vitality of the entire organization. We simply must delegate to increase our discretionary time for high-priority tasks. Time spent delegating, in the long run, is our greatest time saved.

Of course, working through others involves the risk of having things done differently and sometimes done wrong. Instead of rendering judgments directly, Moses had to carefully select and train people and put his faith in them, realizing they might not do it the way he would. They might even make mistakes. Often executives who are unwilling to delegate more than routine matters have faith primarily in their own judgment and way of doing things. They reason, "It has brought me to where I am now. Why change? Why quarrel with success?"

Indeed, some people have extraordinary capacity and ability and can produce amazing results without delegating major responsibilities. However, people and organizations don't grow much without delegation and completed staff work, because they are confined to the capacities of the boss and reflect both personal strengths and weaknesses.

And in the process of delegation, effective managers set up a win-win performance agreement with each employee. One important guideline is the principle of completed staff work.

THE PRINCIPLE: NO COP-OUT

Completed staff work is one of the best ideas to come out of an otherwise militaristic, authoritarian model of management. The principle is that people are to think through the whole problem area, analyze the issue in depth, identify several alternatives and the consequences of those alternatives, and then, finally, recommend one of the alternatives.

This technique causes people to plumb their own resources and put together a specific, final recommendation that represents their best thinking. All a manager must then do is approve or disapprove it. And if he or she decides to approve it, all that remains is to implement the decision or the recommended plan of action. Besides saving the manager's time, completed staff work stops people from copping out in the name of synergy or group-think or in the name of "Let's get together and talk it over."

Decision making by groups may not tap the best resources because in meetings people sometimes take the course of least resistance and merely discuss ideas they haven't really thought through.

The effective executive asks people to think through problems and issues and to make a final recommendation. She is not likely to intercede and intervene in the process and provide people with quick and easy answers, even though they plead for them. She waits until their work is done; otherwise, she cheats people of growth—and they cheat her of time. Moreover, people cannot be held responsible for results if they are "bailed out" in the middle of the fact-finding or decision-making process.

In this the executive must exercise great wisdom. Completed staff work is not a panacea, nor is it applicable to all situations. There is a place for some early brainstorming, especially in the incubation period of a project. There is also a place for synergistic consensus.

But the principle of making people do their homework before coming to the table holds true in most situations. It guards against people bringing half-baked ideas without paying the price to understand the issues and implications. It also guards against the common practice of coming together too early, before people can prepare well-thought-through "white papers."

Now I'll Read It!

When Henry Kissinger was secretary of state, he reportedly required his staff people to bring him their best recommendations. He would then take them, table them for forty-eight hours, and get back to them with the question, "Is this the very best you can do?"

And they'd say, "Well, no. We might think it through a little more; we might document it a little better; and we might present other alternatives and identify the consequences in the event that the people don't take our recommendation."

He'd say, "Well, then, continue to work on it."

And they would bring it back a second time. And the same thing happened. "Is this the very best you can do?" Kissinger would ask.

Now, most people know the flaws of their own presentation. So the principle of completed staff work gives them the responsibility to identify their own flaws and correct them or at least to identify them and suggest some measures for dealing with those flaws.

Invariably Kissinger's staff would identify some minor flaws. He would then tell them to get back to work on it, to improve it, and to strengthen it, which they did.

And they would bring it in the third time. And for the third time he'd say, "Is this the very best you can do? Is this your final recommendation? Is there anything that could be improved?"

And they'd say, "We really feel good about it, but maybe we could tighten the language a little; maybe we could make the presentation a little better."

They'd continue to work on it. And they'd bring it back yet another time and say, "This is the best we can do. We have thought it through thoroughly, and we have clearly identified the alternatives, the consequences, and the recommendations. We have also outlined the plan of action to carry it out in every detail, and we've got it in final shape. We're now convinced that you can present it in full confidence."

And Kissinger would say, "Good, now I'll read it."

This story illustrates that staff people often want to save themselves time and effort, rather than the executive's time and effort. Yet his time is worth so much more than their time—all the more reason for the executive to get the very best distilled thoughts from his staff.

SONY'S MINI-COMPACT DISK PLAYER

Sony got off to a slow start in laser-operated compact disk players, only to beat the competition in bringing out the first successful product to sweep the market. The one man most directly responsible for Sony's success in this area is Kozo Ohsone, a consumer-oriented manager who had overseen the development of the Walkman cassette player.

Ohsone went to his lab one day and made a block of wood about five inches square—the size of a compact disk—and put it out in front of his engineers. To avoid unwanted advice from the top brass, Ohsone didn't tell anyone outside the lab what he was doing. He next brought in some product engineers to help with the design, since the disk players would be so small that researchers needed to know at each step whether their tightly packed circuitry could be mass-produced by robots.

Ohsone told his people that he would not accept the question, "Why this size?" "That was our size, and that was it." His design and production engineers grumbled, but they got to work and completed the project as charged. When Sony's miniversion hit the market, it was one-twentieth the size of the original players, one-third the cost, and infinitely more attractive to consumers.

HOW TO GET COMPLETED STAFF WORK

Use the following five-step process for getting completed staff work.

• First, *provide a clear understanding of the desired results* to set up the psychological contract. That's what Kissinger and Ohsone did so well. Once a person has that, he or she can be set free to work independently or with others to meet a particular deadline for bringing in a final recommendation of what the decision should be, why, and what the alternatives are in the event that the executive wants to go for plan B or C. But the plan of action should be spelled out. Every detail should be thoroughly digested and finalized.

• Second, *give a clear sense of what level of initiative people have:* whether they are to wait until told, ask, make a recommendation, do it and report immediately, or do it and report periodically.

• Third, *clarify assumptions.* If people want some feedback from the executive early to make sure they're not going in the wrong direction, they should bring in their understanding of the assumptions that the executive is making before they complete their work. If they do not clarify assumptions up-front, they could go in an entirely different direction and bring in their final recommendations only to have the chief executive say, "You didn't even understand the premises and the assumptions on which I was operating."

• *Fourth, provide those people charged to do completed staff work with as much time, resource, and access as possible.* Nothing is more frustrating to staff people than the expectation of doing completed work without the necessary information and resources. But if you face a genuine crisis and simply don't have much time to respond, communicate these conditions clearly to your staff.

• *Fifth, set a time and place for presenting and reviewing the completed staff work.* Give your people the chance to make an effective presentation of their work.

Again, this principle is not a panacea. It is simply an effective means for motivating people to do their own thinking and to put their work in as finished a form as possible before they give their final recommendations. My experience is that most staff people welcome the chance to study things out and to show what they are capable of doing. If executed well, completed staff work saves everybody's time in the long run and produces a much higher quality product. That's because the process plumbs the depths of the individual brilliance and talents of people.

APPLICATIONS OF THE PRINCIPLE

Here are just a few of the many applications of this principle.

• *Speeches and presentations.* Spend as much time as necessary in getting the preliminaries together so that the person who is to do the completed staff work knows what resources are available and understands fully what the expectations are. The executive might have to do some work up-front to get the process started. Particularly with speeches and presentations, the executive would need to spell out some things. "These are the basic things I want to touch on in that meeting in two weeks," he might say. "In the meantime, I'm going to be gone on a trip. Let's review your recommendations when I get back."

• *Issue development.* An executive could say to a trusted staff person, "Please think this issue through and bring to me a specific recommendation as to what you think the charter should be and what you should do." In other words, "You do the issue development for me and then write your own contract."

I once did this with a company. I sat in and listened to those staff reports. They were excellent. The chief executive himself just sat back in amazement. He later told me, "I never realized the depth of their thinking."

• *Meeting management.* Completed staff work not only plumbs the genius and talents of good staff people, but also makes for more effective meetings. When people have analyzed an issue in depth, carefully thought through the implications and the alternatives, and responsibly made their recommendations, they make a more powerful contribution to meetings.

• *Synergistic problem-solving.* Once you identify the key issues and prioritize them, you can then set up a small ad hoc committee and give them the challenge of completed staff work.

For instance, you may find that one of the major problems is communications or career development or compensation. Get three or four people from different levels in the organization into a viable working committee and ask them to study in depth that one issue and come up with a specific recommendation to bring back to the executive group: "We recommend this for these reasons. Here are the alternatives. Here are the consequences. And here are the problems we came to understand, along with the causes of the problem." If they have a synergy in their team, you get a strong recommendation representing different points of view. And seldom have I seen top executives turn down such a recommendation.

The process also moderates the extremists—the dissident and negative people who might be riding some hobbyhorse and pushing it. As soon as they've had a free forum—their day in court, as it were—they get all that negative energy out of them. It takes the sword out of their hand, and it moderates them. And it makes for a better win-win solution.

A final word of caution. If this principle is not integrated with others, it could create the perception "Who does the boss think he is? We do his work, and all he has to do is put his name and stamp on it." Or some may say, "He doesn't care; he doesn't want to get involved in the process at all."

But done well, completed staff work develops people and saves the executive's time. It also gives much more responsibility to the staff people. In fact, it increases their response-ability, their ability to choose wise responses to different situations.

Chapter 24

MANAGE FROM THE LEFT, LEAD FROM THE RIGHT

In ORGANIZATIONS, people usually perform one of three essential roles: producer, manager, or leader. Each role is vital to the success of the organization.

For example, if there is no producer, great ideas and high resolves are not carried out. The work simply doesn't get done. Where there is no manager, there is role conflict and ambiguity; everyone attempts to be a producer, working independently, with few established systems or procedures. And if there is no leader, there is lack of vision and direction. People begin to lose sight of their mission.

Although each role is important to the organization, the role of leader is most important. Without strategic leadership, people may dutifully climb the "ladder of success" but discover, upon reaching the top rung, that it is leaning against the wrong wall.

Consider the following historical examples:

• *Automobile industry.* Several years ago, in spite of the counsel of insightful forecasters, American automobile manufacturers continued to build big gas-guzzling cars. Their shortsightedness resulted in a widely known disaster from which they struggled to recover.

• *Steel industry.* The old-line big producers continued to operate our archaic mills while trying to compete with high-technology foreign companies and domestic minimills that can produce high-quality steel at a much lower cost.

• *Semiconductors.* American companies virtually owned the world semi-conductor market until the mid-1970s. During the recessionary years that followed, they cut back production, and by 1979 the U.S. suppliers were at a loss to meet the demand for 16K RAMs. The Japanese had since jumped into the market and by the end of that year had captured almost half the market.

• *Banking.* Most major banks in the United States find their balance sheets held ransom by third-world countries. Conventional wisdom regarded making big loans to developing countries as an excellent way to build a financial statement. Bank executives failed to see that a combination of social unrest, high unemployment, and rapid inflation in most of these countries would make loan paybacks virtually impossible.

• *Transportation.* In the railroad industry, managers lost sight of their essential role—to provide transportation—and instead saw themselves in the railroading business. Then, as they gave their energies to building better railroads, the pipelines, airlines, and truck lines took away most of their business.

• *Accounting.* Managers continue to account almost exclusively for financial and physical resources and neglect accounting for the most important resource of all: people.

We could look at every field of human endeavor and find endless examples of people scrambling to the top of a ladder that is leaning against the wrong wall. Peter Drucker teaches that within a few years of their establishment, most organizations lose sight of their mission and essential role and become focused on methods or efficiency or doing things right rather than on effectiveness or doing the right things. It seems that people tend to codify past successful practices into rules for the future and give energy to preserving and enforcing these rules even after they no longer apply. Indeed, traditional procedures and practices die hard!

MANAGEMENT VERSUS LEADERSHIP

That's why the role of the leader is so crucial to continual success. Leadership deals with direction—with making sure that the ladder is leaning against the right wall. Management deals with speed. To double one's speed in the wrong direction, however, is the very definition of foolishness. Leadership deals with vision—with keeping the mission in sight—and with effectiveness and results. Management deals with establishing structure and systems to get those results. It focuses on efficiency, cost-benefit analyses, logistics, methods, procedures, and policies.

Leadership focuses on the top line. Management focuses on the bottom line. Leadership derives its power from values and correct principles. Management organizes resources to serve selected objectives to produce the bottom line.

Of course, management and leadership are not mutually exclusive; in fact, it might be said that leadership is the highest component of management. And leadership itself can be broken into two parts: one having to do with vision and direction, values and purposes, and the other with inspiring and motivating people to work together with a common vision and purpose. Some leaders have vision but lack team-building talents. Other leaders can inspire people and build teams but lack vision.

As a team builder, the leader attempts to reduce the dysfunctional friction, while recognizing that in a complementary team, strength lies in differences; hence he need not attempt to clone people or make everyone else over in his own image. As long as people have the same goals, it is not important that they have the same roles. When team members regard each other with mutual respect, differences are utilized and are considered strengths rather than weaknesses.

The basic role of the leader is to foster mutual respect and build a complementary team where each strength is made productive and each weakness made irrelevant. The essential role of a manager is to use leverage to multiply the work and role of the producer. A producer rolls up his sleeves and does what's necessary to solve problems and get results.

It is most interesting and instructive to study how well people's jobs fit their personal style or preference with regard to these three roles. For instance, some people may be in a job that requires little production but a lot of management and a little leadership, but their personal style or preference is to be a producer rather than a manager or a leader. Needless to say, a poor fit between job expectations and personal preference will be a source of great frustration as well as criticism from others. And if a job holder has a different perception from that of his boss or peers regarding the relative importance of these three roles in his particular position, his problems will be compounded.

LEFT BRAIN/RIGHT BRAIN

Research on brain theory helps us to understand why some people are excellent producers but poor managers or great managers but weak leaders. The research basically indicates that the brain is divided into two hemispheres, the left and the right, and that each hemisphere specializes in different functions, processes different kinds of information, and deals with different kinds of problems.

Although both hemispheres are involved in logical and creative processes, the left works more with logic, the right works more with emotions. The left deals with words, the right with pictures; the left with parts and specifics, the right with wholes and relationships among the parts. The left deals with analysis, which means to break apart; the right with synthesis, which means to put together. The left deals with sequential thinking, the right with simultaneous and holistic thinking. The left is time-bound, meaning it has a sense of time and goals and one's position in relation to those goals; the right is time free, meaning it might lose a sense of time altogether. The left governs the right side of the body and vice versa.

Using these terms, we might say that we live in a left brain–dominant world, where words and measurement and logic are enthroned and creativity, intuition, and artistry are often subordinated, even punished. This is particularly true with men: the masculine "macho" cultural stereotype, combined with the heavy academic focus on the left side, can often negate or even drive out the more creative, aesthetic, intuitive capacities (often considered feminine).

The Eastern cultures speak of the two parts of man's nature, the yin and yang. The yin is the feminine part and the yang the masculine. Entire libraries have been written on this subject, including organizational books. Many organizations have great management systems and controls but lack heart. Others may have heart but lack mind, good systems, and controls.

The ancient Greek philosophers spoke of influence or persuasion processes in terms of ethos, pathos, and logos. Basically, ethos concerns one's credibility, or what I have called the emotional bank account; pathos deals with the emotions and motivation, which we would here call the right brain; and logos deals with the logical reasoning process, the left brain.

As we apply brain dominance theory to the three essential roles or organizations, we see that the manager's role primarily would be left brain and the leader's role right brain. The producer's role would depend upon the nature of the work. If it's verbal, logical, analytical work, that would be essentially left brain; if it's more intuitive, emotional, or creative work, it would be right brain.

People who are excellent managers but poor leaders may be extremely well organized and run a tight ship with superior systems and procedures and detailed job descriptions. But unless they are internally motivated, little gets done because there is no feeling, no heart; everything is too mechanical, too formal, too tight, too protective. A looser organization may work much better even though it may appear to an outside observer to be disorganized and confused. Truly significant accomplishments may result simply because people share a common vision, purpose, or sense of mission.

Accordingly, my suggestion is this: *Manage from the left, lead from the right.*

Of course, the ideal is to cultivate the ability to have crossover between the right and left sides of the brain; a person could then discern the situation and use the appropriate tool to deal with it. If someone were to ask regarding a game of chess, "What's the best move?" we'd first have to ask, "What's the situation?" Then we could decide what the best move would be. If someone were to ask, "What is the best club to use in golf?" again we'd first have to ask about the lay of the land, lie of the ball, placement of the pin, and so forth. The ability to correctly diagnose the situation comes first, and this itself may require a good combination of left and right brain skills.

To acquire a functional balance, a person may need to exercise the weaker side of the brain. For example, a person who is left-brain dominant should purposely exercise right-brain muscles by learning to communicate through sensing and touching and visual imagery and to listen more with the eyes than the ears, getting involved in artistic endeavors and the creative side of problem-solving and so forth. Those who are right-brain dominant should exercise the latent left-brain muscles through analytical problem-solving processes, communication through words and logic, reading textbooks, and studying scientific and technical material in computer science, law, business accounting, or any of the applied sciences.

Organizations that are devoted to short-term, bottom-line, hard-data orientations usually neglect such leadership development and therefore breed "half-brained" executives who seldom find time, for example, to communicate vision and direction, build teams, develop people, or plan meetings, except in a kind of crisis way.

If leadership issues get on the agenda, they are usually at the bottom, under "Other Business." Executives seldom address leadership issues because they are so fatigued from putting out fires and dealing with the production and management issues at the top of the agenda.

No wonder many individuals and institutions are caught going in the wrong direction, being in the wrong jungle, or leaning against the wrong wall. Strategic leadership can eliminate such misdirection and make things right again.

A strategic leader can provide direction and vision, motivate through love, and build a complementary team based on mutual respect if he is more effectiveness-minded than efficiency-minded, more concerned with direction and results than with methods, systems, and procedures. While all of the producers are hacking their way though the jungle and their managers are sharpening their machetes for them and setting up machete-wielding working schedules and putting on training programs for machete wielders, an enlightened and courageous leader must sometimes cry out, "Wrong jungle!" even though he can expect to receive the answer, "Be quiet! We're making progress."

Chapter 25

PRINCIPLES OF TOTAL QUALITY

CERTAIN UNIVERSAL PRINCIPLES and purposes must be observed in order to obtain total quality of services and products.

When one of our governing values is total quality, we will care not only about the quality of our products and services, but also about the quality of our lives and our relationships.

The paradigm of total quality is continuous improvement. People and companies should not be content to stay where they are, no matter how successful they seem to be. And very few people or companies could possibly be content with the status quo if they were regularly receiving accurate feedback on their performance from their stakeholders. Quality begins with an understanding of our stakeholders' needs and expectations, but ultimately it means meeting or exceeding those needs and expectations.

FOUR AREAS OF TOTAL QUALITY

Total quality is an expression of the need for continuous improvement in four areas:

1. Personal and professional development
2. Interpersonal relations

PS PARADIGM:
FOUR LEVELS OF PRINCIPLE-CENTERED LEADERSHIP

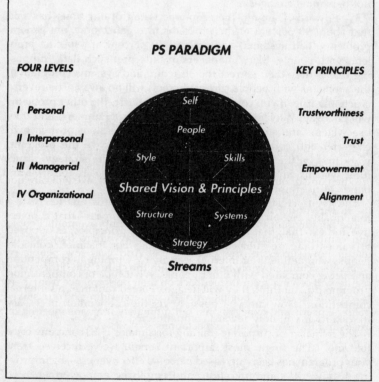

PS PARADIGM

FOUR LEVELS

I Personal

II Interpersonal

III Managerial

IV Organizational

Self

People

Style   *Skills*

Shared Vision & Principles

Structure   *Systems*

Strategy

Streams

KEY PRINCIPLES

Trustworthiness

Trust

Empowerment

Alignment

3. Managerial effectiveness
4. Organizational productivity

• *Personal and professional development.* I've always liked the expression "If it's going to be, it's up to me." In reality you and me are the keys to total quality. It's what I call an inside-out approach to quality. Inside-out means to start first with yourself—your paradigms, character, and motives. This approach often requires personal change—not personnel changes.

W. Edwards Deming, the economic Isaiah of our time, has said that about 90 percent of the problems in organizations are general problems (bad systems)—only about 10 percent are specific problems with people. Many managers misinterpret such data, supposing that if they then correct the structure and systems (programs), the problems with people (programmers) will go away. The reverse is actually true: if you correct the 10 percent first, the other problems will go away. Why? Because people are the programmers, and they use systems and structure as the outward expressions of their own character and competence. If you want to improve the program, work first on the programmer; people produce the strategy, structure, systems, and styles of the organization. These are the arms and hands of the minds and hearts of people.

The key to creating a total quality organization is first to create a total quality person who uses a true north "compass" that is objective and external, that reflects natural laws or principles, as opposed to values that are subjective and internal. For instance, consider people who define their internal security by winning in competition and being compared with other people. What type of compensation program do you think they will design? Forced ranking and internal competition? How can you possibly get the cooperation necessary for quality if you only reward competition?

The manager of corporate training for a major U.S. company once told me, "The single most important benefit we've received from your program has been increased personal effectiveness—by improving teamwork, communication, and employee empowerment, we boosted profits in our overseas operations by 90 percent the first year!" Another executive said that principle-centered leadership "prepares the soil" for the seeds of total quality. His comment suggests that individual executives need to prepare their minds and hearts for a higher level of thinking and their heads and hands for a new way of working before their quality problems can be solved. How people think about their jobs can have more impact than what they actually do.

People who don't make quality their number one priority won't make it through the United States's tough economic times, say winners of the Malcolm Baldrige Award. They've found that the best way to predict the future is to create it, using a compass to navigate the rough, changing terrain. The application of timeless principles of effectiveness will elevate you to a new level of thinking, providing you with a balanced, changeless core. Approaching quality from the human side harmonizes systems with processes, unleashes latent creativity and energy, and creates other benefits that go right to the bottom line.*

Character and skill development is a process of ongoing improvement or progression, a constant upward spiral. The personal side of total quality means total integrity around your value system—and part of that value system means you are always getting better, personally and professionally.

W. Edwards Deming's principle, constancy of purpose, implies that we first *have* a purpose or mission—a statement of what we are about, a vision of what we can become. The common denominator of success is a strong, empowering, guiding, inspiring, uplifting purpose. If you have it set clearly into your mind, if you begin with the end in mind, that purpose will guide everything. It will unleash your creative capacities; because of it, you will tap into your subconscious mind and bring out of it its memory, its contents. You begin to work from your imagination, not your memory. You are not limited or tied to the past but have an unlimited sense of what is possible in the future; your mind-set is prophecy, not just history.

Continuous improvement basically means you are never content with something being half-right. Your customers certainly won't be content. And if you are getting accurate feedback from them, you will be motivated and challenged to improve—either improve or perish.

Many business executives lack the internal security to seek and take feedback from stakeholders—they are threatened by it. Yet feedback is the vital lunch of champions. Champions are continuously getting feedback, and they listen and learn from it. They use it to

---

* For a complimentary audiotape by Stephen R. Covey on keys to implementing quality into your life and your organization, please call 1-800-255-0777.

improve their performance day by day. Personal and organizational improvement programs are built on accurate feedback, not on inaccurate social data. Ironically, the more you care about what other people think of you, the more threatened you are by feedback because your self-image is framed and your security formed in the social mirror. People who act as if they don't care what other people think actually care too much.

• *Interpersonal relations.* Total quality on an interpersonal level means making constant deposits into the emotional bank accounts of others. It is continually building goodwill and negotiating in good faith, not in fear. If you create an expectation of continuous product or service improvement but fail to deliver on that expectation, you will see a buildup of fear and negative forecasting.

A corporate culture, like the human body, is an ecosystem of interdependent relationships, and these must be balanced synergistically and based on trust to achieve quality. If we approach quality with something other than a principle-centered approach on all four levels, our efforts will be necessary but insufficient.

Emotional bank accounts can evaporate fast—particularly when expectations of continuous communication and improvement are violated. If communication doesn't take place, people begin to tap into their memories and into their fears and spin off negative scenarios and start planning based on those scenarios.

In independent enterprises such as a marriage or a business, past deposits will evaporate unless people are continually making new deposits in their partner's emotional bank account. With old friends we don't need to make many new deposits because we have few expectations. We can pick up where we left off and achieve instant rapport. Moreover, with old friends we rarely deal with interdependent jugular issues, only pleasant happy memories. But in a marriage, family, or business, we deal with jugular issues day by day, and these require constant new deposits into the emotional bank account. If we aren't giving twelve hugs a day to some people, we will soon have a withdrawal state because our deposits are essentially evaporative in their nature.

Interpersonal quality means giving those twelve hugs a day— physical hugs, emotional hugs, verbal hugs to the people around us—so that those deposits are constantly being made.

• *Managerial effectiveness*. Managerial quality is basically nurturing win-win performance and partnership agreements—making sure they are "in sync" with what is happening inside that person and what is happening inside the business. These win-win agreements are subject to renegotiation at any time—ideally on a synergistic basis, not a positional bargaining basis, and open to all the dynamics and vicissitudes of the market. So there is a sense of two-way openness.

Win-win thinking creates teamwork. Win-lose thinking creates rivalry. Rivalries are common in established systems as departments develop a life of their own and their own survival mechanisms. Rivalries are very natural when people have limited resources; they perceive their professional world as a limited pie, and they gradually develop win-lose approaches. They sit and talk about "those guys over there" and about what they are going to do to get more internal resources for building their empires. Our fiercest competitors are then right inside our own divisions or departments. And who needs internal competition when we have plenty of it out there in the market?

We need internal unity to get win-win cooperation, loyalty to the mission, constancy of purpose. Win-lose competition is fueled by bad-mouthing other people behind their backs. If you have a problem with somebody, go to them, discuss the problem with them, talk it through, and then get into team building. It is disheveling to the culture to have rivalry.

Most people search for quality in techniques, practices, and processes; they don't realize that quality requires a whole different explanation of the role of management. All the great breakthroughs are break-withs or breakouts of old kinds of thinking. Breakthrough thinking comes not from continuing to look through our glasses at our work but from taking off our glasses and examining the lens.

What is the difference between management and leadership? Management looks through its glasses and does its work, but leadership looks at the lens and says, "Is this the right frame of reference?" Management works within the systems to make them work. Leadership works on the systems. Leadership deals with direction, with vision, with purpose, with principles, with top line, and with people building, culture building, emotional bank account building, strengthening people. Management deals more with control, logistics, and efficiency. Leadership deals with the top line, management deals with the bottom line. The hand can't say to the foot, "I have no need of thee." Both leadership and management, effectiveness and efficiency, are necessary.

Few people give as much emphasis to the people management side of what W. Edwards Deming says as they do to the technical side. But how do you develop the concept of a leader as a coach, as a source of help? How do you remove fear, remove barriers, build cross-functional teams and personal self-worth? The human side is the heart of it because people are the programmers—they produce everything else.

People must know that they are being managed by principles and entitled to due process. You can't manipulate people's lives and play with their rice bowls arbitrarily without making massive withdrawals from their emotional bank accounts. If you must cut costs to remain economically viable and competitive, see that you do it according to due process; otherwise you can become overdrawn immediately. And once fear gets into the culture, everyone wonders what is going to happen to them.

Once the executive vice president of a large company told me, "I've been scared twice in my life—first when I ran up the beaches of Iwo Jima after seeing two-thirds of the first wave killed right in front of me."

"And the second time?" I asked.

"Coming to work in the morning."

"How so?"

He said, "You never know what the old man is going to do. Twice I've seen him move in on people and disrupt their rice bowls. That created such a fear in me that I have never forgotten it. And I can't get over it. I never know when I might be hit."

Even if you only violate a key principle once, you might wound a person deeply, and that one event will effect the quality of your relationship because people never know when you might do it again.

Management's job is empowerment, and empowerment basically means, "Give a man a fish and you feed him for a day. Teach him how to fish and you feed him for a lifetime." When you give people principles, you empower them to govern themselves. They have a sense of stewardship. You have entrusted them with principles to work with; guidelines to work within; resources to draw upon; win-win performance criteria to be measured against; consequences and rewards to work for. When you fully empower people, your paradigm of yourself changes. You become a servant. You no longer control others; they control themselves. You become a source of help to them.

If you want to influence and empower people, first recognize that they are resourceful and have vast untapped capability and potential. Understand their purpose, point of view, language, concerns, customers, boss. Be loyal. Don't do other things that undermine the emotional ties. Maintain credibility. By empowering people, you increase your span of control, reduce overhead, and get rid of unnecessary bureaucracy.

Empowerment takes an abundance mentality—an attitude that there is plenty for everybody and to spare, and the more you share the more you receive. People who are threatened by the successes of others see everyone as competitors. They have a scarcity mentality. Emotionally they find it very hard to share power, profit, and recognition.

• *Organizational productivity.* Proactive leadership springs from an awareness that we are not a product of our systems, that we are not a product of our environments, that those things powerfully influence us, but we can choose our responses to them. Proactivity is the essence of real leadership. Every great leader has a high level of proactive energy and vision—a sense that "I am not a product of my culture, my conditioning, and the conditions of my life; rather, I am a product of my value system, attitudes, and behavior—and those things I control."

Deming continually emphasizes that quality starts at the top—that the leadership of the organization must be intimately involved in the process to see that the quality paradigm is translated into the minds and hearts of everybody in the organization. He notes that the quality crisis is more fundamental than technique and that the solution calls for a new paradigm, a new way of viewing our roles, a transformation of management operations. Quality is not always doing things better—it's doing things differently.

The heart of organizational continuous improvement is problem-solving around stakeholder information. Most organizations do problem solving around financial data and analysis. But the best organizations in Japan and in America are constantly getting information from all the stakeholders—all those who have a stake in the welfare of the enterprise—and they listen intently and fully and then develop solutions based upon that diagnosis. This is why they are in a constant state of improvement. If our paradigm is onetime, seasonal, or unsystematic improvement, we are not moving toward total quality.

In financial accounting everyone is trained in the eight steps: gather data, diagnose data, set up objectives, identify and select and evaluate alternatives, make a decision, implement the decision, study the results against the objectives, and then go back to gathering data. In human resource accounting we often stop at gathering data—one step. Few people know how to diagnose the data, let alone get into prioritization of the objectives and problems around that diagnosis and then into action planning around setting up the criteria of your objectives.

Stakeholder information systems are not set up in most organizations. Sure, management will gather data occasionally through some kind of survey, but that only arouses expectations and creates disillusionment unless the exercise results in change. And the next time they attempt to gather information, they encounter cynicism. The quality in those organizations is hit and miss, often determined by whether individual employees are professionally committed to quality improvement.

Real quality improvements happen when management begins to problem-solve around stakeholder information. Most organizations don't even have the tools to get the data. They don't have a human resource approach to problem-solving; they use a human relations approach—"Be nice to people"—and then it is basically a benevolent authoritarian style. So they don't get a deep buy-in; therefore total quality becomes a program of the company instead of the philosophy and value of every person in the company.

The Procter & Gamble approach to total quality is to understand their consumers—to understand what they require, what they demand, what they want. That's first, and everything is driven by that. The next step is to give them more than they expect, to go the second mile, to give them service, the augmented product that wins such competitive advantage in the minds of customers.

I recommend that every organization develop a stakeholder information system—a feedback system or data base on what shareholders, customers, employees, communities, suppliers, distributors, and other parties want and expect. If done right—if done systematically, scientifically, anonymously, using random sampling of the population—this information will have the same accuracy and objectivity as financial accounting. We should be able to see at a glance the progress we are making with our suppliers, customers, and so forth. I suggest that within five years, any business that does not do this human resource accounting systematically and scientifically and then do problem-solving around this data will not survive its competition.

I also suggest that every organization develop synergistic relationships with customers and suppliers. There is a place for competition, but it's not in areas where you need to cooperate. If you're in an area that requires interdependent teamwork, do everything you can to get rid of competition and to get synergy; reward people for cooperating, for teamwork, for giving their best ideas. Diversity in ideas, not just gender and race, is very powerful, especially when people respect and value the differences in perceptions, feelings, opinions, and backgrounds.

Few people practice synergy because they haven't had models of synergy in their lives. They think synergy means some form of passive cooperation or compromise. They haven't had a personal experience with a synergistic person; they've never been in a synergistic environment, where everyone is transformed. They've never had synergistic relationships and partnerships with suppliers and customers. So in spite of their good intentions and efforts, they've never achieved total quality.

A Total Philosophy

Total quality is a total philosophy, a total paradigm of continuous improvement in all four dimensions. And it is sequential; if you don't have it personally, you won't get it organizationally. You can't expect organizations to improve when the people don't improve. You might improve systems, but how do you get a commitment inside the culture to improve systems? People have to grow and mature to where they can communicate to solve the problems to improve those systems.

Total quality is a principle-centered approach that has come out of the best the world has produced. In our training we emphasize the human side more than the technical side because we believe that the origin and the essence of total quality is empathy with customers, empathy with their motives and buying habits.

Everything is guided by feedback from customers—both internal and external—and from other stakeholders. The key to total quality is to listen to your stakeholders, to seek first to understand and then to be understood.

Why isn't the principle of continuous improvement more fully implemented by individuals and organizations?

• First, we are not yet hurting enough. We had a one-shot economic Pearl Harbor (Black Monday) that shook us up, but generally we are like the frog that stays in hot water heated one degree at a time. In a decade, if present trends continue, we won't govern our economic future—we will be owned. As we experience continuous degradation or deterioration, we can expect to be sold to a higher society. The Japanese are about twice as productive as we are, and in basic research areas they are even farther ahead because of their total quality approach.

• Second, we don't want to change our life-styles. We may know that total quality ultimately involves a change in life-style, but we want quality to be a program or some control at the end of the production line instead of having quality *in* the people on the production line. We don't want to face some hard questions: How are we going to train those people? How are we going to recruit those people? How are we going to get the culture?

• Third, even the best U.S. companies tend to regard quality as a program, a department. It's not integrated in their structure, systems, style, and so forth.

Total quality is rooted in timeless principles:

• faith, hope, humility
• works, industry, research, testing
• constancy, consistency, predictability
• continuous improvement and progression
• feedback based on both measurement and discernment
• virtue and truth in human relations

Without the roots, we don't get the fruits. Without the governing principles of total quality, the methods and techniques alone rarely produce quality products, services, or relationships.

Quality will give any individual or organization a long-term competitive advantage. And if it's in the character of the individual and in the culture of the organization, it can't be duplicated by anyone.

Chapter 26

TOTAL QUALITY LEADERSHIP

THE MOVEMENT toward Total Quality as the operating model for businesses large and small, manufacturing and service industries alike, is increasing at an exponential rate because quality is widely seen as the key to American economic survival and success.

Under whatever variation adopted, the principles and processes of Total Quality represent far more than a passing fad or trendy quick-fix solution to what ails us. Total Quality represents the century's most profound, comprehensive alteration in management theory and practice. Yet most domestic firms are failing, at least not fully succeeding, in their quality improvement efforts. Growing frustration and cynicism in executive, supervisory, and blue-collar worker levels mark the milestones thus far along America's path to Total Quality.

What is the problem? For many, the problem is no foundation. And what is the solution? Over the years our clients have found that Principle-Centered Leadership (PCL) provides the foundation for the successful implementation of Total Quality. They sometimes refer to PCL as "the missing ingredient," or the "leadership and people component," or the "glue that holds Total Quality together," or the "infrastructure on which we build Total Quality," or even the "catalyst that makes the rest of Total Quality work."

262   PRINCIPLE-CENTERED LEADERSHIP

Why has Principle-Centered Leadership and the Seven Habits enabled organizations to achieve previously unrealized successful Total Quality? There's no magic process about it, just the discovery of what W. Edwards Deming has said all along is required to achieve Total Quality: the implementation of essential principles and practices. Any organization can do it.

TOTAL QUALITY: A LEADERSHIP AND PEOPLE PARADIGM

Ironically, the primary elements of Total Quality, as espoused by Deming himself—leadership and people—have somehow been lost in the forest of quality. Corporate executives have focused on the leaves of quality, statistical process control, while ignoring its roots, leadership and people.

How many companies follow a Total Quality program assembled from some combination of the following components?

Automation	New machinery
Hard work	Best efforts
Making people accountable	Management by objectives
Merit systems	Incentive pay
Work standards	Just-in-time inventory
Zero defects	Meeting specifications
Quality control circles	Statistical processes

"Wrong!" says Deming. "All wrong!" None of the above represents Total Quality! But if zero defects, quality control circles, MBO, SPC, inventory are not Total Quality, what is?

Although certain of these elements may contribute to Total Quality (and others undermine it), they by no means assure it. Herein lies the essential understanding of what Total Quality is and how to achieve it through Principle-Centered Leadership. Deming realizes that Total Quality resides effectively in the eye of the beholder—it is what the agent of quality believes it to be. Thus for the line worker quality may be pride of workmanship; for the owner, increasing earnings; for the consumer, reasonably priced, comfortable shoes that look good and wear well over time.

Ultimately, however, the result of quality is what the consumer determines it to be. No other stakeholder of a business enterprise—owners, managers, workers, suppliers—can long survive while ignoring the demands of the judge of quality, the customer. Thus all quality initiatives must be customer-focused. Quality is what consumers judge it to be by voting their purchasing dollars—or yen.

But how to achieve quality in the judgment of consumers? Dr. Deming contends that quality, the result, is a function of quality, the process. And Principle-Centered Leadership provides the principles and application tools necessary to activate the two ingredients most essential to this quality process: leadership and people.

TRANSFORMATION OF MANAGEMENT

Because Total Quality is primarily a paradigm (a way of looking at the world) concerning leadership and people, Principle-Centered Leadership is integral to its success. Overlooked so often in Deming's work is his central premise: The single most important requirement to halt the decline of Western industry and for America to regain worldwide industrial competitive advantage is "to fundamentally transform the Western style of management." And what is the primary transformation that must take place? "The job of management is not supervision, but leadership," says Deming. "The required transformation of Western style of management requires that managers be leaders."

In his book *Out of the Crisis*, he comments, "Most of this book is involved with leadership. Nearly every page states a principle of good leadership or shows an example of good or bad leadership." All of his "14 Points" pertain to leadership in one form or another, and their very purpose is to provide the "basis for transformation of American industry," as well as the criteria to evaluate its success.

The purpose of Total Quality is to bring to the consumer market desirable and continually improving goods and services at ever increasing value, as judged by purchasers, thus providing jobs and benefits to other stakeholders of the enterprise. The purpose of Principle-Centered Leadership is to empower people and organizations to achieve their worthwhile objectives, in essence to become more effective at whatever they do. Thus it incorporates a broader, more encompassing context than Total Quality. When applied to Total Quality theory and methodology, Principle-Centered Leadership enables organizations to achieve their Total Quality objectives. When integrated with Total Quality throughout an organization,

Principle-Centered Leadership becomes fundamental to its success.

Yet Principle-Centered Leadership also applies to individuals and family units—to any human relationship—enabling them to achieve worthwhile purposes of greater love, peace, harmony, cooperation, understanding, commitment, and creativity and to become more effective in all interpersonal and managerial relationships—not unlike certain Total Quality objectives.

Total Quality Leadership

What is the fundamental transformation that Deming believes is required to halt the decline of Western industry? Management must change fundamentally, and transform its attitudes, mind-set, basic paradigms, before total quality can become a reality. He's talking about the way in which American management views itself, its role, its relationship to employees and to all other stakeholders, especially customers and suppliers.

Our current North American management and leadership paradigm is that people are things, "commodities." Give them a fair day's wage and they will return a fair day's labor. Human relations and human resource philosophies have added little of substance to this theory: if we also treat people kindly and ask their opinion once in a while, they will respond more completely with heart and mind as well as back, thus improving their labor's output.

American management has given lip service to tapping the potential of its most important resource—its people. "The greatest waste in America is failure to use the abilities of people," laments Deming. The first fundamental transformation of thinking required of American management is to develop new basic attitudes toward the intrinsic dignity and value of people, of their "intrinsic motivation" to perform to their maximum capabilities.

Management must empower its people in the deepest sense and remove the barriers and obstacles it has created that crush and defeat the inherent commitment, creativity, and quality service that people are otherwise prepared to offer. To receive joy and pride in one's work is the right of all. And it is management practices that prevent it! To achieve total quality managers must become leaders, drawing from their people their greatest capacity to contribute ideas, creativity, innovative thinking, attention to detail and analysis of process and product to the work place. In other words, management must become empowering leaders.

Foundation for Transformation

While Deming's body of Total Quality theory explains the "what" to do and gives a partial explanation of "why" it should be done, there is little practical development of "how" it can be done. Principle-Centered Leadership supplies the missing "how to do it" component of Total Quality: How do you transform the paradigms of people and organizations from reactive, control-oriented management to proactive, empowerment-oriented leadership?

Deming's "14 Points" are more than a mere checklist of things to do to achieve Total Quality. These points are integrated, interdependent, and holistic. They must be viewed and applied as an interrelated system of paradigms, processes, and procedures—a complete framework of management and leadership harnessed to achieve maximum effectiveness and quality of product and service from the people constituting the enterprise.

The Seven Habits, key elements of Principle-Centered Leadership, reflect timeless, fundamental principles of effective human interaction. They are not easy, quick-fix solutions to personal and interpersonal problems. Rather they are foundational principles that, when applied consistently in countless specific practices, become behaviors enabling fundamental transformations of individuals, relationships, and organizations.

As with Deming's 14 Points, the Seven Habits are integrated, interdependent, holistic, and sequential. They build, one upon the other, providing a practical, cohesive basis for successful interpersonal relationships and for organizational effectiveness.

Principle-Centered Leadership incorporates the Seven Habits and related foundational principles. Because Principle-Centered Leadership focuses on basic, fundamental principles and applicable processes, genuine, deep transformation of thinking and character can transpire. Profound, sustainable cultural change can take place within an organization (such as commitment to Total Quality) only when the individuals within the organization first change themselves from the inside out. Not only must personal change precede organizational change, but personal quality must precede organizational quality.

For instance, when skill training focuses on methodology and technique alone, the underlying assumptions and paradigms of individuals rarely change. Thus classes in communication skills to foster team building may have little sustainable benefit when supervisors retain the attitude that their subordinates must be constantly checked and controlled or they will produce inferior work product, or that too much employee empowerment or initiative could threaten the supervisor's job.

Suppose, however, that supervisors develop a new paradigm that employees are capable and desire to make a quality contribution, and that empowerment enhances the supervisor's overall effectiveness. Using principle-centered empowerment methods, supervisors can assist employees to achieve their potential. With these underlying paradigms exercised within aligned systems and structures supporting high-trust levels, teaching the skills of productive communication can be effective over the long term.

Internalizing the Seven Habits and related principles results in the transformation of people and organizations. It is just this transformation that is the key—for many, the missing key—to successful Total Quality.

This article was developed with Keith A. Gulledge of the Covey Leadership Center.

Chapter 27

SEVEN HABITS AND DEMING'S 14 POINTS

A CARDINAL PRINCIPLE of Total Quality escapes many managers: You cannot continuously improve interdependent systems and processes until you progressively perfect interdependent, interpersonal relationships.

Living the principles and processes associated with the Seven Habits enables people to work more effectively together in a state of interdependence—the condition required for maximum communication, cooperation, synergy, creativity, process improvement, innovation, and Total Quality. Interpersonal effectiveness is fundamental to Total Quality tenets such as breaking down barriers between departments, developing partnerships with suppliers, committing everyone to the quality transformation, instituting leadership, achieving continuous improvement and innovation, anticipating customer needs, and so forth.

W. Edwards Deming says that raw data is meaningless without theory to explain and interpret it for necessary prediction. The purpose of statistical analysis is to assist management to develop such theory, to understand, predict, and ultimately control the prime enemy of quality: variation.

Management's key objective is to stabilize all systems and accurately predict process results. Once stable and predictable, processes can be controlled and improved and variation reduced. Statistical analysis is the basic tool to understand, predict, and thus reduce variation in systems and their components. Of all the component resources that make up any business system or process, which is the most important, and also the most variable, unstable, and unpredictable? Of course—it's the people!

People are unique: no two are the same. They are subject to cultural conditioning or scripting; they are emotional beings; their behavior or job performance is frequently a function of their moods, the behavior of others, and the conditions in their environment. Job performance differs from person to person and from day to day, subject to these powerful influences.

And people design, develop, and control all other elements of any system. Deming says that 90-plus percent of all problems in variation or defects are the result of the system rather than the individual. The more people are unstable or subject to variable, unpredictable performance, the more unstable and subject to variation become the systems they design and implement. Anything management could do to stabilize the performance of people, empower them to become more consistent, more predictable, would have a dual benefit. The quality of products would become more consistent, but the systems and processes would also become more stable and predictable. We must understand people, he says, their interaction with each other, and the systems in which they work and learn—their motivations, intrinsic and extrinsic.

An important benefit of Principle-Centered Leadership as applied to Total Quality is that it empowers people to become more intrinsically motivated, more consistent in their personal performance, and thus more readily subject to constant improvement; and it helps to design, implement, and supervise more stable processes and systems in harmony with the Total Quality objectives and strategic path of the organizations. Through applying deep proactivity and living the Seven Habits and related processes, the behavior of people and their interaction with others become a function not of their emotional whims or the conduct of others, but of their commitment to stable, unchanging principles.

SEVEN HABITS TO IMPLEMENT DEMING'S 14 POINTS

Let's analyze each of the Seven Habits briefly as they apply to Deming's 14 Points and other related Total Quality principles. Deming's Points are referenced in parentheses.

Habit 1: Be Proactive—the Principle of Self-Awareness, Personal Vision, and Responsibility

Proactivity is more than being aggressive or assertive. It is both taking initiative and responding to outside stimuli based on one's principles (rather than on one's moods and emotions or the behavior of others). Proactivity rejects the view that people and organizations are controlled by genetic, historical, or environmental forces. Proactive people and organizations are self-aware; accept responsibility for their own actions; don't blame and accuse others when things go wrong; work continuously within their circle of influence; and change and develop themselves first in order to have greater influence with others. They envision their capacity to reject past behavioral scripting and to determine their own destiny, to become exactly what they want to be. They accept the challenge to assist others to do likewise.

Deming recognizes this problem of current management: "Most management today is reactive behavior. You put your hand on a hot stove and yank it off. A cat would do as much." Proactivity forms the basis for successfully incorporating virtually all of Deming's 14 Points, for it is the habit of making decisions and taking action based upon principles and values. Commitment to constancy of purpose (1), adopting the new philosophy throughout the organization (2), decisions to alter inspection procedures (3) and to develop new supplier relationships (4), continuous improvement (5), and all the other points require proactive leadership—and proactive followership.

Imagine the opportunities and consequences in working to break down barriers between departments (9), drive out fear (8), and put everyone to work to accomplish the transformation (14) if all employees, management, and labor accepted responsibilities for their own actions; did not blame or accuse others; and acted according to principles of Total Quality and Principle-Centered Leadership. Initiative, creativity, recommendations for improvement, and acting on those recommendations would flow abundantly, among numerous other benefits.

Habit 2: Begin with the End in Mind—the Principle of Leadership and Mission

Leadership focuses more on people than on things; on the long term rather than the short term; on developing relationships rather than on equipment; on values and principles rather than on activities; on mission, purpose, and direction rather than on methods, techniques, and speed. Developing a personal and organizational mission statement—through special processes to achieve maximum effectiveness—is a key implementation tool for applying this principle.

Deming recently restated his Point 1—"Create constancy of purpose toward improvement of product and service"— to read, "Create and publish to all employees a statement of purpose of the aims and purposes of the company. The management must demonstrate constantly their commitment to this statement."

By assisting hundreds of organizations and thousands of individuals to create mission statements, we have realized their tremendous power to foster commitment, motivation, and clarity of vision and purpose—but only if certain principles and processes are properly observed in their development and deployment. Otherwise the mission statement can deteriorate to nothing more than a cynical object of ridicule—the antithesis of a powerful corporate constitution forming the basis for strategic direction and daily action. Many individuals have found that discovering their personal mission has had a profound effect on their lives. It is not the document alone but rather the process of developing it that becomes so powerful.

Adopting the new philosophy (2), adopting and instituting leadership (7), driving out fear (8), eliminating slogans and exhortations (10), eliminating goals and quotas (11), and putting everyone to work to accomplish the transformation (14) all require the principles of leadership and commitment to a common mission. When organizations and their employees engage in the process of clearly identifying and communicating to each other their respective principles, values, needs, mission, and vision, to the extent of overlap between the company and its employees in these areas, the opportunity for commitment, creativity, innovation, empowerment, and quality becomes activated.

Habit 3: Put First Things First—the Principle of Managing Time and Priorities Around Roles and Goals

Once individuals and organizations make the proactive commitment to act in accordance with their values and principles (Habit 1), then identify and articulate what those values and principles are (Habit 2), in applying Habit 3 they begin to implement or live those values and principles. Most people and organizations approach time management within the context of prioritizing their schedules. It is much more effective to schedule one's priorities that have been identified in conjunction with key roles and goals and determined through assessment of personal and organizational missions. Habit 3 applies the principle of implementing one's action plans to achieve worthy purposes.

As people learn to determine and schedule their priorities, putting first things first, they become more effective in both personal and business pursuits. The organization develops greater capacity for total quality in process, product and service as high-leverage, high-priority activities receive more attention and more timely, significant effort.

Creating constancy of purpose (1), Deming says, wrestles with the problems of today and tomorrow—short-term versus long-term priorities. He says, "It's too easy to stay bound up in the tangled knot of the problems of today." Adopting the new philosophy (2) and putting everyone to work to accomplish the transformation (14) require changes, action planning that Habit 3 assists to implement. To constantly improve systems of production and service (5) again requires management principles and action planning dependent upon putting first things first. It is the application of this habit that enables the principles of Deming's Statistical Process Control and variation analysis to become effectively connected with the other principles of Total Quality and Principle-Centered Leadership.

Habit 4: THINK WIN-WIN—the Principle of Seeking Mutual Benefit

This principle underlies many of Deming's 14 Points and much of his overall Total Quality theory. He discusses in his "Forces of Destruction" the past scripting of Win-Lose experiences received in school, sports, family, politics, business, and education as competition rather than cooperation reigns throughout our society.

In any interdependent relationship, thinking win-win is essential to long-term effectiveness. It requires an abundance mentality, an attitude that says, "There is enough for all." It cultivates the genuine desire to see the other party win as well, the orientation that any relationship should seek mutual benefit for all concerned. Deming believes that our society's competitive, win-lose paradigm is largely responsible for the problems in American management. He advocates Win-Win relations among all business stakeholders—even among competitors.

The implementation of these principles is usually achieved through a Win-Win Performance Agreement among individuals or organizations. Any combination of stakeholders in an enterprise could enter into a Win-Win Performance Agreement developed through communication and trust.

Building quality to eliminate inspections (3), moving toward a single supplier (4), constant improvement of systems (5), instituting training on the job (6), driving out fear (8), breaking down barriers between departments (9), eliminating goals, quotas, and MBO (11), and removing barriers that rob employees of pride of workmanship (12) all require the principles, processes, and application tools of Habit 4, "Think Win-Win." Win-Win Performance Agreements among various stakeholders, such as suppliers, supervisors, and department heads, serve as tangible and powerful implementation vehicles for Deming's principles to become effective.

Habit 5: Seek First to Understand Before Being Understood—the Principle of Empathic Communication

Perhaps the most powerful principle of all human interaction: genuinely seeking to understand another deeply before being understood in return. At the root of all interpersonal problems is failure to thoroughly understand each other. The actual disagreements of substance are magnified and compounded by our inability to see the world not only through another's eyes, but also through his or her mind and heart. We misunderstand and therefore mistrust motives, points of view—we are so ego-invested in advancing our own ideas, defending our position, attacking contrary opinion, judging, evaluating, probing, and questioning—that we normally listen with the intent not to understand but to respond.

Through empathic communication we gain not only clear understanding of another's needs, ideas, and basic paradigms, but also assurance that we are accurately understood as well. True empathic communication shares faithfully not only words, ideas, and information, but also feelings, emotions, and sensitivities. We are raised and scripted to believe that investing the time and emotional energy to understand another deeply—withholding judgment, not defending or attacking—denotes agreement and support. This is not so; but such habits are difficult to break. The new paradigm of seeking first to understand is essential to maximizing total quality.

Habit 5 implements an integrated process known as the Stakeholder Information System (SIS). Through the SIS, management gathers and interprets data beyond that available to traditional financial reporting systems. The "unknown and unknowable" figures that Deming says are the most important to understand in running a business can become more tangible and manageable through SIS.

Every one of Deming's 14 Points rests upon the ability to clearly understand and accurately interpret the interaction of people with each other and with the systems in which they work and grow. Effective communication among people, management, and labor, between the company and its suppliers, and between the customers and the organization is essential to Total Quality.

How can the enterprise achieve constancy of purpose toward improvement of product and service (1) if clear communications among all levels of employees are not constant and consistent? How can the business innovate products and services (1) unless it seeks first to understand the marketplace? How do we motivate employees to adopt the new philosophy (2), or put everybody to work to accomplish the transformation (14), if through unclear communications they do not understand the new philosophy or mistrust the desired transformation?

How do we remove barriers to pride of workmanship (12), or successfully eliminate goals and quotas, including MBO (11), or eliminate slogans and exhortations (10—requires clear communication, Deming says), much less break down barriers between departments built over many years (9)? Only through sincere, genuine, and accurate two-way empathic dialogue may the parties involved thoroughly understand exactly what is happening and why, how they are benefited, and what their responsibilities and opportunities are because of it. Adopting and instituting leadership (7), achieving continuous improvement (5), implementing training (6, 13)—all require maximum clear understanding and communications effectiveness at every level.

Leadership and people—the dual cornerstones, the basic paradigm, of Total Quality—require empathic communication at all levels. Yet communication skills alone are not enough! Thus the necessity of Habit 5 is empathic communication. Not until management becomes principle-centered through proactivity, acting according to values instead of external stimulus (Habit 1); not until common mission and purpose are identified and mutual commitments are made interpersonally and with the organization (Habit 2); not until management begins not only to walk its talk, but to live its values, becoming sufficiently trustworthy to merit the trust of employees (Habit 3); not until the spirit of mutual benefit, thinking win-win, is consistently implemented (Habit 4)—not until these conditions have been developed will communications among people and within and among organizations achieve maximum effectiveness and the Total Quality objectives flowing therefrom be achieved.

Habit 6: Synergize—the Principle of Creative Cooperation

The sum is greater than the whole of its parts—attained through synergy, fostered and nurtured through empowering management styles and supportive structures and systems (all developed through applications of Principle-Centered Leadership). In an environment of trust and open communication, people working interdependently are able to generate creativity, improvement, and innovation beyond the total of their individual but separate capacities.

As employees and managers live the spirit of win-win, practice empathic communication, exhibit trustworthiness, and build trusting relationships, synergy becomes the fruit of such efforts—and with synergy comes the crowning achievement of Total Quality: continuous improvement and constant innovation.

Every issue addressed in each of Deming's 14 Points—as well as overcoming the Deadly Diseases, surmounting the Obstacles, and withstanding the Forces of Destruction—is resolved more readily and satisfactorily through interdependent synergy than by independent action. Through synergistic problem-solving, the thorny issues of today and tomorrow are addressed with constancy of purpose (1). Synergy enables new market analysis and design and production processes to replace mass inspection to achieve quality (3). Partnering with suppliers to establish new relationships, including creating Win-Win Performance Agreements, requires effective synergy (4).

How does the enterprise improve forever the system of production and service (5), except through creative, synergistic leadership? Removing the inhibitors to good work and developing the most appropriate training programs possible to maximize using the abilities of people is the result of effective synergy (6). To drive out fear (8), trust must be developed—and trust grows through synergistic interaction among people. When performance interviews become synergistic coaching, mentoring, and problem-solving experiences, rather than judgmental, finger-pointing inquisitions, trust and confidence replace fear and doubt, opening further opportunities for greater creativity and more synergy (8, 12). If departmental turfism and barriers are to be replaced by cross-functional cooperation and communication, synergy must become the catalyst to generate the necessary coordination and effectiveness (9).

Habit 7: Sharpen the Saw—the Principle of Continuous Improvement

People and organizations have four major needs or characteristics: 1. physical or economic; 2. intellectual or psychological; 3. social or emotional; and 4. spiritual or holistic. Developing within human beings and organizations consistent commitment and continued performance in refining and expanding their abilities in these four areas is the key to overall continuous improvement in all other areas. Principle-Centered Leadership focuses on how individuals and organizations are able to develop their abilities and meet their needs in these arenas. Ever learning, growing, developing new capacities and expanding old are the vehicles through which continued success in applying related principles and using needed tools is made possible. Applying Habit 7 is the principle that enables maximum effectiveness in living all the other habits.

Habit 7 applied at the organizational level results in what Peter Senge of MIT calls "the learning organization." *Kaizen* is the umbrella of continuous improvement under which Total Quality of organizational systems, processes, and finally product and service is implemented. Through practicing this process and principle of Habit 7, the organization itself is improved and increases capacity in all areas to further increase its capacity.

Deming's Point 5—"Improve constantly and forever the system of production and service"—is the obvious direct application of Sharpening the Saw. Utilizing Habit 7 incorporates all the elements of how to implement this improvement process. Greater consistency in employee output is not only achieved through instituting training (6) and the application of Habit 7, but all the elements of Principle-Centered Leadership result in stability and consistency in the performance of people. Deming's requirement to institute a vigorous program of education and self-improvement (13) is activated by applications of processes and principles learned through Principle-Centered Leadership's Habit 7, Sharpen the Saw.

The practical effective benefits of living Principle-Centered Leadership while cultivating Total Quality are demonstrable and substantial. Principle-Centered Leadership makes Total Quality work. To elicit from every employee his or her deepest commitment, continued loyalty, finest creativity, consistent excellent productivity, and maximum potential contribution toward achieving the mission of the organization—toward continuous improvement of process, product, and service—is the challenge of leadership. This is the requirement of Total Quality and the result of Principle-Centered Leadership.

This article was developed with Keith A. Gulledge of the Covey Leadership Center.

SUMMARY OF DEMING'S 14 POINTS

1. • Create *constancy of purpose* toward improvement of product and service, with the aim to be competitive, to stay in business, and to provide jobs.
   • Create and publish to all employees a *statement of purpose* of the aims and purposes of the company or other organization. The management must demonstrate constantly their commitment to this statement.
2. • *Adopt the new philosophy*—top management and everybody. Western management must awaken to the challenge of a new economic age, learn their responsibilities, and take on leadership for change.
3. • *Cease dependence on inspection* to achieve quality. Eliminate

the need for mass inspection by building quality into the product initially.
- Understand the *purpose of inspection*, for improvement of processes and cost reduction.
4. • End the practice of awarding business on the basis of price tag alone. Instead, minimize total cost. *Move toward a single supplier* for any one item, based on a long-term relationship of loyalty and trust.
5. • *Improve constantly and forever the system of production and service,* to improve quality and productivity, and thus constantly decrease costs.
6. • *Institute job training,* to develop skills in new hires, to assist management to understand all processes of the organization.
7. • *Teach and institute leadership.* Supervision of management and production workers should help people and machines, working together, to do a better job.
8. • *Drive out fear* to increase everyone's effectiveness. Create trust. Create a climate for innovation.
9. • *Break down barriers* between departments.
    • *Optimize* toward the aims and purposes of the company the efforts of teams, groups, staff areas.
10. • *Eliminate slogans,* exhortations, and production targets for the work force.
11. • *Eliminate numerical goals and quotas* for production. Instead, learn and institute methods for improvement.
    • *Eliminate management by objective.* Instead, learn the capabilities of processes and how to improve them.
12. • *Remove barriers* that rob hourly workers, as well as management, of their *right to pride of workmanship. Eliminate the annual rating or merit system.*
13. • Institute a vigorous program of *education and self-improvement* for everyone.
14. • *Institute an action plan, and put everybody in the company to work to accomplish the transformation.*

Chapter 28

TRANSFORMING A
SWAMP INTO AN OASIS

IMAGINE IN YOUR MIND'S EYE a swamp—very murky, dark, dank, and unstable, full of mud, water, weeds, even quicksand. You see insects skidding about on the surface of the swamp. You also see crocodiles, alligators, bugs, spiders, snakes, and other animals suited to that environment. The water is stagnant; no fresh water is coming in or going out. You can see the fungus growth and moss, and the stench is very offensive. The water is putrid, stale, filled with disease and decaying vegetation.

Now, imagine the gradual transformation of that murky swamp into a magnificent oasis. See the swamp being drained of the old water. The swamp begins to dry up; fresh water is introduced with inlets and outlets, so that the water is gradually purified. The ground becomes more stable; the stench is gone; vegetation begins to grow again; lovely blossoms and flowers create an entirely new fragrance, the aroma of which is soothing and satisfying. You see beautiful vegetation, trees, lagoons.

Finally the swamp becomes a true oasis—one that has shade under beautiful trees from the sun and pooling areas and clear, pure water.

You could even drink the water, it is so clean. The oasis is now an attractive place to rest and to work and to relate with others. If you were to describe it in quality terms, you would say that it was beautiful, lovely, excellent, attractive, enchanting, resplendent, magnificent, peaceful.

Transforming Your Situations

How might you transform a swamp—a bad situation or condition you face—into a lovely oasis? What do you do to transform a swamp into an oasis? It is the result of several smaller transformations.

First, your organization should be a farm, not a school. It should be centered on natural laws and enduring principles because those laws are going to operate regardless.

You can't transform a politicized swamp into a total quality culture unless and until you build basic habits of personal character and interpersonal relations based on principles; otherwise you will not have the foundation to make quality and other reform initiatives work.

Imagine: if you could transform a swamplike culture based on adversariness, legalism, protectionism, and politics into a kind of oasis culture based upon natural laws or principles, your payoffs would be enormous. You would save big bucks by increasing span of control and tapping the energies and talents of people. But how?

Basically you have to build a sense of internal security so that the organization can be flexible in adapting to the realities of the marketplace. The less internal security people have, the less they can adapt to external reality. They have to have some sense of security, some sense that the ground will not shift on them, some predictability. They may try to get it out of the structure and systems, but that only creates bureaucracy. It tends to fossilize organizations and make them incapable of quick adaptation to shifts in the marketplace.

People won't willingly change with commitment, with desire, unless their security lies inside themselves. If their security lies outside themselves, they view change as threat. We must have a sense of permanency and security. We can't live on unstable ground all the time. It's like living through an earthquake every day. So we create something that is stable, predictable, often by forming structures and systems, rules and regulations. But rules and regulations only stifle the organization from adapting by closing off the stream of fresh water (new ideas). Swamplike conditions begin to develop. The water stays shallow and stagnant; it stinks (and people know it), but if the competition is in the same condition, we survive. When new competition comes under the scene—competition having a culture of high trust, teamwork, hard work, and a commitment to quality and innovation—we may study their methods and try to imprint them into our culture, but if the foundation isn't there, we're still stuck in the swamp.

What happens when people get into a political environment and come to feel that the compensation is unfair? They cry for redress of the perceived wrong. They may form a union, seek social legislation, or offer collective resistance. These measures tap the social need to belong and be accepted and the psychological need to use creative energies and talents and to have a cause, a purpose. But often the organization becomes a place where politics run the show and where people are constantly reading the tea leaves.

This kind of culture breeds dependency, and you can't empower people who are dependent. That's why most empowerment initiatives don't work. People may act as if they are independent and empowered, but they are often loose cannons—and when they go off in the wrong directions, executives pull back that power and get into the control mode, using coercive or utility power—"If you'll do this, we'll do this." But old successful methods don't work with new challenges. Today, nothing fails like past success.

If you are principle-centered, you will tend to have principle-centered relationships, even with people who have a political paradigm. It's hard to be around a principle-centered person for very long and not feel the power of that kind of integrity. Politically oriented people will either shape up or ship out. They can't stand that much integrity, particularly if the principle-centered person just models it quietly. And as the politicians either shape up or ship out, you see a transformation take place inside that culture, from swamp to oasis.

Principle-centered leaders create a common vision and a set of principles and work on decreasing the restraining forces. Managers focus primarily on increasing the driving forces. If you increase the driving forces—the muscle of an organization (its financial and human capabilities), temporarily you can make some improvement. But these improvements create tensions—and the tensions break out in new problems, requiring new driving forces. Performance tends to slip back, and it can even go all the way back and lower, particularly as the organization becomes fatigued and cynical. Management by drives will lead to management by crises. Because so many balls are in the air, so many urgent problems to be addressed, it consumes all the energies of people just to meet day-to-day demands and the urgencies. "Hope springs eternal," however, and there is always new hope born with new initiatives.

The oasis of "total quality" represents the desired state. Quality initiatives are based on the principle of continuous improvement, not only of products and processes, but also of continual innovation, which is the anticipation of customer wants and needs before the customer has asked. It's going beyond satisfaction. It builds deep loyalty.

The ideas of W. Edwards Deming found fertile soil in Japan after World War II. He showed the Japanese how to transform their culture. Japan was devastated and left with few resources, except people. And they rapidly learned under those humbling circumstances that the only way they could survive and prosper was to get people to work hard and work together. In their schools and in their corporations they make an enormous investment in the human resource. Interdependency, the upper end of the Seven Habits maturity continuum, became the predominant social norm.

Economic transactions may take place in dependency cultures, but not core transformations—not fundamental shifts in the way the organization is managed. Most organizations won't take this message seriously until they are hurting seriously. Of course, many are hurting: every major industry is hurting. And almost every major company is going through a metamorphosis.

TRANSFORMATIONAL LEADERSHIP

One of the more popular lines of toys for children in past years has been the Transformers. These colorful units are really two toys in one: they change like chameleons from one thing to another—from robot to jet plane, for example—simply by maneuvering certain parts.

In the corporate world, "transformers" are also quite popular. At least in the management magazines one encounters them on nearly every page—and with good reason. "We all have a need to reinvent what we're up to," says John Naisbitt, author of *Megatrends*. "It's a matter of survival."

Certainly the world is undergoing revolutionary changes. Any careful observer will note the metamorphosis that is taking place in virtually every industry and profession. In *The Aquarian Conspiracy*, author Marilyn Ferguson describes it as a great shuddering, an irrevocable shift, a new mind—a turnabout "in consciousness in critical numbers of individuals, a network powerful enough to bring about radical change in our culture."

It is a change so fast, so profound, so complete, that it will almost overwhelm the careful observer. Reportedly, more change will take place in the next few years than has taken place in the past few centuries. Yet some people are oblivious of it. Like fish who discover water last, they fail to perceive the obvious. They do not sense the difference between then and now, today and tomorrow.

In my opinion these revolutionary changes will alter forever the way many companies operate. People and products that are not in touch with these changes will fast become obsolete.

TRANSFORMING WITH THE TRENDS

While some cynics may accept obsolescence as an inevitable consequence of change, proactive executives innovate and increase market share. The trick is first to identify the trends and then to transform with the trends.

For example, *PC* magazine reported that the microcomputer, even more than the mainframe and minicomputer before it, will "transform computing, those who use computers, and even the nature of our society and life in this century."

The "megacomputing trends" suggest that by the end of this century "there will be a computer on almost every desk—and at least as many computers as TV sets in the home. The personal computer will increase personal productivity by 20 percent; executives will begin using the computer more enthusiastically; and voice input will play an important role—transforming every telephone into a full-fledged computer terminal for both input and output."

The effective executive will note the computing trends and make necessary transformations. Many social observers are describing the "megatrends" and giving us a sense of how dynamic and radical these changes are. To simplify matters, I will consider three categories—economic, technological, and social/cultural—and contrast traditional and emerging patterns within these categories.

Traditional	Emerging
Economic	
Industrial-age rules	Information-age rules
Stable seconomy	Uncertain economy
Stable markets/suppliers	Fluid markets/suppliers
Assembly-line production	Personalized delivery of services
Domestic competition	International competition
Brawnpower	Brainpower
Technical	
Mechanical technology	Electronic technology
Predictable technological innovation (10 years)	Rapid, unpredictable technological innovation (18 months)
Social/Cultural	
Acceptance of authoritarian hierarchical roles	Rising expectation of employee involvement
Stable male workers	Women, minorities, baby boomers
Growing birthrates	Declining birthrates
Externally driven/material values	Internally driven/quality-of-life values
Corporate drift from dominant social/economic values	The reaffirmation of dominant social/economic values

The scope and scale of these emerging trends require leaders of organizations to adopt a transformational style.

IMPLICATIONS FOR MANAGERS AND EXECUTIVES

Implied in these changes is the need for a major shift in management thought and practice. Many companies and their managers are not transforming with the trends. For example, our society values democracy, yet most companies practice autocracy; our society values capitalism, but many organizations practice feudalism. While our society has shifted to pluralism, many companies seek homogeneity. Perhaps the most fundamental need is to understand man's full nature. Motivational theory has shifted its organization from stomach (physical and economic) to heart (good human relations, good treatment) to mind (identify, develop, use, recognize talent) to spirit (a sense of transcending purpose or meaning).

An enlarged concept of man's nature triggers another shift in the role of the manager from hero to developer, from commander to consultant, from order giver to mentor, from decision maker to value clarifier and exemplar. The new manager is moving away from confrontational dialogue to empathic dialogue, from retaining power to sharing power, from adversarial relationships (win-lose) to collaborative relationships based on mutual interests (win-win).

We might think of this "paradigm shift" in terms of a continuum, with external control on one side and internal control or commitment on the other side—from superficial human relations to full utilization of human resources.

The new leader is learning to "read" each situation and to adopt accordingly. An excellent model of this new leadership style is Ken Blanchard's "Situational Leadership II." As he describes it, this model suggests that the leader must adapt his style to suit the ability and maturity (competence and commitment) of his people. Such a leader must have good diagnostic skills and a large repertoire of management styles, with the courage and flexibility to use the appropriate one.

PERSONAL PRECEDES ORGANIZATIONAL CHANGE

It's almost axiomatic to say that personal change must precede or at least accompany management and organizational change; otherwise the duplicity and double-mindedness will breed cynicism and instability. Life's imperative is to grow or die, stretch or stagnate.

Attempting to change an organization or a management style without first changing one's own habit patterns is analogous to attempting to improve one's tennis game before developing the muscles that make better strokes possible. Some things necessarily precede other things. We cannot run before we can walk or walk before we can crawl. Neither can we change our management styles without first changing personal habits.

Psychologist William James suggested that to change personal habits, we first make a deep internal commitment to pay whatever price is necessary to change the habit; second, we grasp the very first opportunity to use the new practice or skill; and third, we allow no exceptions until the new habit is firmly imbedded into our nature.

Of course, change—whether it's personal or organizational—carries some degree of risk. Because of that risk and the fear of failure, many people resist change. Those who adapt well to changing environments generally have a set of changeless values within them and are congruent in behavior with those values. This integrity boosts their self-esteem and provides a bedrock of security from which they deal effectively with changing circumstances.

Companies on the "cutting edge" often enjoy a competitive advantage. Not surprisingly, these are often young companies, trendsetters.

While well-established companies like U.S. Steel or General Motors won't transform in the same way, all companies must, as John Naisbitt says, "reinvent" or transform themselves. Those driven by momentum and memory may find themselves going right over a cliff.

Transactional Leadership

Transformational leadership is not the same as transactional leadership. The former basically means that we change the realities of our particular world to more nearly conform to our values and ideals. The latter focuses on an efficient interaction with the changing realities. Transformational leadership focuses on the "top line" and is principle-centered. Transactional leadership focuses on the bottom line and is event-centered. Transformational and transactional leadership may be contrasted in other ways, as the chart on the following page shows.

Transformational Leadership

- Builds on man's need for meaning
- Is preoccupied with purposes and values, morals, and ethics
- Transcends daily affairs
- Is oriented toward meeting long-term goals without compromising human values and principles
- Separates causes and symptoms and works at prevention
- Values profit as the basis of growth
- Is proactive, catalytic, and patient
- Focuses more on missions and strategies for achieving them
- Makes full use of human resources
- Identifies and develops new talent
- Recognizes and rewards significant contributions
- Designs and redesigns jobs to make them meaningful and challenging
- Releases human potential
- Models love
- Leads out in new directions
- Aligns internal structures and systems to reinforce overarching values and goals

Transactional Leadership

- Builds on man's need to get a job done and to make a living
- Is preoccupied with power and position, politics, and perks
- Is mired in daily affairs
- Is short-term and hard-data oriented
- Confuses causes and symptoms and concerns itself more with treatment than prevention
- Focuses on tactical issues
- Relies on human relations to lubricate human interactions
- Follows and fulfills role expectations by striving to work effectively within current systems
- Supports structures and systems that reinforce the bottom line, maximize efficiency, and guarantee short-term profits

Obviously both kinds of leadership are necessary. But transformational leadership must be the parent, as it provides the frame of reference, the strategic boundaries within which transactions take place. Without a clear picture of what kind of transformation is needed, executives and their managers will tend to operate on social and political agendas and timetables.

The goal of transformational leadership is to "transform" people and organizations in a literal sense—to change them in mind and heart; enlarge vision, insight, and understanding; clarify purposes; make behavior congruent with beliefs, principles, or values; and bring about changes that are permanent, self-perpetuating, and momentum building.

I am personally convinced that one person can be a change catalyst, a "transformer," in any situation, any organization. Such an individual is yeast that can leaven an entire loaf. It requires vision, initiative, patience, respect, persistence, courage, and faith to be a transforming leader.

Chapter 29

CORPORATE CONSTITUTIONS

A WRITTEN CORPORATE CONSTITUTION can be a priceless document for both individuals and organizations. As Thomas Jefferson said about the Constitution of the United States: "Our peculiar security is in the possession of a written Constitution."

Mission statements, whether personal or corporate in scope, empower people to take control of their lives and thereby gain more internal security.

In writing a mission statement, you are drafting a blueprint, raising a standard, cementing a constitution. The project deserves broad involvement. In my experience every company that has conscientiously involved their people in formulating a mission statement has produced a fine constitution. The principle is basic to our society: govern (manage) by the consent of the people. People have a sense of what is right and, if involved, will come up with a noble document.

For example, at the Pillsbury Company—a fast-growth, diversified corporation that almost tripled in size during the last decade—executives woke up one day with "the uneasy feeling that our concern with financial goals had come at the expense of helping our people adapt to the dramatic growth of the company. We decided there had to be some statement, a public declaration of what Pillsbury should stand for. It would have to be simple, short, give people permission to dream dreams, take risks, and think creatively and signal a change in our culture from conservative, cumbersome, and bureaucratic to people-oriented, innovative, and supportive of individual initiative."

Pillsbury took one year and involved their top two-hundred managers with participation throughout the company to create a one-page constitution, their mission and values statement.

And what difference has it made? Reports Virginia Ward, vice president of human resources, "We now feel a sense of ownership throughout the company for our mission and values. We are more effective in our management of people because of the principles inherent in our mission and values. There is a spirit of optimism and excitement about the future."

Such is the power of a corporate constitution. We have in America a glorious Constitution. John Adams said that the Constitution of the United States was written for a moral people. Most corporate mission statements also assume there is a basic morality, integrity, and sense of social responsibility in people.

A mission statement focuses your energies and lets you enjoy a sense of orientation, being, purpose. It prevents you from being distracted and sidetracked. It also focuses your personal energies and resources. You don't spend time and money and effort on things that don't return and aren't related to your reason for being.

Use your mission statement to direct and unify your life. You build more internal security by being more self-directed. If you build your own security around the weaknesses of others, you allow their weaknesses to control you. If you build on weaknesses of your competitors, you actually empower them. On the other hand, if you operate from your own statement of mission and values, your life is not so buffeted by external forces. In fact, your focus will begin to shape the events of your life.

The mission statement becomes a framework for thinking, for governing.* Review it periodically and ask, "Are we doing the best we can to live by this? Are we preventing problems? Management by quick fix leads to management by crisis. Crises come one after an-

* For additional examples of personal, organizational, or family mission statements and a worksheet to develop your own, please call 1-800-255-0777. There is no cost to you.

other just like a pounding surf. Troubles come so frequently that life begins to blend into one huge problem. Cynicism and fatigue set in.

For example, we once worked with a business that wanted to create cost-consciousness. So the company put on a drive, and everyone became cost-conscious and forgot new business. Then the new drive was to get new business. Everyone went out to get new business and neglected internal relationships. The next frantic drive was human relations. One drive followed another. Cynicism became pervasive, until people would no longer support a drive. Their energies were diverted into politicking, polarizing, and protecting turf.

This can also happen in families. Too many families are managed on the basis of quick-fix, instant gratification, not on sound principles and rich emotional bank accounts. Then, when stress and pressure mount, people start yelling, overreacting, or being cynical, critical, or silent. Children see it and think this is the way you solve problems—either fight or flight. And the cycle can be passed on for generations. By drafting a family constitution, you are getting to the root of the problem.

If you want to get anywhere long-term, identify core values and goals and get the systems aligned with these values and goals. Work on the foundation. Make it secure. The core of any family is what is changeless, what is always going to be there. This can be represented in a family mission statement. Ask yourself, "What do we value? What is our family all about? What do we stand for? What is our essential mission, our reason for being?"

If you identify your essential purpose and set up shared vision and values, you can be successful with any situation that comes along. The mission excites people. It gets them to deal with problems and to talk them through in a mature and reasonable way. If there is a dream, a mission, a vision, it will permeate that organization and shape its actions.

Principles are timeless, universal laws that empower people. Individuals who think in terms of principles think of many applications and are empowered to solve problems under myriad different conditions and circumstances. On the other hand, people who think in terms of practices tend to be limited in effectiveness to specific conditions under which the practice is effective.

Principles have infinite applications, as varied as circumstances. They tend to be self-validating, self-evident, universal truths. When we start to recognize a correct principle, it becomes so familiar to us, it is almost like "common sense." The danger is that we may cast it off early instead of looking deeply into how the specific principle may be valuable in our current circumstance.

This can be seen easily when we talk about the principles involved in developing personal and corporate "constitutions." Certain underlying principles are applied whether in the life of an individual or in the life of an organization. Processes grow out of principles and give life to principles.

A mission statement helps people achieve success because it answers key questions like "What do I want to do?" and "What do I want to be?" Becoming the kind of person you want to be and doing the things that you desire to do actually define success.

The same is true with an organization. Unless organizations have some identity, some compelling mission, they accomplish far less that they might. To accomplish things based on objectives is not enough. To unleash the productivity in an organization, the focus needs to be not only on what you want to do but on what you want to be. Thus the corporate constitution deals with the questions of why.

For example, our firm has done some work with the Walt Disney Company. Initially, of course, Walt was the catalyst for the whole Disney organization. Since his death over twenty years ago, the Disney Corporation has worked to complete his ambitious dream, the Epcot Center. After completing the center, the production and design team went from 2,200 engineers, artists, and technicians to around 500. Morale was low.

To create new growth, a group prepared a mission statement for the company, but few bought it because they weren't involved. Then they began a months-long process of writing a mission statement, involving all levels of the organization. Today they are motivated by a new mission. The spirit of the new Disney approach is "We seek not to imitate the masters; rather, we seek what they sought." Clearly this was needed to move forward.

A corporate mission statement provides meaning for the enterprise. Meaning is the challenging need of the modern worker. It's not enough to work to eat or stay on the job because you're treated well. Nor is it enough to have an opportunity to contribute your talents and to unleash some of your potential. People want to know why. Meaning is the essential ingredient in modern times to organizational success.

The same thing applies to nations. The Declaration of Independence and the Constitution of our country define what we're about, what we're trying to achieve, and why. The underlying principles of constitutionalism, individualism, and volunteerism are still the cornerstones of our society. Many things that we value are manifest in the Declaration of Independence and the Constitution.

How to Write Your Own Constitution

There are some specific steps individuals and companies must go through in developing a constitution: first, expand perspective; second, clarify values; third, test it against yourself; and fourth, test yourself against it.

• *Expand perspective.* We become so involved, both individually and organizationally, with the day-to-day preparations of life that it's usually necessary to stand back to gain or expand perspective and remind ourselves what really matters.

These "perspective experiences" may be planned or unplanned. Unplanned experiences may include the death of a loved one, a severe illness, a financial setback, or extreme adversity. At such times we stand back and look at our lives and try to ask ourselves some hard questions. What do we consider to be really important? Why are we doing what we're doing? If we didn't have to do what we do to get money, what would we do? Through this self-evaluation process, we tend to expand our perspective.

Proactive people can expand their perspective through such planned experiences as gathering the views of others involved in the organization or situation. They start contemplating, "What is most important to organization? What contribution can we make? What is the meaning of what we do? What are we about? What do we want to be? What do we want to do?" The many views expand perspective. As individuals search for the best within them and the best within the organization, real synergy takes place. Synergy is the process of valuing the differences and creating the best possible solution.

"Management by wandering around," a common practice at Hewlett-Packard, is another good way to expand views on the organization. Often people are reluctant to provide much open information because they do not feel part of the governing body of the organization; they question whether their values or their views are really needed or appreciated; or they feel at risk in sharing those views. One way to overcome this reluctance is to put together some questions and have buzz groups discuss them and submit their findings. Those can be compiled, considered, and responded to. When people see that what they contribute is taken seriously, they tend to want to contribute more.

This process of expanding perspective, of gathering the views of others and trying to get a handle on what is the best, highest, and noblest within the organization, is a process that should not be rushed. It takes time, several months in a large organization.

• *Clarify values.* After perspective has been expanded and many new views contemplated, some individuals need to be charged with the responsibility to write a draft of an organizational mission statement, taking into account what has been gathered, and seen, and shared so far.

This draft then needs to be sent back to the members of the organization with the caption "We don't like it either." It is the exact wording that clarifies and gives tremendous focus to the mission statement. One that is not well defined and refined will not be as valuable and useful in decision making. The best mission statements are the result of people coming together in a spirit of mutual respect, expressing their different views, and working together to create something greater than any one individual could do alone.

• *Test it against yourself.* Take a more final draft of the mission statement or constitution and test it by asking, "Is this in harmony with my values? Does it inspire and motivate me? Does it capture the heart and soul of the company? Does it represent the best within the organization?"

Think of the constitution in terms of two overlapping circles. One circle can represent the value system of the organization, and the other circle can represent the value system of individuals. The more the circles of the individuals and the organization overlap, the more effective the organization tends to become. The mission statement needs to be tested for fit.

• *Test yourself against it.* After the mission statement has been through this process, most people now need a chance to live with it for a while and to test the organization against it. Since these shared values are the heart and soul of the company, all policies, programs, strategies, structure, and systems should be in harmony with them.

Over time, this process of writing and refining a mission statement becomes a key way to improve the organization. You do it periodically to expand perspective, shift emphasis or direction, and amend or give new meaning to timeworn phrases.

By having a constitution, you have continuity. This is one of the major benefits of managing and leading by a mission statement developed by a participative process. It provides long-term continuity and helps executives maintain a long-term competitive advantage because they have direction and purpose. And when individual values are harmonized with those of the organization, people work together for common purposes that are deeply felt. They contribute more as a team than they would individually. Productivity doesn't just get a little better, it gets dramatically better.

AN ONGOING PROCESS

As you change and grow, your perspective and values may undergo metamorphosis. It's important that you keep your mission statement current and congruent with your values. Here are some questions to help you:

- Is my mission statement based on proven principles that I currently believe in?
- Do I feel this represents the best within me?
- Do I feel direction, purpose, challenge, and motivation when I review this statement?
- Am I aware of the strategies and skills that will help me accomplish what I have written?
- What do I need to do now to be where I want to be tomorrow?

Keep in mind that you can never build a life greater than its most noble purpose. Your constitution can help you be your best and perform your best each day.

Chapter 30

UNIVERSAL MISSION STATEMENT

YOU MIGHT WANT TO pattern your personal and professional mission after a twelve-word universal statement. The universal mission statement is an expression of meta (not macro or micro) leadership.

Meta. Meta leadership deals mainly with vision and stewardship—with what is being entrusted to you as a leader and as a manager.

Macro. Macro leadership deals with strategic goals and how you organize structure and systems and set up processes to meet those goals.

Micro. Micro leadership deals with relationships, with building the emotional bank accounts so that you have legitimate authority with people—people then *choose* to follow and align themselves with your vision or mission.

Effective senior executives give most of their time and energies to issues at the meta and macro levels of leadership. They focus on maintaining and enhancing relationships with the people they work with most.

The universal mission statement is intended to serve leaders of organizations as an expression of their vision and sense of stewardship. It attempts to encompass, in one brief sentence, the core values of the organization; it creates a context that gives meaning, direction, and coherence to everything else.

To be functional, mission statements should be short so that people can memorize and internalize them. But they also need to be comprehensive. These appear to be contradictory concepts. How can something be short *and* comprehensive? By being simple, general, generic. We see in the computer world, for example, that the more advanced the technology becomes, the simpler the product becomes. The same thing can happen with a mission statement. And if the mission statement represents your "software," you will begin to see and deal through it.

This doesn't mean that the mission statement will take the place of your organizational goals. But it will direct those goals and provide context and coherence for everything else.

The universal mission statement should deal with all aspects of a person's responsibility, with the long run and short run. It could apply to all organizations, as a common denominator that leaders of organizations could consider as they develop their own mission statements. It reads like this:

> To improve the economic well-being and
> quality of life of all stake-holders.

THREE PARTS

I will now comment on the three key phrases of the statement.

1. *Economic well-being*. Why do we address the economic dimension first? Because organizations are established primarily to serve economic purposes. Employment is the way people derive their livelihoods. It does not take the place of families or churches or fraternal organizations. Jobs are to produce wealth, to produce things that people can use and consume in their daily lives—and, ideally, enough money to pay taxes, tuition, and everything else.

We sometimes lose sight of this simple fact. That's what Abraham Zaleznik, my former professor at Harvard Business School, suggested in his article "Real Work" (*Harvard Business Review*, January–February 1989). Tom Peters and Bob Waterman said the same thing in their book, *In Search of Excellence*: Companies exist to make and sell products. And Ted Levitt, author of *Marketing Management*, said that companies exist to get and keep customers. Simple ideas.

2. *Quality of life.* Individuals and organizations sometimes feel that they cannot deal with quality-of-life issues unless they are relatively affluent. Historically that's been the case; probably 90 percent of all people have not dealt with quality-of-life issues, only with survival issues. Even in the United States today, perhaps only 50 percent of us have and take the time to address quality-of-life concerns. That's one reason we have so many legislative and social movements toward more recreation, continuing education, fitness, wellness, leisure, travel, and tourism. In large measure these quality-of-life industries have developed in America in the last forty-four years, since World War II.

Business executives should be concerned with the overall quality of life of their stakeholders, but their primary responsibility is to enhance the quality of *work life*; there are other institutions—school, family, church—that deal more with private life.

I see five dimensions to quality of life:

• *Acceptance and love.* People have a need to belong and be accepted, to join with others in common enterprises, to engage in win-win relationships, and to give and receive love.

• *Challenge and growth.* People also have a need to experience challenge and opposition, to grow and develop, to be well utilized, to be informed, and to be creative. The vast majority of the work force possess far more capability, intelligence, resourcefulness, and initiative than their present jobs allow or require them to use. Such a waste! Such a low quality of life! Leaders must identify, develop, use, and recognize talent; otherwise people will go elsewhere, physically or mentally, to find their satisfaction and their sense of growth.

• *Purpose and meaning.* People also have a need for purpose and meaning—for making a contribution to that which is meaningful. People can make good money and have all kinds of growth experiences and good relationships, but if their work is not intrinsically satisfying or if the outcome does not contribute constructively to society, they won't be motivated in the highest and deepest sense.

The economic dimension is extrinsic. But you don't work just for money. Money is a means to an end. You also work for intrinsic satisfactions—meaning that the nature of the work, the relationships at work, and the sense of contribution to something meaningful are satisfying in and of themselves.

• *Fairness and opportunity.* The basic principles in the field of human motivation emphasize *fairness* regarding economic rewards and *opportunity* regarding intrinsic rewards. Frederick Herzberg, a University of Utah professor who is an expert in the field of motivation, talks about "dissatisfiers" and "satisfiers," or motivators. A dissatisfier would be a sense of inequity regarding economic rewards. When people become dissatisfied, when their higher-level needs are not met, they fight the organization in one way or another in order to give their lives cohesion and meaning. That's why a person's "economic well-being" and "quality of life" are closely interrelated.

• *Life balance.* Now, if people have fairness, justice, and equity regarding economic rewards, but they lack challenge and meaning in their organizations, what will they do? They'll press for more money, more benefits, and more time off—because with money and time they have opportunity to satisfy their interests and find their intrinsic satisfactions off the job. Therefore the real challenge of leadership is to recognize that these are not only needs of people, they are capacities. And if any of these needs are not fulfilled, the neglected capacity will work *contrary* to their organization.

For instance, if people have a mission statement that focuses only on the economic side and not on the social, psychological, and spiritual sides, the mission may actually encourage them to moonlight or to use their talent and energy to try to get more money and a better deal for themselves so they can have more time and find more fulfillment off the job.

3. *All stakeholders.* This universal mission statement deals with all stakeholders. And who is a stakeholder? The best way to answer that is to ask, "Who will suffer if the enterprise fails?"

Who suffers depends on what the situation is. If the owners have plowed their life savings into the enterprise and are at risk right up to their ears, they'll probably be hurt the most if the enterprise fails. Other people can go and get jobs. But the owners may be wiped out and have to start again. They may have to pay off tremendous debts for a long period of time. If, however, the owners are wealthy and have many diversified assets, they may not be hurt if a particular investment or enterprise fails. But the employees might suffer tremendously, especially if they are specialized professionals stuck in a one-industry town with the wrong training and skills. Also, the suppliers may suffer terribly. And the domino effect could be damaging to many other people in the community.

It takes a lot of judgment, discernment, and sense of stewardship about all stakeholders—all who have a stake in the welfare or success of the enterprise—including customers, suppliers, distributors, dealers, the community, and the public at large. Because if business leaders become exploitative, they help create a cynical climate, get the media on their backs, and hurt many other companies in the same industry. They may even cause special legislation to avoid dirty dealing on the part of "big business."

The leaders of corporations should have a high sense of responsibility about some social problems and get involved and encourage high involvement by members of the organization. For example, John Pepper, president of Procter & Gamble, once asked me to speak to the Cincinnati School Board about some issues that concerned him. Many other organizations want their people involved in volunteer work with social and educational programs because they know that this affects some stakeholders directly and the entire business climate indirectly.

Stakeholders means more than just the shareholders. Most mission statements are geared more to the shareholders—and, more specifically, to the short-term quarterly dividend. One reason is that many organizations are owned by small shareholders who count on that income; losing it could be very dislocating. But the whole "goose and golden egg" phenomenon is in operation here: if we focus on the short term and kill the goose, we won't have more golden eggs—and that hurts not only the shareholders, but all stakeholders.

Consider the story of the entrepreneur who takes his prime employees to a scenic site that overlooks a beautiful valley and tells them, "I appreciate what you've done all these years, and if you continue your devotion and industry, I just want you to know that someday all of this will be mine." That's just about how some mission statements are worded. One large organization basically had as its mission "to enhance the asset base of the owners."

I asked the CEO, "If you put that on the wall, would it inspire the devotion of your employees and the commitment of your customers? Would it communicate that you really care about them?"

There is a kind of conscience in organizations, social as well as private, that defines equity and fairness. Any time you have people putting in a greater investment than they are rewarded for, you will have many negative consequences. Or, if there are more rewards than investment, that too is an injustice in the social ecology—and it will eventually have a negative impact on other things.

That's why meta leadership requires a sense of stewardship about the whole package and a careful balancing of many different interests. Meta leadership is not a transactional approach. The human resource movement defines people as assets, as resources; they are that and more—they are intrinsically valuable in and of themselves, not just as assets. If you don't see that people have intrinsic worth, you get into a utilitarian approach. You are "nice to them" as important assets, but you violate their spiritual nature and their sense of intrinsic worth. Ultimately the human resource approach to leadership is *transactional*—it is not transforming or synergistic.

The principle-centered approach to leadership is *transformational* because it gives people the conviction that they (their respective fates in the company) are a function not of arbitrary personalities but of timeless, correct principles, particularly if principles are embedded in the mission statement and emanate to management style, practices, procedures, policies, strategy structure, systems, and so forth. People then gain confidence that "this place is run by principles" and that everyone, including the top people, are accountable to those principles as well as to each other.

In fact, I would like to see a new organizational chart: in the center of the chart are correct principles and on the perimeter would be the different stewardships. The chairman and everyone else are accountable to those principles.

What I'm suggesting is that the universal mission statement, whether it is written or not, is already operating. It's like a natural law: you cannot violate it—or this sense of total economic community—with impunity.

FIVE MAJOR BENEFITS

I see five basic virtues of this universal mission statement.

- *Ecological balance*. The universal mission statement helps you to think ecologically about all stakeholders. You know that by constantly attending to the transforming principles, all stakeholders will enjoy synergistic benefits.
- *Short- and long-term perspective*. The universal mission state-

ment suggests that if you try to take the short-term approach, you will over the long term compromise or kill the goose that lays the golden eggs.

- *Professional challenge.* The twelve words of the universal mission statement embody enough challenge for leaders throughout their entire professional careers.
- *Management context.* Within the parameters of the universal mission statement, you can better set policies and procedures, strategy, structure, and systems.
- *Personal sense of stewardship.* The universal mission statement generates a sense of stewardship with respect to people and other resources.

Again, I see this as a generic mission statement for leaders, not necessarily for organizations, although leaders might want to build these concepts into their organizational mission statements. They may also want to apply these concepts to their personal and family mission statements. The universal statement doesn't preclude the need for a personal, family, or corporate statement in any way. Every organization should have its own mission statement. But it might well be an extension of the universal mission statement:

> To improve the economic well-being and
> quality of life of all stakeholders.

Chapter 31

PRINCIPLE-CENTERED LEARNING ENVIRONMENTS

THE PRESENT CONDITION OF education might be visually described as a land-mined wilderness. The future direction of education, in general, remains virtually uncharted. Defining and predicting educational success is, at best, inexact and uncertain. Such unpredictability creates land mines of controversy.

Controversy diverts educators from their focused task. They sincerely want to prepare the next generation, but there are many conflicting expectations. It is as though society wants education to handle all of its basic ills, its deeper problems. The educational system is expected to address and compensate for the failures that take place in the home and other institutions such as the church, the government, and so forth.

All these conflicting expectations exist because the level of trust is low. When trust is low, communication processes deteriorate. We see a great deal of adversarial communication, interpersonal conflicts, and interdepartmental rivalries. People develop a siege mentality. Often they turn to a legalistic approach to legislate their wishes. They lobby pressure groups and push for what they want.

One group is always in conflict with another. The net effect is a downward spiral of trust. People start to feel increasingly frustrated. They develop a sense of futility and hopelessness. Many educators care and try their best, but because they are vulnerable and exposed, eventually they burn out.

Educators often develop a kind of survival mentality. They ask themselves, "What can we do just to make it through the day?" They go through the motions. Sometimes they withdraw to their individual classrooms. The only deposits to their emotional bank account come from within the classroom walls. They feel unappreciated and undervalued. Many administrators also feel this way. One of the deepest hungers of the human soul is to be appreciated, to be valued, to be recognized. So little of this is taking place. Consequently this negative cycle feeds upon itself, intensifies, and develops its own momentum.

LACK OF COMMON VISION BLOCKS CHANGE

Another mentality often present is what we call the scarcity mentality. Since there are so few resources and so many demands, there is a great sense of scarcity. People think, "If I don't get mine, someone else might," or, "If someone else gets some large resource or even recognition in some way, it takes something from me." Consequently they begin to think adversarially, to think win-lose, to be protectionist, and to think defensively. This atmosphere of low trust, defensive communication, and conflicting expectations has become a major problem in our society, with many negative ramifications.

Society uses many approaches in its attempts to address education problems. Multiple programs are devised; however, they often contribute to the confusion and an attitude of compartmentalization. Why? There is no common vision. Without the same set of criteria, frame of reference, and overall vision, people become adversarial, with a great deal of fighting, rivalry, and polarization breaking down the culture.

Without a common vision, various groups push for their own special kind of legislation. The public presses for more accountability. Teachers press for more freedom from restraints placed upon them, and parents press for more measurement, more explicit, definable, quantifiable standards by which to make judgments. This entire process is a massive energy cycle that feeds upon itself and causes demoralization among teachers and administrators. It causes excessive criticism and fosters a spirit of accusation.

What kind of common vision do teachers and educators need? Teachers can learn to assist in the empowerment process of students. Through the facilitator concept, they can better meet the individual needs of students. Once empowered, students become more responsible for their own learning process. Teachers are not limited by their own knowledge, and the paradigm shifts.

This new common vision liberates teachers, allowing their creative energies to be maximized, alleviating the burden of constant pressure to perform. It creates a return to the attitude of learner rather than master. Whenever someone feels like a master of something, learning seems to stop. When learning stops, people begin to protect the status quo and adopt behaviors antithetical to good positive relating. When good relating is limited, the learning environment is affected.

Ultimately it is children who suffer in an emotionally toxic environment. They become the victims of a reality filled with low trust, adversarial relations, high pressures, and conflicting expectations. In fact, not only are they victimized by this environment, they are powerfully modeled by it. They begin to look at it and unconsciously absorb its approaches and methods of problem-solving. People are trained to think win-lose and lose-win. Consequently their response is to give up, fight, or flee.

In fact, the whole image children may have of the teaching profession often discourages them from going into teaching themselves. If throughout society the teaching profession loses its reputation and its tremendous capability to influence, young people will not be empowered to be responsible for their own learning and lives because they will have seen too much blaming, too much criticism, too much transfer of responsibility, and too much abdication of power to the weaknesses of other people or to institutions.

It is important for teachers and leaders in education to begin with the end in mind. Begin with a personal mission statement or a vision statement that deals basically with two things: 1) What is it your life is about? and 2) How are you going to go about it? In other words, purpose and principles. This is a very difficult and sometimes agonizing process. But there is no more powerful intervention to improve a person's life—to strengthen a marriage, a family, or any organization—at any level than the development of a mission statement.

NATURAL LAWS OF CHANGE

Personal integrity develops strength of character. "Walk your talk"—particularly if one of the values that you are trying to secure is to become increasingly competent, to be regularly involved in both personal and professional development. With character and competence, a foundation of trust and trustworthiness is secured, which in turn produces more trust. And if trust is present, you have an empowerment approach as an administrator or as a teacher. You also have a larger circle of influence that can begin to have some impact on the design and structure of the system.

Initially you may live in a hostile environment. You'll have to get your security primarily through your own integrity to your personal value system, rather than from outside reinforcement. This will take great courage; it will also take great empathy and great patience. It is a process, not a quick-fix approach. In spite of all the success literature to the contrary, there is no one easy way of getting what we desire in some simplistic success formula.

The more we can build our own lives around natural laws or principles, and become principle-centered in ourselves, and then live by those principles in our relationships with others, the more our mutual trustworthiness grows and deepens. This kind of trust enables our circle of influence to become, little by little, increasingly large.

You can start to have pockets of excellence, even in seas of mediocrity. You can see this if you go around the country and observe many different school settings. There are proactive people out there—people who are inwardly directed by their own value systems—and they have the internal discipline and the commitment to live by that value system.

THE TRIM-TAB FACTOR

Buckminster Fuller used to talk about the "trim-tab" factor. On the rudder of a huge ship there is another minirudder called the trim-tab.

By moving the trim-tab ever so slightly, the rudder is slowly moved, which eventually changes the whole direction of a huge ship.

In your own personal mission statement, see yourself as a trim-tab factor. See yourself as a change catalyst. By making some changes in your part of the ecosystem and believing that through a process of patience and diligence you begin to have reverberations on other parts of that ecosystem, you will become a person we call a "transition figure": one who stops the transmission of tendencies from one generation to another. For instance, you may see some tendencies in your children that you do not like, but these tendencies are already in you. You may also see some of those same tendencies in your parents or their parents.

Transition figures, those who are trim-tab factors inside a family, can stop the transmission of undesirable tendencies if they will internally develop their proactive, empathic, synergistic, and self-renewal muscles. They can become an enormous source of influence in causing their small inner circle of influence to get larger and larger.

Some might say it will take forever; however, it is amazing how rapidly such transition figures, such change catalysts, such trim-tab factors, start to influence an entire culture. Sometimes change occurs in a matter of a few months, sometimes in a year or two, sometimes in just a few weeks. Try it in your home for thirty days. You will start to see the whole ecosystem altering because of this positive energy source. This can also be energizing in the classroom!

SHARED RESPONSIBILITIES

We refer to this as developing the "Principle-Centered Learning Environment." Historically, the pressure in education has all been directed toward the student-teacher relationship. Educational system stakeholders blame and put all the responsibility on students and teachers. In a Principle-Centered Learning Environment we shift and align that energy to focus on the learning environment, thereby entrusting and empowering the student.

Collective bargaining in education has eroded trust to the point where it no longer exists between teachers and administrators, between parents and the community, or in the performance of the educational system. The student is the one who suffers. Most people see the learning environment as simply teacher and student. Conse-

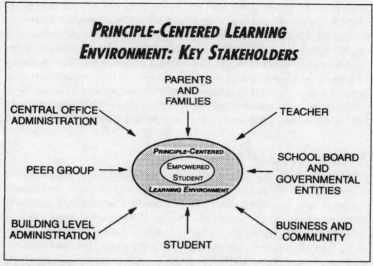

PRINCIPLE-CENTERED LEARNING ENVIRONMENT: KEY STAKEHOLDERS

PARENTS AND FAMILIES

CENTRAL OFFICE ADMINISTRATION

TEACHER

PRINCIPLE-CENTERED
EMPOWERED
STUDENT
LEARNING ENVIRONMENT

PEER GROUP

SCHOOL BOARD AND GOVERNMENTAL ENTITIES

BUILDING LEVEL ADMINISTRATION

BUSINESS AND COMMUNITY

STUDENT

© 1990 Covey Leadership Center

quently society only evaluates how well a particular teacher is doing with a particular student.

With a principle-centered learning environment, we identify all the stakeholders. Each stakeholder has and shares equal responsibility for providing the best learning environment for children to grow and become empowered. For instance, the educational family includes the central office administration, the school board, the building level administration, and the teacher. Each of these stakeholder entities has an individual set of responsibilities that contributes to the learning environment. Each has certain things to do. Each has ownership in providing resources and seeing that those resources stay at a high level. Parents within the private community and business leaders within the public community also have a vested interest in the learning environment.

In working with parents and educators, we talk about the "paradigm of readiness." Readiness is a popular word in education. Most states are looking at readiness programs: whether a student is ready for kindergarten or for first grade. Readiness programs are often implemented between the first and second grades. If a student is not quite ready for second grade, he is not placed in a retention program; rather, he goes into a readiness room and gets ready for the second grade. Readiness in a parent's paradigm should be providing such students with a home environment that encourages them to work effectively in their learning environment every day. Envision this as placing a moving bubble around a child. Everywhere he goes, he is surrounded in an enriched learning environment. This "moving bubble" is the ideal of the principle-centered learning approach.

AN ECOSYSTEM FOR LEARNING

Children learn from peer groups and family. They certainly learn academics and other things, both positive and negative, at school. Students have responsibilities to the learning environment. Fulfilling those responsibilities maximizes the available experiences. This is why it is so important for students to have their own "private victories," to be proactive, to do things that increase their self-esteem, their self-confidence, and their self-awareness and maximize their potential in the learning environment.

We have also included the peer group in the learning ecosystem. As children become responsible for themselves, they experience private victories. Students may responsibly dare to differ, dare to counsel each other, and dare to put themselves on the line for their fellow friend and peer. When children have self-confidence and self-esteem, they do themselves justice by their own individual choices and consequences. Strengthened in private victories, they can go to a friend and say, "Are you really sure you are making the right decision here?" In a group situation they can ask, "Do we really want to be doing this on Friday night? Is this really the best thing that we can do?"

We've got to deal with the learning environment so that a student can become empowered and nurtured and grow in that environment. The ecosystem is such that when students learn the Seven Habits and then return to a contaminated environment, they can act as catalysts and start to impact the whole ecosystem. Even though the entire organization doesn't get involved vertically, the Private Victory starts to build self-esteem and raise self-awareness, and the student begins to take personal responsibility for learning. The natural fruit of that situation is the impact on the teacher as students become more learner driven. If students are engaged with the teacher, the teacher is actually going to be more empowered. It is a virtuous cycle instead of a vicious cycle. So even working independently with one element can affect the whole ecosystem.

We're saying to the school, "If you move toward the Principle-Centered Learning Environment, parents are as vital as teachers in that new structure. How students view their peer groups, their feelings about peers, their influence over peers, and how they react to the environment are all very important. We build upon each one as it contributes to the scenario. While not all are equally weighted, each contributes to the well-being of a student and the environment." We can be leaders in educational reform across the nation. Principle-centered learning environments are the key to effective reform.

DRIVING FORCES VERSUS RESTRAINING FORCES

This is the power of the inside-out approach. Educators have been bombarded with external driving forces like curriculum. Most states have some form of character education in the curriculum as an intervention program, which is an outside-in approach. The principle centered learning approach is an inside-out approach to deliver character education. If we create the environment that models the characteristics that we want in students, we never have to teach integrity, honesty, or trustworthiness. When these characteristics come through a system that models them, students will develop those traits automatically. Students will be enhanced as they come through a principle-centered system.

Educators will find this isn't another curriculum they have to go in and teach; rather, it is something that will change the culture if they dedicate themselves to and do it over a three- to five-year period. Then lots of other things will occur. An educator in Chicago said, "You know, through the Seven Habits, not only will we help the character traits of the kids, but if we create an environment to practice the principles, we'll also see dramatic rise in academic scores."

We gave a workshop in Chicago, Illinois, and we were talking about proactivity, the circle of influence, and the control of oneself. A young black girl stood up in the audience and told us, "Prior to my freshman year I was a C-D-F student, averaging a low D. Registering for my sophomore year, I can remember looking over the course offerings and making the choice that I was going to maximize my education rather than continue to just throw it away. Every semester since I made that decision, I've been on the Dean's List. I'm graduating with honors." As a high school student, her goal was to graduate and attend Northwestern School of Law. She said she could remember consciously making the decision to be proactive. It was the paradigm shift that affected her behavior.

Educators will find that focusing on the Principle-Centered Learning Environment will make the restraining forces more identifiable. Focusing will help them meet their goals so they can design their own in-service and renewal programs to eliminate those restraining forces. They decide what a Principle-Centered Learning Environment is to them, then build their mission statement and everything else around that determination.

In a very real sense, do you know what Principle-Centered Learning does? It gives everybody inside an organization the same compass. They all know where the true north is. Those are the natural laws or principles, and they are essentially self-evident and indisputable. Unlike the great debate that surrounded value clarification, these are basic principles that you will find everyone will recognize.

We work with scores of organizations and find it is easy to identify the underlying natural laws and principles. Once people have a compass inside them, they can negotiate the wilderness. Many of those land mines are no longer there, simply because all the stakeholders participated in the development of the compass. The spirit of adversariness is gone. The spirit of synergy has come back. While many things are not anticipated, true north is clearly defined and understood. Having the ability inside to know where we are really going and on what principles we operate enables people to deal with all kinds of unforeseen obstacles and hidden land mines. Again, this will take a great deal of courage, balanced with consideration. That is the essence of the mature leader. It will also take considerable patience because it is a process. It is not a quick fix, but it is extremely powerful and effective.

Implementation

In working with school districts across the nation, we have developed a well-defined process of implementation. This process depends upon the following five prerequisites:

- The principles of the Seven Habits and the sequential process of dependence, to independence, to interdependence must be well understood.
- Stakeholders understand the importance of the private victory and the concepts "The key to the ninty-nine is the one" and "If you think the problem is out there, that is part of the problem."
- Implementation of the principle centered learning environment is a long process requiring coaching, supportive groups, and renewal programs. This is *not* a quick-fix program.
- Alignment and conditions to ensure success are as important as understanding content.
- Stakeholders involved in the process must *walk their talk*.

The model that seems the most successful would begin training at the highest organizational level possible. Here's how Principle-Centered Learning Environments have been incorporated in schools across the nation.

- In the North Montgomery School Corporation in Indiana, the training began with the board of education and the superintendent, followed by the administrative team and the instructional staff.
- In the state of Ohio, a joint effort is being developed among the local school districts, the state Department of Education, and a major corporation to participate in the training of the Seven Habits.
- In many districts in the state of Utah, training is starting with individual buildings within a district and then moving horizontally and vertically through the district. In Utah, the Principle-Centered Learning Environment is a delivery system for *character education*.
- In Joliet, Illinois, the Joliet Township School Corporation began training with a cadre of educators made up of students, parents, and administrators, followed by training for the central office and building level administration and division chairs.

Common to these examples is the unique relationship formed between the Covey Leadership Center and state and local districts to implement reform. In all of the above cases, Covey Leadership Center staff provided initial workshops, an implementation plan, and certified trainers within the district. It is the center's goal to empower a district to train itself. Through the empowerment process it can better develop its own internal systems of coaching supportive groups and renewal programs that will further move the success of Seven Habits training.

The implementation of this program depends upon personal commitment of individual staff members who understand that this approach is

- inside-out
- principle-centered
- personal empowerment.

We do not know of a more exciting challenge than for educators to exercise a positive, beneficial effect by influencing and modeling the Principle-Centered Learning Environment for our children and future generations.

This article was developed with Chuck Farnsworth of the Covey Leadership Center.

Epilogue

FISHING THE STREAM

FOR MANY YEARS I've subscribed to the following bit of philosophy:

> Give a man a fish and you feed him for a day.
> Teach him how to fish and you feed him for a lifetime.

It's an old axiom, but it's as timely as ever. In fact, we currently use the principle in our training. The goal is always to teach executives how to "fish the stream" for themselves.

Streams represent the environments—the ever-changing realities of the marketplace—that you and your organization are working in. You may be fishing many streams—the corporate network, the parent industry, the market, the government, and the community. There are many currents and many streams that affect the success of your organization. To the degree that the strategy, systems, and shared values are in harmony with the streams, your organization is more likely to achieve success.

RULE ONE, RULE TWO

On the surface a stream appears easy enough to read, and indeed the fundamentals are quickly learned. But, as in fishing, the finer points can take a lifetime.

In teaching executives how to fish the stream, I often refer to a simple rule of thumb. I call it "rule one, rule two." The basic idea is that the shared values or governing principles of the organization ought to be primary considerations—that's rule one. Rule two suggests that everything else—the strategy, structure, systems, skills, and style—are derivatives, that is, they ought to flow with, not against, core values and stream realities.

In the PS model on the facing page, we see that the shared values are central and are considered in the context of the stream. To understand the derivatives, you have to study the source. In fact, executives who are clear on shared values (mission, roles, and goals) can better afford to study the stream because they have something that never changes—their value system, their principles. They can afford to study the stream because their security does not come from the hard S's; their security comes from their value system.

But if organizations don't have a central value system based on correct principles, they build on a foundation of sand—their strategy, structure, and systems. It gives them a sense of security. But it's false security. They may have a nice set of flies and trophies on the wall, but all that doesn't matter much if they are out of "sync" with the stream. They will borrow strength from the past and by doing so will build weakness.

After presenting the PS model and the idea of rules one and two to executives at a large insurance company, they said, "We've got to build a fundamental security source of shared values in order to have the freedom and strength we need to change whatever we're doing that must be changed."

We have now helped them do that by getting them to formulate their mission statements. And once it gets into their minds and hearts, people won't go back to the old ways. It's also very unsettling and unpopular with some executives. One executive told me that he struggled with it, but he's coming to realize that he's got to manage by principles. It's the only way to "fish the stream" effectively over time.

FISHING & MANAGING

I've long been impressed with the many parallels between fishing and managing. In reality, senior-level executives are really fishing the stream. That is, they're looking at the business in the context of the

PS PARADIGM:
FOUR LEVELS OF PRINCIPLE-CENTERED LEADERSHIP

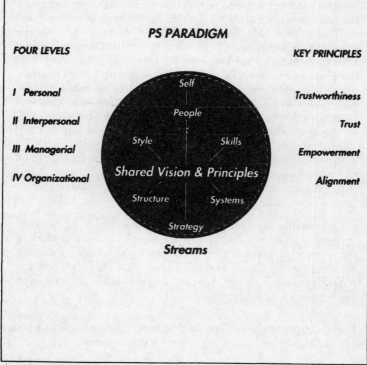

PS PARADIGM

FOUR LEVELS

I Personal

II Interpersonal

III Managerial

IV Organizational

KEY PRINCIPLES

Trustworthiness

Trust

Empowerment

Alignment

Self

People

Style   Skills

Shared Vision & Principles

Structure   Systems

Strategy

Streams

total environment and devising ways to "reel in" desired results.

As I see it, there are basically two ways to fish, reactively and proactively. The reactive method is a "waiting game," as described here by Gene Hill:

> I like fly fishing as a nice way to pass time—waiting. It is a respectable thing to do as opposed to being purely idle, stretched out in a hammock or taking a nap on the couch. You at least look serious and industrious—a vest full of instruments, polarized glasses, wading staff, and net, perhaps a small canvas creel, and the busy little hum of the fly line slicking through the rod guides.
>
> "There," you say, "is a serious man," if you should see me poised like a heron in some stream. Far from it. There you see an idler in costume, a man wondering where the time went. Not the past hour or so while exchanging nods with a duck or mulling a two-penny philosophy about a mud-colored snake, but the past five or ten years. He is thinking about his work that has been left undone, his loves unknown, and that just yesterday, he was only a boy.

In truth, some executives are like this fisherman—idlers in costume. On the other hand, proactive executives better fit the following description:

> Consistently successful anglers are not locked in to fixed responses to situations; rather they are flexible, constantly reading the water to discover the best place from which to cast into each lie. They, in fact, learn to think like a fish. Often they will approach the water slowly, keeping a low profile, perhaps even casting from a kneeling position.

That's sound advice for any angler: keep a low profile and kneel while casting. Here's more, right from the handbook:

> Many contemporary anglers are imitationists with a penchant for minutiae and measurements and with an eye for surface details. But they might be better off if they never weighed, measured, or recorded their catches. The experts are usually too busy fishing or observing to count and measure things.

Effective executives constantly read the stream. They look carefully at the business trends and the cultural "megatrends," since these are like the currents. They tune in to knowledgeable forecasters—people like Naisbitt and Yankelovich—who monitor the stream and report periodically on current conditions. They get a sense for themselves of what the basic trends are and what will likely happen as a result of those trends.

All of this reading of trends in the environment, like the forecasting of weather, is done for a clear purpose: to better get through the day and prepare for what's to come tomorrow. If you're caught in a rainstorm by surprise, you can look pretty foolish. In a downpour, it's nice to have an umbrella and a water-repellent coat. Likewise, in a downturn, it's nice to have the right apparel and repellents to avoid getting soaked.

Back to the handbook:

> Match line, leader, and tackle to the type of fishing you do, taking into account such things as the speed of the current, the depth of the water, and the rate of retrieve. If you fish different waters, have more than one line. And give careful thought and attention to the leader, the most important link in the tackle system.

Once you see that the trends are starting to turn, the trick is to adapt—to make your internal operations harmonious with the external environment. The most important trends to look for are opportunities and threats. If the stream starts turning away from your product line, that's a threat. If the stream turns toward a new product line, a new technology, or new market, that's an opportunity. But an opportunity could be a threat if you don't adapt to it.

One of the main problems that I find with organizations is that they don't adapt their structure and systems to the stream. In fact, they're often looking at the stream through their existing structure and systems. Consequently they don't know where the catch is. They don't see the threats and opportunities because they're looking through the wrong lens.

Even if they can sense a shift, they may be stuck with the wrong equipment, weighed down by high overhead, or burdened by bureaucracy. Whatever the reason, the result is the same—they can't move. Something—be it myopia or debt load or deadwood "fat"—is keeping them from being flexible and having the freedom to move to adapt to a new stream.

Again, the handbook says:

> To be successful over time, an angler must have some under-standing of history, biology, geography, stream ecology, and, of course, fishing strategy and tactics. Moreover, most could ben-efit from a crash course in entomology, because imitating the natural food source is the name of the game when fly fishing for trout. Trout are smart, tentative, cautious, hard to fool, and stubborn about not taking flies that look like Easter hats instead of caddis fly nymphs.

For example, it's not likely that General Motors was ignorant of the trends when the low-price, high-quality Japanese cars started gain-ing market share. Detroit was aware of the trend, but the main problem was that they had all of their systems, particularly their compensation systems for their top executives, geared toward selling big cars. So they continued to manufacture big cars to feed that system.

They didn't adapt to the stream, and their existing structure and systems were ill suited to the new game—it was like playing golf with a tennis racket.

Now, in retrospect, GM executives are talking about how they've learned some hard lessons from the stream and how they've gone through many years of team building to regain their competitiveness and recapture a measure of the world market. And they're saying that anybody who's really serious about competing long term is go-ing to have to go through that kind of pain to get the gains. And it's true. Every industry—from steel to health care—must learn to fish the stream.

How? First, they should not look at the hard S's as being sacred cows. Those are all paper concepts, and they can be changed. They are programs. People often don't want to change them because it may mean leaving a comfort zone or entering uncharted waters. But not changing them may be the greatest risk of all.

Nothing Fails Like Success

I'm reminded of another axiom: Nothing fails like success. We can abridge all of history into a simple formula: challenge/response. The successful response works to the challenges.

As soon as the stream changes, the challenge, the one successful response, no longer works. It fails. Nothing fails like success. It's intriguing, and it's true. Historian Arnold Toynbee documented it throughout history. He noted that as new challenges arise—as the stream changes—the response stays the same because people don't want to leave their comfort zone. They have their perks, their life-style, and they don't want to change. They're too tied to it.

Just as an expert fisherman reads the stream, so the professional executive considers the ambient conditions—the light, the tempera-ture, the time of day, the total environment—before selecting tackle and lure. But perhaps nothing in his current tackle box, no bait or lure, is appropriate to the stream. Maybe all an executive has inside his tackle box is old stuff. He sees competitors out there using the searchlights and dynamite, and all he's got is the fly rod.

I once observed a fascinating scene on the banks of the Yellow-stone River. On one side of the stream was a young man, obviously a tourist, who was diligently casting out a variety of lures and bait from a scenic spot overlooking the river. He wasn't having any luck in the venture, but the very activity of "fishing the stream" seemed to satisfy him—that is, until another man started fishing the stream from the opposite side.

From his decorated cap and vest to his hip-boot waders, I could tell that this man was no stranger to the stream. Moreover, he was catching fish—so many fish, in fact, that he had to let them go because he already had his limit. Now he was fishing for the sport of it.

Meanwhile the hard-luck tourist didn't even get a bite during the time I observed him. Yet he was fishing the same stream, same spot, same day. As time passed he grew so frustrated that he was about to wade in and try to catch a fish with his bare hands.

The problem is that most newcomers aren't interested in waiting years to learn the art and craft of fly fishing—they want to pass over the fundamentals quickly and get out on the water and start reeling in impressive results. Some schools even cater to such ambition.

They promise their students that in no time they'll know all about the different lines and leaders.

Seasoned professionals, however, know that there is simply no short cut to developing the capability to handle with excellence almost any situation or condition that might occur on the water. Real excellence does not come cheaply. A certain price must be paid in terms of practice, patience, and persistence—natural ability notwithstanding.

Here's one more bit of advice from an old sage:

> Often a strike can only be detected by watching for a slight twitch or pause in the drift of the line. A major fault of most fishermen, novice and expert alike, is striking too hard, suddenly and violently stressing the leader, snapping the line, and breaking off the fish. Set the hook smoothly by simply lifting the rod tip and tightening the line. Keep the point sharp, and in all ways, be gentle.

FEEDING FOR A LIFETIME

I once worked with a large restaurant organization that wanted to make their management style consistent with the philosophy "Give a man a fish and you feed him for a day; teach him how to fish and you feed him for a lifetime."

This company had hundreds of restaurants, and each had its own manager. While these managers seemed to have full authority and responsibility for running fairly sizable restaurants and employing large numbers of people, they were really only resident assistant district managers.

Almost all of the significant decisions regarding employment and other business practices were made by the district managers who supervised them. Every time they encountered a problem, they ran to the district manager for a "fish." Since the district managers only supervised a few restaurants and were supervised themselves by regional managers, they were trapped in a constant problem-solving or management-by-crisis mode.

This method of operation created a picture of a single career path in most people's minds. The procedure was to begin at the bottom, eventually become a restaurant manager, and then get promoted up the line. Usually the higher one went in the organization, the more one traveled. And the more managers traveled, the more marriage and family problems resulted. Once they reached the top of the ladder, they realized it was leaning against the wrong wall. They weren't doing what they enjoyed doing or living where they wanted to live. But such was the price for success.

The restaurants, moreover, tended to be managed on the basis of company rules and procedures rather than consumer needs and wants, because managers lacked the flexibility and incentive to develop and use their own judgment, ingenuity, and initiative to solve or prevent problems. The entire hierarchy was more methods-oriented than results- or consumer-oriented, even though "customer relations" was the theme of almost every management meeting. Company politics so dominated the minds of the managers that many decisions were made on political or social criteria.

Remarkably, in spite of all this, the company was doing well relative to their competition, but the people at the top throughout the entire organization knew that there must be a better way.

After diagnosing the problems with them, we reached a general agreement that the operation needed to be decentralized by pushing the authority and responsibility for decision making as far down the corporate ladder as possible and by strengthening the role of the restaurant manager. It was further recognized that more management training and development was needed to make decentralization feasible and financially profitable.

The change process started slowly and continued over a number of years. The renewed commitment to the importance of the individual manager was communicated not only through the rhetoric in company meetings and literature, but also through an increased investment in planning, training, and career counseling programs. In addition, the compensation system was adjusted to reward managers for training the people who reported to them.

It soon became apparent that true decentralization would require managers at all levels to develop new skills. When entire levels of line management and overhead were removed, restaurant managers started supervising about twenty restaurants instead of five or six, making it impossible for them to be involved in day-to-day operating decisions. The resident managers now made those decisions, and they needed training in decision making and in carrying the full responsibility for managing the restaurant.

The serendipitous effect of this decentralization was to create a dual-career path: the traditional one up the line and a second one that provided resident restaurant managers with more community status and recognition and with more financial incentive for building up the restaurant and developing people inside to take over other restaurants in the corporation. Incidentally, making this second option more attractive to resident managers reduced the number of marriage and family problems in the company.

In the upper echelons of the company, executives were no longer directing, controlling, motivating, evaluating—practices they had been heavily involved in up to this point. Instead their energies shifted to training and development, counseling, coaching, and responding to requests for guidance. Essentially they began training their managers "how to fish" and stopped giving them a "fish" a day.

This liberated them to focus more upon planning, organizing, and developing people—responsibilities that had been neglected during the management-by-crisis days.

Perhaps the biggest benefit of the decentralization effort was that it uprooted many of the top people who had served earlier as pathfinders and entrepreneurs and exposed their deeply imbedded but ineffective ways of delegating, communicating, and developing people.

When these pioneers moved on to other endeavors, many wondered what the effect would be. To the surprise of some, the transition not only went smoothly, but created a sense of upward mobility, excitement, enthusiasm, and gratitude. Within three days the organization was essentially reorganized, and soon the quality and depth of leadership was evident to everyone. People were being called to assume more responsibility, trained in the applications of correct principles, and found equal to the task.

On a personal level, however, this transition was not easy or simple. It involved a great deal of gut wrenching, uprooting, and growing pains at all levels. But because everyone knew that it would be the best in the long run, both personally and organizationally, and because the people at the top were committed to the strategy, it worked.

In fact, as the vision of what the company could become was transmitted—almost by osmosis—throughout the organization, a strong sense of mission developed within the company. In effect, the company culture changed as new stories and anecdotes were shared continually to confirm the vision.

Such far-reaching results come naturally from the practice of managing and leading an organization by correct principles.

A Personal Note

IN A VERY REAL SENSE there is no such thing as organizational behavior. There is only individual behavior. Everything else flows out of that.

The main sticking point between Sigmund Freud and Carl Jung dealt with conscience. Freud believed the conscience or superego was basically a social product. Jung believed it primarily to be part of the collective unconscious, transcending the mortal overlay of culture, race, religion, gender, or nationality.

I believe Jung was right and Freud was wrong. In working with thousands of organizations and individuals around the world in preparing mission or value statements—assuming four conditions are present, namely 1) enough people; 2) interacting freely; 3) well informed about the realities of their situation; 4) feeling safe to express themselves without fear of censure, ridicule, or embarrassment—*then* the values or principles part of the mission statement all basically say the same thing, even though different words are used, regardless of nationality, culture, religion, or race.

Gandhi emphasized: "A person cannot do right in one department whilst attempting to do wrong in another department. Life is one indivisible whole." John Wesley's mother taught her son, "Whatever weakens your reason, impairs the tenderness of your conscience, obscures your sense of God, takes off your relish for spiritual things, whatever increases the authority of the body over the mind, that thing is sin to you, however innocent it may seem in itself."

Further, I believe God is the true name and source of the collective unconscious and is therefore the ultimate moral authority in the universe. The daily prayerful study of His revealed word is the single most important and powerful discipline in life because it points our lives, like a compass, to "true north"—our divine destiny.

It also sets us on a life of service and I fear, unless enough of us capture the spirit of the following conviction of George Bernard Shaw, that the social problems of today will overwhelm the economic machine and discombobulate all of society.

"This is the true joy in life, being used for a purpose recognized by yourself as a mighty one.

"Being a force of nature instead of a feverish, selfish little clod of ailments and grievances complaining that the world will not devote itself to making you happy.

"I am of the opinion that my life belongs to the whole community and as I live it is my privilege—my *privilege* to do for it whatever I can.

"I want to be thoroughly used up when I die, for the harder I work the more I love. I rejoice in life for its own sake. Life is no brief candle to me; it is a sort of splendid torch which I've got a hold of for the moment and I want to make it burn as brightly as possible before handing it on to future generations."

ACKNOWLEDGEMENTS

Even though I take full responsibility for the ideas expressed in this book (with the exception of the five collaborated chapters), I gratefully give full credit to my friend and colleague Ken Shelton for making it all possible. For almost eight years, he has served as editor of our newsletter, *Executive Excellence*, from which this material was taken. He listened to countless speeches, conducted extensive interviews, edited many writings, and then prepared final drafts for my approval of most of the articles collected for this book. He and Greg Link, my "make it happen" friend and affirming, creative associate, together with the valued encouragement and professional expertise of Bob Asahina, Vice President and Editorial Director of the Summit Division of Simon & Schuster, were all instrumental in the vision and editing of this book.

This work is the fruit of the principle-centered, interdependent, synergy of my 170 associates at the Covey Leadership Center and our many stakeholders—clients, suppliers, customers. Their commitment to our mission, principle-centered living, quality, and excellence provide me continuous inspiration, support, and opportunity to learn and improve. To them, I express my deepest admiration and gratitude for their tremendous contributions to humankind.

Specifically I thank these special people who contributed to this book:

Dr. Blaine Lee for his chapter, "Principle-Centered Power," and for his friendship and instrumental contributions to our firm and our clients.

A. Roger Merrill for his chapter, "Organizational Control Versus Self-Supervision," and his wise synergistic efforts and friendship.

Keith Gulledge for his chapters, "Total Quality Leadership" and "Seven Habits and Deming's 14 Points," and his thirst for learning and attention to detail.

Chuck Farnsworth for his chapter on "Principle-Centered Learning Environments," and his passionate dedication, along with my loyal brother, John Covey, in applying principle-centered leadership to future generations through our educators, students, and their parents.

Robert Thele for his supportive friendship and for his splendid management of the firm that provides the margin so necessary to forward our mission; my assistants Marilyn Andrews and Boyd Craig for second-mile help, and to my dear son, Stephen, for his liberating emphatic support and "walking the talk."

INDEX

ABOUT THE AUTHOR

Stephen R. Covey, husband, father, and grandfather, is an internationally respected leadership authority, family expert, teacher, organizational consultant, founder of the former Covey Leadership Center, and co-chairman of Franklin Covey Company. He has made teaching Principle-Centered Living and Principle-Centered Leadership his life's work. He holds an MBA from Harvard and a doctorate from Brigham Young University, where he was a professor of organizational behavior and business management, and also served as director of university relations and assistant to the president. For more than thirty years he has taught millions of individuals and families and leaders in business, education, and government the transforming power of principles or natural laws that govern human and organizational effectiveness.

Dr. Covey is the author of several acclaimed books including *The 7 Habits of Highly Effective People*, which has been at the top of the best-seller lists for over seven years. More than ten million copies have been sold in twenty-eight languages and seventy countries. His books *Principle-Centered Leadership* and *First Things First* are two of the best-selling business books of the decade.

Dr. Covey and other Franklin Covey authors, speakers, and spokespersons, all authorities on leadership and effectiveness, are consistently sought by radio and television stations, magazines, and newspapers throughout the world.

Among recent acknowledgements, Dr. Covey has received the Thomas More College Medallion for continuing service to humanity, the Toastmaster's International Top Speaker Award, *Inc.* magazine's National Entrepreneur of the Year Lifetime Achievement Award for Entrepreneurial Leadership, and several honorary doctorates. He has also been recognized as one of *Time* magazine's twenty-five most influential Americans.

Stephen, his wife, Sandra, and their family live in the Rocky Mountains of Utah.

ABOUT FRANKLIN COVEY

Stephen R. Covey is co-chairman of Franklin Covey Company, a four-thousand member international firm devoted to helping individuals, organizations, and families become more effective through the application of proven principles or natural laws. In addition to working with and creating products for individuals and families, the company's client portfolio includes eighty-two of the Fortune 100 companies, more than two-thirds of the Fortune 500 companies, thousands of small and midsize companies, and government entities at local, state, and national levels. Franklin Covey has also created pilot partnerships with cities seeking to become principle-centered communities, and is currently teaching the 7 Habits to teachers and administrators n more than three thousand school districts and universities nationwide and through statewide initiatives with education leaders in twenty-seven states.

The vision of Franklin Covey is to teach people to teach themselves and become independent of the company. They encourage organizations to be family friendly, and they teach skills and provide products to help people balance work and family life. To the timeless adage by Laotzu: "Give a man a fish and you feed him for a day; teach him how to fish and you feed him for a lifetime," they add: "DEvelop teachers of fishermen, and you lift all society." This empowerment process is carried out through programs conducted at facilities in the Rocky Mountains of Utah, custom consulting services, personal coaching, custom on-site training, and client-facilitated training, as well as through open enrollment workshops offered in over three hundred cities in North America and forty countries worldwide.

Franklin Covey has more than seven thousand licensed client facilitators teaching its curriculum within their organizations, and it trains in excess of 750,000 participants annually. Implementation tools, including the Franklin Day Planner, the 7 Habits Organizer, and a wide offering of audio- and videotapes, books and computer software programs enable clients to retain and effectively utilize concepts and skills. These and other family products carefully selected and endorsed by Franklin Covey are available in more than one hundred Franklin Covey 7 Habits Stores throughout North America and in several other countries.

Franklin Covey products and materials are now available in twenty-eight languages, and their planner products are used by more than fifteen million individuals worldwide. The company has over twelve million books in print, with more than one and a half million sold each year. *Business Week* lists Dr. Covey's *The 7 Habits of Highly Effective People* as a number one best-selling trade business book of the year and its First Things First time management book as a number three.

For information on Franklin Covey 7 Habits Store or International Office closest to you, or for a free catalog of Franklin Covey products and programs, call or write:

Franklin Covey Organisation Services Ltd
PO Box 1000
Newcastle-upon-Tyne
NE85 2BS, UK
Tel: (44) 0870 600 0226
Fax: (44) 0870 600 0212

FRANKLIN COVEY COMPANY® GLOBAL OFFICES

Australia
Brisbane Office
Franklin Covey Pty Ltd
GPO Box 2769
Brisbane, QLD 4001
Tel: (61-7) 3259-0222
Fax: (61-7) 3369-7810
Info@franklincovey.com.au

Sydney Office
Franklin Covey Pty Ltd
Suite 4802, Level 46
MLC Centre
19-29 Martin Place
Sydney, NSW 2000
Tel: (61-2) 9221-5311
Fax: (61-2) 9221-7811

Bahamas
P.O. Box SS-5679
Nassau, Bahamas
Tel: 242-322-1605
Fax: 242-364-0171
Mdrqs@batelnet.bs

Canada
60 Struck Court
Cambridge, Ontario
N1R 8L2 Canada
Tel: (519) 740-2580
Fax: (519) 740-8833
Canada@franklin.com

China
The Gateway, Suite 7-00
10 Yabao Road
Chao Yang District
Beijing 100020 China
Tel: 8610 6594 2288
Fax: 8610 6592 5186

Estonia
7 Habite Eestl
Narva mnt 7
10117 Taillnn, Estonia
Tel: 372 672 2625

Hong Kong
Room 1502
15/F Austin Tower
22-26A Austin Avenue
Tsimshatsui
Kowloon, Hong Kong
Tel: 852 2541 2218
Fax: 852 2544 4311

India
301-B
Eden-3
Hiranandani Gardens
Powal, Mumbai 400076
India
Tel: 91 22 570 0005
Fax: 91 22 570 1383

Indonesia
Jl. Bendungan Jatiluhur 56
Bendungan Hilir
Jakarta, Indonesia 10210
Tel: (62-21) 572-0761
Fax: (62-21) 572-0762

Ireland
5 Argyle Square
Donnybrook
Dublin 4, Ireland
Tel: (353-1) 668-1422
Fax: (353-1) 668-1459
Sales@covey.ie

Japan
Marumasu Koujimachi
Building 7F, 3-3
Chiyoa-Ku, Tokyo
102-0083 Japan
Tel: 81-3-3237-7830
Fax: 81-3-3237-7820

Korea
11F J insung Building
996-1 Daechi-Dong
Tel: (82-2) 6245-7000
Fax: (82-2) 6245-8001
Klc@nuri.net

Latin America
107 N. Virginia Ave.
Winter Park, FL 32789
Tel: (407) 644-4418
Fax: (407) 664-5919
Franklincoveyla@fcla.com

Argentina
Corrientes 881 Sto. Piso
2000 Rosario, Argentina
Tel: (54-341) 440-8765
Fax: (54-341) 449-5646
Franklincoveyar@fcla.com

Bermuda
4 Dunscombe Road
Warwick, Bermuda WKD8
Tel: (441) 236-0383
Fax: (441) 236-0192

Chihuahua Office
AMI Chihuahua S.C
Ranoho Santa Clara # 7222
Col. Pradero, Dorada
Cd. Juarez Chihuahua CP 32650
Tel: 52 16 230 488
Fax: 52 16 230 468
Amioh2@chih1.telmex.not.mx

Chile
Alcontara No. 410
Las Condes
Santiago, Chile
Tel: (56-2) 374-3140
Fax: (56-2) 228-5699
Franklincoveych@fcla.com

Colombia Office
Calle 90 No. 11-A34
Oficina 206
Santa Fe de Bogota, Colombia
Tel: (57-1) 610-0396/0385
Fax: (57-1) 610-2723
Franklincoveyco@fcla.com

Curacao Office
Ajaxway 3, Willemstad
Curacao, Netherlands Antilles
Tel: (599) 97-371284/1286
Fax: (599) 97-371289
Franklincoveycu@fcla.com

Ecuador Office
Malecon 305 y Padre Aguirre
Edifiolo El Fortin 15 B
Guayaquil, Ecuador
Tel: (593-9) 752-664
Fax: (593-4) 303-006
Franklincoveyec@fcla.com

Panama Office
Centro Aventura
Tumba Muerto, Oficina 113
Panamá, Republic de Panamá
Tel: (507) 260-9534/8763
Fax: (507) 260-0373
Franklincoveypa@fcla.com

Puerto Rico Office
Urb. Altamira, 546,
Aldebaran St.
Guayanbo, PR 00988
Tel: 787 273 6 750
Fax: 787 783 4594
Franklincoveypr@fcla.com

Uruguay Office
Avenida 19 de abril 3420
Montivideo, Uruguay 11700
Tel: 59-82-601-7194
Fax: 59-82-209-8317
Franklincoveyur@fcla.com

Venezuela Office
Calle California Con Mucuchles
Edif, Los Angeles, Piso 2
Ofic. 5-6B, Las Mercedes
Caracas, Venezuela
Tel: (58-2) 993-8550/3639
Fax: (58-2) 993-1763
Franklincoveyve@fcla.com

West Indies Office
#23 Westwood Street
San Fernando
Trinidad, West Indies
Tel: (868) 652-6805
Fax: (868) 657-4432
Lcg@carib-link.net

Malaysia/Brunei
J-4, Bangunan Khas,
Lorong 8/1E
46050 Petaling Jaya
Setangor, Malaysia
Tel: (60-3) 758-6418 X21
Fax: (60-3) 755-2589
Covey@po.jaring.my

Mexico
Monterray Office (head office)
Edificio Losoles D-15
Avenida Lazaro Cardenas
#2400 Pte.
San Pedro Garza Garcia
NJ 666220 Mexico
Tel: (52-8) 363-2171
Fax: (52-8) 363-5314
Fqmexventas@infosel.net.mx
Fqseminarios@infosel.net.mx

Mexico City Office
Florencia #39 Tercer Pisa
Col. Juarez
Delgacion Cuahutemoc
Mexico DF 06600 Mexico
Tel: (52-5) 533-5201/5194
Fax: (52-5) 511-9103
Fcmex@infosel.mx

Mexico Licensee
Jose Maria Rico 121-403
Colonia del Valle
03100 Mexico D.F. Mexico
Tel: (52-5) 534-1025/1945
Fax: (52-5) 524-5903
Franklincoveyme@fcla.com

Middle East
Egypt Office
122 Mohi El-Din Abou El-Exx Str.,
Mohandesen, Glza
Egypt
Tel: 202 336 8911
Fax: 202 347 4658
Fc_eltc@soficom.com.eg

Lebanon Office
Sarraf Building, 10th Floor
Independence Avenue
Ashrafieh
P.O. Box 167089
Beirut, Lebanon
Tel: 324923 204081
Fax: 324923 204081
Starman@cyberia.net.lb

Saudi Arabia
LADA International
P.O. Box 89806
Riyadh, Saudi Arabia 11557
Tel: 966-1-4628271
Fax: 966-1-4628526

Turkey
I.D.E.A., A.S.
Building 7, Cayirova
Istanbul, Turkey 81719
Tel: 90-2164-232426
Fax: 90-2164-232433

New Zealand
21 William Pickering Drive
Albany
Auckland, New Zealand
Tel: (84-9) 415-3891
Fax: (64-9) 415-4966
Delivery Address:
Private Bag 300981
Albany
Auckland, New Zealand

Nigeria
Plot 1654 Oyin Jolayemi St
(4th Floor)
Victoria Island, Nigeria
Tel: (234-1) 470 5124
Fax: (234-1) 288 0883
Restral@infoweb.abs.net

Philippines
G/F Hoffner Building
KATI Punam Ave
Quezon City, 1108
Philippines
Tel: (63-2) 426-6121
Fax: (63-2) 426-5935
Mcar@pusit.admu.edu.ph
Philippines@covey.com

Singapore
19 Tanglin Road
#05-18 Tanglin Shopping Ctr
Singapore 247909
Tel: 65 838 9206
Fax: 65 838 9211
Covey@singnet.com.eg

South Africa
Johannesburg Office
18 Crescent Road
Parkwood 2193
Johannesburg, South Africa
Tel: (27-11) 442-4596
    (27-11) 442-4589
Fax: (27-11) 442-4190
Covey@pixie.co.za

Johannesburg Office #2
45 De La Rey Road
Rivonia 2128
South Africa
Tel: (27) 11-807-2929
Fax: (27) 11-807-2871
Covey@iafrica.com

Cape Town Office
20 Krige Street (courier service)
Stellenbosch 7600
South Africa
Tel: (27-21) 886-5857
    (27-21) 883-8080

Cape Town Office #2
P.O. Box 351 (for letters)
Stellenbosch 7599
South Africa
Tel: (27-21) 866-5857
Fax: (27-21) 883-8080
Csa_cst@iafrica.com

Taiwan
7F-3, 165, Cheng Hsiao
E. Road
Sec. 4 Taipei
Taiwan R.O.C.
Tel: (8862) 2751-1333
Fax: (8862) 2711-5285
Sns@pts1.seed.net.tw

UK/Europe
Grimsbury Manor
Grimsbury Green
Banbury, Oxfordshire
OXI6 3JQ England
Tel: (44) 1295 274 100
Fax: (44) 1295 274 101
Training@franklincovey.co.uk

Customer Service:
Franklin Covey Europe Ltd
P.O Box 1000
Newcastle-upon-Tyne
NE85 2BS, UK
Tel: (44) 0870 600 0226
Fax: (44) 0870 600 0212
Customer.orders@franklincovey.co.uk

FIRST THINGS FIRST

Stephen R. Covey, A. Roger Merrill with Rebecca R. Merrill

In the first real breakthrough in time management in years, Stephen R. Covey and A. Roger Merrill apply the insights of *The 7 Habits of Highly Effective People* to the daily problems of people who must struggle with the ever-increasing demands of work and home-life. Rather than focusing on time and change, Covey and Merrill emphasise relationships and results. And instead of efficiency, they emphasise effectiveness.

First Things First shows:

Why your previous attempts to manage time failed.

How to overcome the tremendous gravity of habit.

What the connections are between time management and money management.

How to turn your resolutions into reality.

How to delegate without losing control.

Where the winners really spend their time.

How to rediscover your power and passion.

How to lead your life, not just manage your time.

With the wisdom and insight that has made *The 7 Habits of Highly Effective People* a massive international bestseller, *First Things First* will empower you to define what is truly important; to accomplish worthwhile goals; and to lead rich, rewarding and balanced lives.

0684858401   £10.99
Also on audio read by Stephen Covey – 0671853228   £8.99

THE 7 HABITS OF HIGHLY EFFECTIVE FAMILIES
Stephen R. Covey
Foreword by Sandra Merrill Covey

The long-awaited new book that offers precious lessons in creating and sustaining a strong family culture in a turbulent world.

With the same profound insight, simplicity, and practical wisdom that propelled *The 7 Habits of Highly Effective People* to worldwide acclaim, Stephen R. Covey now focuses on a primary concern of society today – the family. No family is free from challenges from its own members or from the outside world and the 7 Habits create a powerful framework of timeless, universal, and self-evident principles that enable family members to communicate effectively, set goals and find creative, meaningful ways for solving problems and improving their relationships.

True happiness does not come from possessions or fame: it comes from the quality of your relationships with the people you love and respect. *The 7 Habits of Highly Effective Families* will help you find answers to such common family difficulties as:

- How can you have quality time for the family when both parents (or the only parent) are working simply to keep food on the table?
- How can you build harmony in the family when everyone is criticising and putting one another down?
- How can you influence a family member who just won't listen to you at all?
- How can you strengthen your family to withstand destructive influences in society?
- How can you discipline without punishing?
- How can you rebuild a broken relationship when the feeling is no longer there?
- How do you create and maintain order and a spirit of co-operation in the family yet give family members the freedom and autonomy they need to grow and find fulfilment?
- How do you create a spirit of fun, adventure, and excitement in the family?

0684860082   £10.99

All of these titles are available, or can be ordered from your local bookstore. If difficulties are encountered, it is possible to buy through mail-order:

CODE	TITLE	PRICE	QUANTITY REQUIRED	TOTAL PRICE
BEPB7HB	7 Habits Book	£10.99		
BEPB1ST	First Things First book	£10.99		
BEPB8CL	Principle-Centred Leadership book	£10.99		
BEPBDAI	Daily Reflections book	£4.99		
	7 Habits . . . Families book	£10.99		
AE1S7HB	7 Habits audio	£8.99		
AE1SLIV	Living the 7 Habits audio	£8.99		
AE1SIST	First Things First audio	£8.99		
AE1S8CL	Principle-Centred Leadership audio	£8.99		
AE1SDAI	Daily Reflections audio	£8.99		
			p&p (£1.60 per book, 50p per tape)	
			Grand total	

Send your order to Franklin Covey Europe Ltd, PO Box 1000, Newcastle-Upon-Tyne NE85 2BS, UK. Alternatively call (44) 0870 600 0226 to place your order. Please be ready to quote the relevant code number(s) for the item(s) you require. Mastercard, Visa and American Express are accepted. You can also fax your order on (44) 0870 600 0212.

For a full list of the many business and positive development books and tapes available from Simon & Schuster, please write to Simon & Schuster Business Books, Africa House, 64-78 Kingsway, London WC2B 6AH, United Kingdom.